EVERYDAY ISLAMOPHOBIA

Spaces and Practices of Justice

Series Editor: **Agatha Herman**, Cardiff University

Geographies of justice investigate the spatialities of (in)justice and its impacts on practices, relations, discourses and experiences. This book series explores and analyses the exciting nexus offered by a focus on (in)justice for interdisciplinary work and so draws on engagements from across sociology, politics, international relations, urban studies, anthropology, rural studies, cultural studies, criminology, development studies and human geography.

Also available in the series:

Researching Justice
edited by **Agatha Herman** and **Joshua Inwood**

The Practice of Collective Escape
by **Helen Traill**

Arctic Justice
edited by **Corine Wood-Donnelly** and **Johanna Ohlsson**

Landscapes of Hate
edited by **Edward Hall**, **John Clayton** and **Catherine Donovan**

Find out more at:
bristoluniversitypress.co.uk/spaces-and-practices-of-justice

EVERYDAY ISLAMOPHOBIA

Peter Hopkins

First published in Great Britain in 2025 by

Bristol University Press
University of Bristol
1–9 Old Park Hill
Bristol
BS2 8BB
UK
t: +44 (0)117 374 6645
e: bup-info@bristol.ac.uk

Details of international sales and distribution partners are available at bristoluniversitypress.co.uk

© Peter Hopkins 2025

The digital PDF and ePub versions of this title are available open access and distributed under the terms of the Creative Commons Attribution-NonCommercial-NoDerivatives 4.0 International licence (https://creativecommons.org/licenses/by-nc-nd/4.0/) which permits reproduction and distribution for non-commercial use without further permission provided the original work is attributed.

British Library Cataloguing in Publication Data
A catalogue record for this book is available from the British Library

ISBN 978-1-5292-3267-7 paperback
ISBN 978-1-5292-3268-4 ePub
ISBN 978-1-5292-3269-1 OA PDF

The right of Peter Hopkins to be identified as author of this work has been asserted by him in accordance with the Copyright, Designs and Patents Act 1988.

All rights reserved: no part of this publication may be reproduced, stored in a retrieval system, or transmitted in any form or by any means, electronic, mechanical, photocopying, recording, or otherwise without the prior permission of Bristol University Press.

Every reasonable effort has been made to obtain permission to reproduce copyrighted material. If, however, anyone knows of an oversight, please contact the publisher.

The statements and opinions contained within this publication are solely those of the author and not of the University of Bristol or Bristol University Press. The University of Bristol and Bristol University Press disclaim responsibility for any injury to persons or property resulting from any material published in this publication.

Bristol University Press works to counter discrimination on grounds of gender, race, disability, age and sexuality.

Cover design: Blu inc
Front cover image: unsplash/Jr Korpa

For Chris

Contents

Series Editor's Preface		viii
List of Figures and Tables		ix
Acknowledgements		x
1	Introduction	1
2	What is Everyday Islamophobia?	13
3	The Islamophobia Industrial Complex	33
4	Global Islamophobia, Nation-States, and Politics	51
5	Transnational Networks and Media	74
6	Communities, Public Spaces, and Mobility	92
7	Mosques and Institutions of Education and Employment	112
8	Home, Family, and the Body	124
9	Impacts and Solutions	139
References		154
Index		178

Series Editor's Preface

Agatha Herman

Justice refers to a broad concern with fairness, equity, equality and respect. Just from the daily news, it is readily apparent how questions of justice or, in fact, the more obvious experiences of *injustice* shape our everyday lives. From global trade to our own personal consumption; living or dying through war and peace; access to education; relations in the workplace or home; how we experience life through a spectrum of identities; or the more-than-human entanglements that contextualize our environments, we need to conceptualize and analyse the intersections between spaces and practices of justice in order to formulate innovative and grounded interventions. The Spaces and Practices of Justice book series aims to do so through cutting across scales to explore power, relations, and society from the local through to international levels, recognizing that space is fundamental to understanding how (in)justice is relationally produced in, and through, different temporal and geographical contexts. It is also always practised, and a conceptual focus on these 'doings and sayings' (Shove, 2014) brings a sense of the everydayness of (in)justice but also allows for analysis of the broader contexts, logics, and structures within which such experiences and relations are embedded (Jaeger-Erben and Offenberger, 2014; Herman, 2018).

References
Herman, A. (2018) *Practising Empowerment in Post-Apartheid South Africa: Wine, Ethics and Development*, London: Routledge.
Jaeger-Erben, M. and Offenberger, U. (2014) 'A practice theory approach to sustainable consumption', *GAIA*, 23(S1): 166–174.
Shove, E. (2014) 'Putting practice into policy: reconfiguring questions of consumption and climate change', *Contemporary Social Science*, 9(4): 415–429.

List of Figures and Tables

Figures

3.1   The Islamophobia industrial complex   49

Tables

2.1	Categories of Islamophobia	30
3.1	Conspiracy theories that promote Islamophobia	36
5.1	Key groups involved in the Islamophobia industry in Canada	79
5.2	Strategies used to promote Islamophobia	80
6.1	Media strategies to help mainstream and platform the extreme far right	107
9.1	Ten dominant counter-narratives to Islamophobia	147

Acknowledgements

Many thanks to those whom I have closely collaborated with on research projects and/or on writing together about issues connected with Islamophobia, racism, refugee experiences, and related topics. These include Rowena Arshad, Jen Bagelman, Matthew Benwell, Katherine Botterill, John Clayton, Mattias de Backer, Kevin Dunn, Robin Finlay, Malcolm Hill, Kathrin Hörschelmann, David Howard, Rik Huizinga, Elisabeth Kirndörfer, Kawtar Najib, Anoop Nayak, Elizabeth Olson, Raksha Pande, Rachel Pain, Michael Richardson, Gurchathen Sanghera, Susan J. Smith, Ilse van Liempt, and Joel White. A special thank you to Heather Smith for our ongoing work together on issues of anti-racism in teaching, research, and engagement.

I have been very lucky to work with and learn from some very sharp and insightful postdoctoral researchers over the last ten years. Many thanks to Katherine Botterill, Robin Finlay, Malene Jacobsen, Kawtar Najib, and Joel White. Many thanks to Kawtar for her helpful comments and points of clarification on my discussion on the French context, and to Joel and Malene for insightful observations on an earlier draft. And many thanks too to those who have supported my thinking or work in other ways, through conversations, writing groups, or other forms of mutual support, including Iman Atta, Jen Bagelman, Smajo Beso, James Carr, Kelechi Dibie, Amina Easat-Daas, Soudeh Ghaffari, Simon Guy, Majid Khosravinik, Elaine Lopez, Djermana Seta, Sonja Sharma, Liz Todd, and Irene Zempi. Many thanks to Jessa Loomis, Ingrid Medby, and Emma Ormerod for setting up the weekly writing group meetings in Geography and to the 'writing superheroes' group, including Sonja Marzi, Rachel Pain, and Zuriatunfadzliah Sahdan for writing support, motivation, and inspiration. A massive thank you is also due to Georgina Weaver for her outstanding copyediting work. Finally, many thanks to the ongoing support of Emily Watt, Anna Richardson, and Angela Gage at Bristol University Press.

I am very thankful indeed to the Leverhulme Trust for the award of a Major Fellowship [MRF-2022-112], without which I would not have had the time to commit to writing this book. The Arts and Humanities Research Council [grant number AH/K000594/1] supported the work on the everyday geopolitics of ethnic and religious minority young people (with Katherine Botterill, Gurchathen Sanghera, and Rowena Arshad). The research on Muslim youth and political participation (with Robin Finlay) was funded by the Institute for Social Renewal at Newcastle University. The work to undertake an inquiry into Islamophobia in Scotland was supported by the Economic and Social Research Council, Impact Acceleration Account Grant [ES/T501827/1] at Newcastle University.

1

Introduction

Islamophobia – anti-Muslim racism – has become a daily occurrence for Muslims around the world and those who are mistaken for being Muslim (Runnymede Trust, 2024). The United Nations (UN) Special Rapporteur on Freedom of Religion or Belief reported that Islamophobia has 'escalated to epidemic proportions' (Shaheed, 2021: 1). In this context, I set out what *everyday Islamophobia* is and introduce the *Islamophobia industrial complex* that empowers its distribution, enables its operation, and keeps it going. Rather than seeing everyday Islamophobia as some sort of *low-level* or mundane, daily form of Islamophobia – and thus in contrast to the more international forms of Islamophobia that may be regarded as more spectacular – I offer an expansive review of everyday Islamophobia, which considers the diverse factors that shape it from global and national politics through to issues of the media and stereotypes of gender, migration, and the body. I consider the impact it has on its victims and on wider society, explore responses to this, and review strategies for addressing it.

Recorded Islamophobic incidents are so numerous that this book can only attempt to outline a few examples that highlight the nature and severity of the issue at hand. On 14 September 2015, a 14-year-old student, Ahmed Mohamed, was attending MacArthur High School in Irving, Texas.

> The young student of Sudanese descent was an aspiring engineer, who brought a clock he built to impress his teachers. Instead, one of his teachers accused him of making a bomb, leading to his arrest. Ahmed was released and the case received national attention, getting Ahmed invitations to the White House and talk shows. (Selod et al, 2024: 24)

Ahmed's clock was confiscated by his teacher, and he was sent to the office of the school principal. He was later handcuffed and quizzed by the police for 90 minutes at a juvenile detention centre, where he had his fingerprints and photograph taken. He was also given a three-day suspension from school (Jangbar, 2022). Several factors interconnected here to lead to Mohamed being treated with suspicion, including his name, his skin colour, the events of 9/11 (for example, Elfenbein, 2021) when the religion of Islam was 'hijacked' (Iftikhar, 2016: xiii) leading to the subsequent 'war on terror', and the general lack of trust and wariness of Muslims and those who may be perceived to 'look Muslim'.

A few years after Ahmed experienced Islamophobia at school in Texas, on 15 March 2019, in Christchurch, New Zealand, Brenton Tarrant killed 51 people and injured at least another 50 during Friday prayers at Al Noor Mosque and Linwood Islamic Centre. He live-streamed his attack, declaring 'Europa rises!' He was a fitness instructor who lived in Dunedin in New Zealand and had previously lived in New South Wales, Australia, and embodied what Poynting (2020: 76) refers to as a 'form of white nationalist anti-Muslim racism'. The Australian white supremacist had produced a 74-page manifesto that was called 'Great Replacement' and contained key points from some of the main conspiracy theories that are reinforced by white supremacists, such as the 'white genocide', which I discuss in Chapter 3. This document was 'highly reminiscent of the longer "compendium" of mass murderer Anders Behring Breivik' (Poynting, 2020: 75), who killed eight people by detonating a van outside the government headquarters in Oslo and then killed scores of teenagers in a massacre at a summer camp on the island of Utoya on 22 July 2011, leaving 77 people dead, most of whom were in their late teens (Bangstad, 2014).

Ten years after the Breivik massacre, Nathaniel Veltman deliberately drove a truck at high speed into a Pakistani Muslim family in London, Ontario, Canada on 6 June 2021, killing four people and three generations of the same family as they were out on an evening stroll through their local neighbourhood.

> Police called this deadly incident an Islamophobic hate crime and stated that the Afzaal family, hit by a speeding truck, were targeted because of their Muslim faith. A nine-year-old boy survived the attack but was left hospitalized with serious injuries. This was the second mass murder of Canadian Muslims in four years, following the shooting in a Quebec mosque on 29 January 2017, where six Muslim men were killed after their evening prayers. (Zine, 2022a: 14–15)

In 2023, Germany reported unprecedented levels of Islamophobia: a 140 per cent increase on the previous year (Goldmann, 2024). And in the year to February 2024, there was a 335 per cent increase in hate incidents against Muslims in the UK (Runnymede Trust, 2024). More recently still, in August 2024, the UK witnessed Islamophobic rioting in several towns and cities, when far-right demonstrators caused widespread civil unrest, arson, looting, racist graffiti, violence, and brutality targeted at immigration centres, hotels housing asylum seekers, and at least 14 mosques.

It might be easy for some to dismiss these high-profile incidents as one-offs, conducted by a 'lone wolf' or as exceptional and out of the ordinary, unlikely ever to happen again. However, they are accompanied by widespread negative societal discourses and views expressed about Muslims and Islam. Although it is difficult to provide exact numbers of incidents and participants because of the challenges of under-reporting and different systems of monitoring such events in different countries, there is widespread agreement that Islamophobia is a matter of increasing concern (Shaheed, 2021). For example, in surveys conducted in Europe in 2018 and 2019, an average of 37 per cent of the population reported that they held unfavourable views of Muslims. The European Union Agency for Fundamental Rights (2024) reported on their survey of 9,604 Muslims living in 13 member states of the European Union that half of those surveyed felt discriminated against in the last five years and 38 per cent said that they had done so in the last year. Key areas in which Muslims experienced racial discrimination in the last five years were employment (39 per cent when looking for work and 35 per cent when at work) and housing (35 per cent). In 2017, some '30 per cent of respondents to a survey conducted in the United States of America viewed Muslims in a negative light' (Shaheed, 2021: 2). Green (2015: 2) reports that 63 per cent of citizens in the Netherlands felt Islam was incompatible with modern life; in France, 74 per cent felt that Islam was opposed to French society; and, in the UK, fewer than one in four people felt that Islam was compatible with life in the UK. Further, '[a]n Amnesty report found that between 2013 and 2015, there was a nearly 87 per cent increase in violent racism crimes primarily targeting German Muslims' (Iftikhar, 2021: 82). In the United States, '53 percent of Americans hold views of Islam described either as "not favorable at all" or "not too favorable"' (Green, 2015: 2). In a survey in the UK, Jones and Unsworth found that 25.9 per cent 'feel negative towards Muslims. This compares with 8.5% for Jewish people, 6.4% for black people, and 8.4% for white people' (Jones and Unsworth, 2024: 10). They also note that, alarmingly, 18.1 per cent of respondents supported a 'Muslim ban', and this was between 6.3 per cent and 3.4 per cent higher than a ban for any other ethnic or religious grouping (Jones and Unsworth, 2024).

Muslims report awareness of these sentiments; 63 per cent in the UK felt that there was more prejudice against them than there was against any other religious group (All-Party Parliamentary Group on British Muslims, 2018). This is highlighted in a recent piece by Al-Sabawi et al (2024) who refer to a recent Gallup report that found that at least one in four Muslims thought they were not treated fairly in countries where they are a minority. Indeed, even in contexts where the Muslim population is very small – such as in

East Central Europe – higher rates of Islamophobic attitudes can be found (Narkowicz and Pedziwiatr, 2017; Kalmar, 2024).

In recognition of the situation, the UN declared 15 March – the day of the deadly attacks in Christchurch in 2019 – the International Day to Combat Islamophobia, and on 15 March 2024 the UN General Assembly passed a resolution on measures to counter Islamophobia (A/78/264). The European Commission has a Coordinator for Combating anti-Muslim hatred, the Canadian government has a Special Representative on Combatting Islamophobia, there is a Special Envoy to Combat Islamophobia in Australia, and there are many voluntary and community groups, charities, and other organizations that seek to measure, monitor, and map Islamophobic incidents, while some also offer support and advice to victims. Examples include TellMAMA in the UK, the Islamophobia Register Australia, the Council for American Islamic Relations, the Muslim Anti-Racist Collective in New Zealand, the Collective for Countering Islamophobia in Europe, and CLAIM (Alliance Against Islamophobia and Anti-Muslim Hate) in Germany, to name only a few.

Researching Islamophobia

As a middle-class white academic who researches Islamophobia, I am often asked what brought me to research this topic. Usually in a well-intentioned manner, I am quizzed about my interest in the topic, why and how I research it, and how I encourage people to speak to me about their experiences. Others still question the validity of my research as an outsider to the community and make assumptions that Muslims only speak to other Muslims and not to anyone outside their community. As such, the focus of my research has generated a fair amount of intrigue from some but has also been accompanied by rejection and dismissal by others.

As I have written about elsewhere, the multiple positions occupied by a researcher in relation to the communities in which they work are often a lot more complex than those that see a person as simply a complete outsider or insider (Hopkins, 2009). Most people occupy positions of inbetweenness that locate them in neither of these positions, even if they are perceived by some to be a complete insider or outsider (see Sanghera and Thapar-Bjoker [2008] for a useful discussion of related issues). For example, in my earlier work, I made the point that I was an outsider as a non-Muslim and as a white person but shared characteristics with my young Scottish male research participants as I am also a Scottish man and was relatively young at the time of doing the research. My view remains that what I am researching and why I am doing it is more important than evaluating the quality of research based only on perceptions of the position of a researcher as a fixed insider or outsider. This is why I continue to focus on issues that I think are important – such as those associated with the unfair and unjust exclusion of people stemming from Islamophobia – and to do so from a position that is motivated by anti-racism and prioritizes the lived experiences of those involved.

To provide some further context to my interest in and motivation for doing this work, I here consider some of my lived experiences in relation to the topic of this book. I grew up in the south side of Glasgow, Scotland's largest city, in the 1980s and 1990s and attended a large non-denominational state-funded (that is, not private) secondary school that was one of the most ethnically diverse schools in Scotland (Hopkins, 2024). The primary schools that feed into this secondary school – and the local neighbourhoods where they are located – comprise the catchment area of the secondary school I attended, which include several working-class areas and a smaller number of middle-class neighbourhoods, although some wealthier middle-class parents send their children to private schools such as the nearby Hutcheson's Grammar that was attended by both Humza Yousaf, the former Scottish First Minister, and Anas Sarwar, the leader of the Scottish Labour Party. Some of these areas are ethnically diverse, such as Pollokshields and Govanhill, where around half of the local population have a South Asian ethnicity and approximately 40 per cent identify as Muslim (Hopkins and Smith, 2008). In several of my classes, Scottish Pakistani Muslims were the largest grouping (Hopkins, 2024), and I recall sitting a Latin exam, aged 16, in a large examination hall with the other 20 or so mostly white students in my class. At the other side of the examination hall, just as many students (and possibly more accommodated elsewhere) – almost all of whom were Pakistani Muslims – were writing their responses to their Urdu examination.

There was a short period of unrest in 1992 when pupils of the school were attacked by a gang armed with knives and baseballs bats. Some pupils in my year were injured, and local shops – such as the newsagent near where my late grandmother lived – were wrecked and the stock stolen or damaged. These events and the tensions that existed in the local community at the time contributed to my interests in social inequalities and injustices, particularly those focused on issues of race and religion. Alongside this, one of my favourite subjects at school was religious studies, for which the curriculum at the time covered issues such as feminist theology and Christianity and Marxism as well as focusing on another of the world religions. In the school I was attending, the world religion we studied was Islam. From this, I learnt a lot about the basic principles and foundations of the Islamic faith, including the five pillars, I completed a special project focusing on Hajj, and our teacher took us on a trip to visit the local mosque. What I learnt in these classes sparked an interest in Islam and Muslim identity, and I quickly realized that what is essentially a religion that promotes peace was frequently misrepresented, regularly demonized, and often misunderstood.

Shortly before I commenced my doctoral studies at the University of Edinburgh in 2001, the events of 9/11 changed the world, especially for Muslims, as much research has demonstrated. So, while I had initially planned to study Asian youth identities in contemporary Scotland, I was drawn to focus my research on the lived experiences of young Muslim men, given that much research had already focused upon the accounts of young Muslim women in research in geography (Bowlby et al, 1998; Dwyer, 1999; Mohammad, 1999; Bowlby and Lloyd-Evans, 2009). So, I ended up completing a doctoral study that used focus groups and interviews to explore the identities and experiences of young Muslim men in Scotland, with an important focus being their experiences of, and responses to, racism and Islamophobia following the events of 9/11 (Hopkins, 2007). Since this work in the early 2000s, my interest in Islamophobia has continued, and I have supervised several doctoral projects and worked on some individual and many collaborative studies on issues relating to Muslim identities, racism, Islamophobia, social exclusion, and social justice.

So, part of my motivation for writing this book comes from my own lived experiences alongside the individual and collective scholarship I have been engaged with mostly in the UK and what I have learnt about through conferences, thesis examining, and other forms of academic engagement. Based on my reflections on researching Islamophobia over the last 25 years in the UK – as well as collaborative work in France and Australia – and the recent public inquiry into Islamophobia in Scotland (Hopkins, 2021), I have become increasingly dissatisfied with the ways in which Islamophobia is discussed and debated, and the barriers that present themselves or work to close down open conversation on this topic when it arises.

Contributions

There are five interconnected sets of contributions that I hope to make in writing this book. First, this book contributes by offering clarity around the meaning of Islamophobia and how it operates. Part of my intention in this book is to explore the key debates about Islamophobia, what it means, and the forms it takes. I want to move beyond public and political debate that often operates to discredit the very idea of Islamophobia and to recognize this as an everyday issue that has serious consequences in the lives of many people who are Muslim and others who are assumed to be Muslim. To constantly discuss terminology only restricts further discussion about the nature of Islamophobia, how it operates in everyday life, and how it can be challenged and overcome. I have no issue with ensuring that terminology is used properly and that problems are well defined and clearly set out. However, despite there being several carefully articulated definitions of Islamophobia in circulation, I too often find myself in contexts where the definition itself becomes the sole focus of conversation, with little or no attention given to important issues such as how to challenge Islamophobia, how to report it, or how to resist or overcome it. There seems to be an obsession with the 'phobia' part of the word (Birt, 2009), yet the same level of attention is rarely given to terms used similarly, such as 'homophobia', 'xenophobia', 'Romaphobia', or 'fatphobia'. Moreover, other forms of discrimination, exclusion, and harassment, such as sexism, ageism, classism, or antisemitism are rarely questioned to the same extent. As such, one of my motivations for writing this book is to place everyday Islamophobia centre stage and to focus on its operation, giving it the in-depth attention it warrants without being distracted or sidelined by debates about terminology.

I introduce the idea of the Islamophobia industrial complex to help explain the ways that everyday Islamophobia operates. My aim here is to demonstrate that everyday Islamophobia is not low-level, banal, or trivial but is instead embroiled in a much larger and more complicated set of relationships with global geopolitics, the media, and the international network of funders working to promote Islamophobia. It is crucial to understand this to appreciate how it operates and, as Manzoor-Khan (2022) notes, the work that Islamophobia does. 'And how understanding its function is central to understanding how we can build a world that is safe for all oppressed, exploited and marginalized people, rather than a world that is "secure" for nation-states to repress, and imperialist capitalist interests to accumulate profit' (Manzoor-Khan, 2022: 3).

Second, in exploring everyday Islamophobia, I hope that this book contributes to several key fields of inquiry. First, the principal contribution here is to the interdisciplinary field of Islamophobia studies, which is an engaged and critical field of inquiry focused on exposing the complex workings of Islamophobia in different contexts (for example, Sayyid, 2014; Zempi and Awan, 2019; Zine, 2022a). Added to this, my exploration of everyday Islamophobia contributes to debates in ethnic and racial studies, to ethnic and migration studies, and to explorations of the intersections of race and religion. Most work in these fields is about Islamophobia in Muslim minority contexts, and this book largely draws upon this context in setting out what everyday Islamophobia is. The point about interdisciplinarity is important here, as the specific ways in which Islamophobia is studied mean that there are sometimes quite disparate sets of fields exploring the issue on their own terms and within their own frames of reference with little mention of other disciplines or across different domains. For example, some studies prioritize a focus on issues of counterterrorism and are deeply embedded within the logic, debates, and issues arising in this field. This work is important but sometimes only focuses on these issues and thereby plays down or overlooks the everyday lived experience of Islamophobia. Other studies prioritize the provision of rich critiques of policy interventions or political strategies, often doing so in a highly sophisticated way with relatively little attention outside the policy domain. Rather than being limited by a specific disciplinary focus or domain, my intention is that this book will speak across disciplines and research foci, providing a focus on the diverse operation of everyday Islamophobia.

Third – and building upon my second point – there is a sometimes a tendency to focus both on the *global* and *transnational* issues, and in so doing pay attention to the big picture, and the more sensationalized incidents of Islamophobia such as some of the incidents I referred to in the Introduction. Both tendencies can work to make invisible the everyday, trivialize people's everyday experiences, emotions, feelings, and practices (Horschelmann, 2007; Pain and Smith, 2007; Hopkins, 2022). Focusing only on the *big* issues can work to place Islamophobia in the limited spaces of international political platforms or transnational affairs, or in the contexts of global geopolitics. This assumption sees Islamophobia happening 'up above'. The second tendency locates Islamophobia in locations where specific terrorist incidents have taken place, whether that be New York in the case of 9/11, Paris in the case of the *Charlie Hebdo* shootings, or in London given the events of 7/7. Except for those who live in these places, such an approach places Islamophobia 'over there' and therefore positions it at a distance, far away, remote, and isolated. Combined, these two tendencies risk placing Islamophobia as a remote outlier, positioned as it is 'up above' and 'over there'. Such an understanding depersonalizes, externalizes, and distances Islamophobia rather than seeing it as something that happens here and now, intimately and in close quarters. My view is that there is a continuing need to challenge the prioritization of the global in a fixed hierarchy of influence without downplaying the significance of specific political decisions and geopolitics. One of the many intentions of this book is to demonstrate the complex relations between and within the global and the intimate, the transnational and the body, and the geopolitical and the everyday. There are the rich, textured, and detailed accounts of everyday Islamophobia that pay attention to the ways in which it is experienced on the ground, including how it is felt and embodied, and how it is resisted and contested. Such work is more likely to be informed by feminist research or activist work. I am eager to platform such work but to do so in way that contextualizes it within the broader Islamophobia industrial complex that is crucial to its operation. Added to this are case study-based examples of research in which the focus tends to be around a specific issue – such as a mosque proposal or a political or terrorist incident – and to have a relatively localized or national frame of reference.

While my work has constantly been drawn to the complex ways in which Islamophobia is experienced in specific contexts, the significance of the everyday, localized, and interpersonal nature of Islamophobia has been a key focus. This context is referred to in some existing work, a lot of which I cover in this book, but there is a tendency to draw more attention to the nation-state, to transnational issues, global politics, or geopolitical contestations, which downplays, marginalizes, or excludes and omits the significance of the everyday lived experiences and negotiations of Islamophobia on the ground and in everyday life. The experiences of those who encounter Islamophobia are grounded in the everyday, experienced on the street, in the school playground, or on public transport; these experiences are intimate, deeply personal, and felt on and in the body. However, these experiences are shaped by a complex set of issues, including those circulating globally and transnationally as well as those shaped by national policy or informed by state politics. My hope, then, is for a more integrative focus that brings together these different domains so that everyday Islamophobia can be appreciated as a complex phenomenon that is not only grounded in everyday lived experience but is shaped by a diverse set of interweaving factors, including global politics and events, transnational and supranational issues, national politics and state policy initiatives, as well as issues occurring regionally, in cities, suburbs, and rural and remote contexts, in local communities, neighbourhoods, and homes.

Fourth, I am eager to consider how Islamophobia intersects and overlaps with other forms of discrimination and marginalization alongside the ways in which it alters according to specific national, regional, and local contexts. As I make clear in Chapter 2, we know that Islamophobia is experienced in very different ways by Muslim women and by Muslim men (for example, Easat-Daas and Zempi, 2024) and shaped by other markers of social difference such as those associated with ethnicity, sexuality, class, and migration status. Throughout this book, I point to the ways in which everyday Islamophobia works against different groups of Muslims including, for example, Muslim women, Muslim refugees, and Muslims running community organizations, to demonstrate how it operates as it intersects with other identity categories and forms of power and oppression.

Fifth, I am insistent that it is crucial to consider what can be done to address Islamophobia. I do not see the study of Islamophobia as simply an academic exercise, but one that should ideally connect with those experiencing it and with those seeking solutions to its harmful presence. I think it is crucial to consider the impact that everyday Islamophobia has on Muslims and those perceived to be Muslim, as well as possible ways to challenge, tackle, and overcome it. I agree that it is important to include the voices of those who endure Islamophobia in our research, and most of the studies I use in this book draw upon the lived experiences of Muslims and other ethnic and religious minority groups mistaken for being Muslim. Moreover, I agree that we must take the perspectives of Muslims seriously in studies of Islamophobia (Kozaric, 2024). However, in addressing the challenges presented by everyday Islamophobia, it would be highly problematic to leave the victims of Islamophobia to address it on their own. I stand with Manzoor-Khan when she says, 'Islamophobia is not a problem for Muslims alone, and cannot be tackled on its own. It is not a single-issue struggle but a problem for the world, related to all racisms, all forms of oppression, border violence, policing, war, environmental catastrophe, gender-based violence and injustice' (2022: 2).

Despite the negativity and suspicion that have sometimes been directed towards me as someone from outside the Muslim community, I have remained committed to conducting ethically sound, grounded research about Islamophobia, given my commitment to anti-racism. My hope is that this book will inform and enable others to be better informed about the complex operation of Islamophobia and thereby be strongly positioned to tackle it.

The structure of this book

Following this introduction, in Chapter 2 I discuss key literatures about Islamophobia and work towards outlining an understanding of everyday Islamophobia. This includes an exploration of some of the key facets of Islamophobia, focusing upon processes of racialization and its relationship to debates about Orientalism, empire, ethnonationalism and the ways in which Muslims and/or Islam are othered. I also examine how Islamophobia can operate as a form of stigmatization, a hate crime, a form of discrimination, and how it can be articulated through its absence or through silence. I consider some of the different categories of Islamophobia and offer an account of everyday Islamophobia.

I set out what I call the Islamophobia industrial complex in Chapter 3. Specific stereotypes that are often employed in Islamophobic discourse are then discussed before I explore the key conspiracy theories that are used to advance racist interpretations of Islam and Muslims. I consider key mechanisms used to circumvent the existence of Islamophobia or to downplay significantly its overall importance. I then examine how extreme far-right ideas and narratives have become increasingly mainstreamed in recent years, which provides an ideal platform for the sharing of anti-Muslim sentiment. I end this chapter by outlining the key components of the Islamophobia industrial complex – the financial transactions, companies, organizations, and related forms of commerce that make up the 'Islamophobia industry' (Lean, 2012) and generate significant profits by promoting Islamophobia. I look at the main actors involved in this and touch upon the ways in which they work in collaboration as a powerful engine promoting Islamophobia globally.

After this third chapter, the book is organized into five main chapters that explore how everyday Islamophobia operates across a range of different domains. These five chapters are best read in order, as they build upon each other, and Chapters 4 and 5 set out some of the key mechanisms that support the operation of everyday Islamophobia and so provide for understanding how everyday Islamophobia works in the context of the issues discussed in Chapters 6, 7 and 8.

Concerns about global issues, the global 'war on terror' and related counterterrorism initiatives, in addition to Islamophobic state-sponsored strategies and policies, are the focus of Chapter 4. I draw attention to Trump's Muslim ban in the United States and China's treatment of Uyghur Muslims as specific examples of explicit Islamophobia being enacted on a nationwide scale. In contrast to this – and to provide an example of the denial of Islamophobia – I look at France to consider how the promotion of a specific form of secularism can lead to the closing down of debate about the very existence of Islamophobia as a phenomenon and the forced closure of a respected organization set up to monitor and challenge Islamophobia.

In Chapter 5, I discuss the role of powerful and highly influential transnational networks that actively promote Islamophobia and constitute the 'Islamophobia industry' (Lean, 2012) and I look at how these work in the United States and Canada. I provide specific examples of how such networks operate, including the controversy they helped to generate around the so-called Ground Zero mosque. I also focus on the role of think tanks in promoting Islamophobia, pointing to the very close relationship that these often have with both the media and with politics and government, and then I consider the role of the media, including social media, print and broadcast media, and the impact of trigger events. Together, Chapters 4 and 5 explore the key actors in the Islamophobia industrial complex, who often work together to promote, platform, and share Islamophobia.

The three chapters that follow focus on the areas that are more traditionally associated with everyday Islamophobia. Experiences of Islamophobia in community settings and local neighbourhoods, in public spaces and in daily mobility practices – such as the journey to school or work, or negotiations of airport security – are the focus of Chapter 6. I explore initially the ways in which everyday Islamophobia manifests through the segregation versus integration debate, before setting out how anti-Muslim narratives feature in discussion about refugee dispersal, resettlement, and integration. I then turn to daily mobility practices and the encounters with Islamophobia that are a feature of these before touching upon the mechanisms by which Muslims are often racially profiled as they negotiate airport security. Attention is then drawn to the explicit experiences of everyday Islamophobia through Islamophobic riots and public protests such as Quran burning.

Maintaining a focus upon the local context, in Chapter 7, I turn my attention to contestations over the location and presence of mosques and religious venues and experiences of Islamophobia in educational institutions and places of work. The ways in which Islamophobia features in the process of seeking approval for new mosques are discussed before I consider how mosques and religious buildings have become key targets for those wanting to directly express Islamophobia. I then explore spaces of education and the promotion of anti-Muslim sentiment through national policies inspired by the global war on terror, which result in the surveillance of Muslim students. Finally, I examine how Islamophobia can be produced through problematic workplace cultures.

In the penultimate chapter, Chapter 8, I examine the ways in which Islamophobia is experienced on the body, in the context of the home and family relationships, and how it can be encountered through misrecognition, as those bodies that are read as Muslim but are not experience Islamophobia as a result. I consider the impact of the 'Punish a Muslim Day' letters and expand upon the idea of embodied Islamophobia (Mansson McGinty, 2020) that was referred to in Chapter 2. A key concern of this chapter is the obsession with clothing and the focus on the veil as an overdetermined marker of difference.

In Chapter 9, the final chapter, I consider the impact of Islamophobia and possible ways to tackle it. First, I explore some of the impacts that everyday Islamophobia has on its victims. These include social, emotional, and spatial impacts, as well as the medical and health-related problems resulting from regularly experiencing Islamophobia. In the second half of this chapter, I turn to focus on what is being done to challenge, resist, and ideally overcome everyday Islamophobia, emphasizing the need to abolish the Islamophobia industrial complex by working either to eliminate completely key parts of it or by constraining and minimizing the influence of other aspects. I end by exploring possibilities for collaborative and collective working in partnership with Muslim communities, many of which have developed sophisticated strategies of resistance in response to the harmful presence of everyday Islamophobia.

2

What is Everyday Islamophobia?

In this chapter, I explore what Islamophobia is by offering some definitions of the word and touching on some of the contestations in relation to it. I explore the factors that shape it, explaining processes of racialization that provide its foundation. I also consider issues of Orientalism, empire, and ethnonationalism as additional factors that shape contemporary Islamophobia, and which often intersect and interact with processes of racialization. I then discuss the principal manifestations of Islamophobia, which include stigma, discrimination, and hate crime, as well as the ways in which Islamophobia can present through absences and silences.

To set out a clear approach to everyday Islamophobia, I first explore the different categories of Islamophobia that have been the subject of research, including historical, institutional and structural, intellectual and political, interpersonal, internalized, representational, intersectional, spatialized, and embodied Islamophobias. Although these categories are not always distinct from each other – and indeed, many of them overlap and interconnect in powerful ways – it is important to appreciate each of these to understand everyday Islamophobia. Drawing inspiration from Essed's (2002) work on everyday racism, I then offer an account of everyday Islamophobia.

What is Islamophobia?

Although the word 'Islamophobia' 'first appears in its French form, *Islamophobie*, in a book by the painter Etienne Dinet in 1918' (Green, 2015: 9), the history of the idea suggests that it was a combination of the 1979 Iranian revolution and the end of the Cold War and collapse of the Soviet Union in 1991 that resulted in Muslims and Islam becoming a key focus of global concern (Bazian, 2018).

> The watershed moment for the emergence of Islamophobia ... all-encompassing and undifferentiated in terms of sect and group, is directly

connected to the collapse of the Soviet Union, the immediate outcome of the 1st Gulf War, and the Palestinian uprising which provided the stage for problematizing Islam and Muslims as a single threatening subject. (Bazian, 2018: 5)

However, it was not until the late 1990s that the term became more widely used. The Runnymede Trust (1997) published its landmark report on Islamophobia in the late 1990s, and its definition is referred to in much research in Europe, North America, and Australia (for example, Dunn et al, 2007; Poynting and Mason, 2007; Allen, 2010; Esposito and Kalin, 2011): 'The term Islamophobia refers to unfounded hostility towards Islam. It refers also to the practical consequences of such hostility in unfair discrimination against Muslim individuals and communities, and to the exclusion of Muslims from mainstream political and social affairs' (Runnymede Trust, 1997: 4). Several examples were provided that characterized open and closed views of Islam. Open views of Islam focused on it being diverse, interactive, sincere, and considered, whereas closed views considered it monolithic, separate, inferior, and manipulative. While the Runnymede Trust (1997) admitted that this definition was not ideal, and insightful critiques have been offered of the open and closed approach (for example, Allen, 2010), Vakil (2010) confirms that there was a new set of everyday experiences and realities that needed naming and acting upon. Similarly, Green (2015: 3) notes that 'Islamophobia refers to the fear, hatred, and hostility toward Muslims and Islam'.

Prior to 9/11, understandings of Islamophobia had focused more on issues of anti-Muslim discrimination, with little explicit reference to issues of race or racialization, but a follow-up report by the Runnymede Trust (Elahi and Khan, 2017: 2), 20 years after the Trust's initial definition, states specifically that 'Islamophobia is anti-Muslim racism'. It further offers a longer definition that builds on the United Nations' definition of racism.

> Islamophobia is any distinction, exclusion, or restriction towards, or preference against, Muslims (or those perceived to be Muslims) that has the purpose or effect of nullifying or impairing the recognition, enjoyment or exercise, on an equal footing, of human rights and fundamental freedoms in the political, economic, social, cultural or any other field of public life. (Elahi and Khan, 2017: 2)

It is now widely recognized that these issues of race and racialization play a central role in Islamophobia. 'Although the original application of the term centred on a fear of Islam, several scholars have articulated the ways that race and racism are central to the concept, allowing it to capture anti-Muslim racism' (Selod et al, 2024: 5).

In 2018, the All Party Parliamentary Group on British Muslims in the UK parliament collected evidence and reviewed submissions to develop a working definition of Islamophobia. It found three key factors as being crucial. First, there are *processes* of Islamophobia. Second, there are specific *actions* that are Islamophobic, and third, there is the *impact* of Islamophobia. It notes that 'Islamophobia is rooted in racism and is a type of racism that targets expressions of Muslimness or perceived Muslimness' (All Party Parliamentary Group on British Muslims, 2018: 11). This last point is echoed by Younis (2024: 33), who sees Islamophobia as the 'management of ideal Muslim subjectivity', or, put differently, Islamophobia is about the ways in which different aspects of being a Muslim – or measures or performances of Muslimness – are policed.

Since its coming into general use, there have been contestations over and objections to the term 'Islamophobia' from a range of sources. Shaheed (2021) points out that 'Islamophobia' is often the preferred term among policy makers, scholars, and activists, but that in some quarters there is a preference for 'anti-Muslim hatred', given the concern that 'Islamophobia' can be seen to prevent any critique of Islam. It is important to note, of course, that 'one can disagree with and criticise the beliefs and practices of Muslims without being Islamophobic' (Green, 2015: 20). However, there are those who challenge and contest this alternative term, arguing that it omits those who employ anti-Islamic discourses. Others prefer the term 'anti-Muslim racism': 'Often the term "anti-Muslim racism" is preferred over Islamophobia, as it is seen to better capture the phenomenon of discrimination against Muslims and solves the problem that critics of Islamophobia hold by separating out criticism of Islam' (Zine, 2022a: 17). Further critiques of the term 'Islamophobia' include suggestions that it overlooks anti-black racism because the concept has been rooted in the experiences of Arabs and South Asians (Beydoun, 2017).

There is validity, certainly, in raising awareness of the issues implicit in terminology: 'The definitional debates surrounding Islamophobia are important to consolidate its meaning and intelligibility and because language and discourse are constitutive of social relations' (Zine, 2022a: 13). However, although a number of definitions exist – many of which focus on similar issues – and alternatives have been offered, there is a tendency in some quarters to question the very legitimacy of specific definitions.

> Many critiques have been levied against the terms Islamophobia over the years: it's not a racism; it's not irrational; it conflates a critique of Islam with hate towards Muslims; it doesn't focus enough on Islam; it restricts freedoms of speech etc. ... Of the criticisms, one stands out for the purpose of our discussion: incoherence. As Vakil (2010: 271) relates, Islamophobia is 'essentially contested as both phenomenon and term, both in what it names and as a name'; Vakil reminds us,

however, that the lack of consensus in definition and inconsistency can be found in every concept. (Younis, 2024: 35)

I agree with Younis (2024) here and feel that the focus on debating definitions of Islamophobia acts a distraction from addressing its operation and impacts. Arguing that a specific definition is too complex is a denial, which leads us to what Lean (2019: 13) refers to as an 'unnecessary etymological roundabout', where we spend lots of time debating the history, development, authenticity, and meaning of a phrase or term, and essentially end up going round in circles and not moving forward in our attempts to address the issue itself. The constant debate about the term is itself a form of Islamophobia. The Runnymede Trust (2024: 5) makes the point that a key method used to discredit Islamophobia is through 'semantic diversion'. Indeed, I have found myself in countless meetings and fora where much of the time and a lot of the debate – including in in-person meetings or on the online 'chat' – are about definitions of Islamophobia and preferences for specific phrases or terms rather than there being a focus on the experiences of it on the ground or on actions to tackle it. This can generate a kind of groupthink in which questions about Islamophobia – or any resistances to the term – are met with a quiet form of consensus among the group rather than leading to a critical conversation about Islamophobia and how to address it.

So, Islamophobia is a form of anti-Muslim racism, and an act is Islamophobic if it targets Muslims, or people who are perceived to be Muslim, even if they are not religious or are following another religion. There are many examples of the types of actions or behaviours that constitute Islamophobia, and it is useful to refer to some here. Islamophobia includes promoting the harming or killing of Muslims and promoting generalized and homogenizing stereotypes of Muslims that demonize them, for example, promoting the myth that all Muslims are terrorists or that all Muslim women are oppressed. Being Islamophobic includes holding all Muslims responsible for an event, problem, issue, or challenge that is deemed to have been caused by a Muslim. The result here is that Muslims can be scapegoated and essentially held responsible for specific social ills. Islamophobia also includes suggesting that Muslims are disloyal to the 'West' and/or more committed to the Islamic world than they are to the places in which they live. It includes the employment of symbols, images, or representations that are anti-Muslim or Islamophobic, or the denial of access to a venue, space, group, or context, or the provision of services, based on a person's perceived identification as a Muslim or their perceived affiliation with Islam. Insisting that Muslims actively condemn in a public forum the specific actions of others is also Islamophobic, as is the use of negative, derogatory, hateful, or harmful words, visual imagery, or other form of representation that target Muslims or Islam.

Racialization

Central to understanding and appreciating Islamophobia as anti-Muslim racism is understanding the processes and practices of racialization (for example, Sayyid, 2014; Carr and Haynes, 2015; Gardell, 2015; Selod, 2015, 2019; de Koning, 2016; Meer and Modood, 2019; Modood, 2019; Vakil and Sayyid, 2023; Aziz and Esposito, 2024; Uddin, 2024). Omi and Winant (1986: 111) define racialization as 'the extension of racial meaning to a previously racially unclassified relationship, social practice, or group'. Part of the challenge here is appreciating the complex ways in which racialization often operates, given its relationship to racism, which is itself fluid and ever-changing. This is about the processes 'by which bodies become racial in their lived realities' as different 'cultural, biological, and embodied qualities and traits end up resulting in the denial of equal treatment in society' (Selod, 2018: 23).

> Racialization is a concept that allows for an understanding of how groups of people are read and understood in racial terms ... racialization enables us to think about how a religious identity acquires racial meaning without relying only on phenotypical or biological factors, like skin tone, which allows for its use in countries that do not acknowledge racial classifications. (Selod et al, 2024: 13)

What happens here is that specific practices – such as wearing a headscarf, walking to the mosque, or eating a curry – are read through the lens of race and racialization. Indeed, even those who are white but engage in such activities are racialized as Muslims (Moosavi, 2015; Hyokki, 2022). Hence, there is now widespread agreement that Islamophobia is a form of racism. Kundnani (2015: 11) refers to the 'racialization of Muslimness' and explains that 'since all racisms are socially and politically constructed rather than reliant on the reality of any biological race, it is perfectly possible for cultural markers associated with Muslimness (forms of dress, rituals, language, etc.) to be turned into racial signifiers' (Kundnani, 2015: 11).

Part of the challenge of appreciating processes of racialization is that there are often multiple, complex, and diverse logics of racialization at play, and these processes often interact with other identity characteristics in ways which can make them difficult to detect. These logics also work differently in different places, so the specific operation of racialization in Australia may be very different from how it plays out in Norway, Canada, or Singapore. Further, these logics change over time. Consider this example:

> A racialised Black Muslim man (who sports a beard, for example) will find themselves within *several* logics of racialisation ... the association

of Blackness with gangs, like stop and search policies. Their blackness increases the likelihood of being stopped by the police, but it is their Muslimness which opens the door for a counter-terrorism referral. (Younis, 2024: 26)

Likewise, Selod et al argue that

> racialization is a better theoretical analysis because it allows us to show how religion is racialized and interacts with other identities, such as religion, gender, race, ethnicity, sexual orientation, ability, class, etc., in unique ways ... racialization of religious identity via Muslim men as terrorists and Muslim women as cultural threats justifies security practices that are deeply racialized. (Selod et al, 2024: 6)

They are clear that racism against Muslims is 'part and parcel of racism at large' (Selod et al, 2024: 6), and they go as far as to suggest that 'Muslim racialization is a better way to understand and theorize a 21st century racism that is global' (Selod et al, 2024: 7). Moreover, the racialization of Muslims is also complicated by the fact that, when experiencing Islamophobia, Muslims are also 'encountering racism and racist structures' (Selod et al, 2024: 14); Muslims are racialized in and of themselves but are also often using, encountering, and being part of wider racist structures and systems.

A key point to note here is that Islamophobia is not only about Muslims and is therefore not simply a 'Muslim problem'. There is now quite a long tradition of work that points to the ways it threatens the lives of many ethnic and religious minority groups, including those of different faiths and those without faith (Sanghera and Thapar-Bjokert, 2007; Hopkins et al, 2017; Awan and Zempi, 2020b). This is a result of the ways that markers of Muslim identity have been racialized to the extent that anyone with brown skin, a beard, or a headscarf will be assumed to be Muslim, even though they may be Sikh, Hindu, Christian, or indeed of no faith. For example, Sanghera and Thapar-Bjokert (2007), among others, note that the Sikh community was victimized following 7/7, with gurdwaras being targeted with racist graffiti.

It is also important to emphasize that Muslims – and those mistaken for being Muslim – are racialized in many ways, some or all of which they may not be aware of. I have been in many meetings where specific members of the Muslim community express their frustration with terms like 'Islamophobia' and 'anti-Muslim racism', noting that Muslims are not a race. Indeed, some of the strongest opposition from within specific segments of the Muslim community to the definitions discussed earlier comes from those who express strong distaste at discussions about race and racism. Here, I find Younis' (2024: 25) point useful, that 'Muslims are thus racialized – that is, made sense of – in ways which go beyond their understanding of themselves'.

The racialization of Muslims is, of course, frequently more obvious and less concealed:

> The racialization of Muslim in the 21st century is global in nature. Although the terrorist attacks that incited this war took place in the United States, this new war, one that is waged against terror as opposed to a nation-state, has allowed for counterterrorism law and policies that rely on the construction of a Muslim as a threat to both national security and cultural values to be reproduced and cross borders. (Selod et al, 2024: 2)

'For this to occur, Muslims have been continuously racialized as a threat' (Selod et al, 2024: 15), and it is here that we see the explicit racial profiling of Muslims in the workplace, in educational institutions, and at airports (Considine, 2017).

Finally, racialization processes flow across the globe into specific countries and contexts, sometimes changing and transforming as they do so. Ganesh et al (2024: 899) note that 'flows of Islamophobia' include those connected with migration, information, symbols, and money: 'the first is about flows of people and objects, the second about flows of signs, texts, and images, the third about flows of facts, events, and data. The fourth is about circuits and infrastructure, and the last is about flows of money, resources, and commodities' (Ganesh et al, 2024: 899). They are specific in their use of the term 'flow', as they are eager to appreciate 'Islamophobia as something that circulates and moves along pathways of complex systems of actors, materials, calculation, and protocols' (Ganesh et al, 2024: 899).

They propose that there are several modalities of Islamophobia, of which racialization is one:

- Racialization – The construction and articulation of essential, inherent 'qualities' of Muslimness that apply to a group of people or an internal enemy.
- Group-making – The construction and articulation of an identity under threat from Muslims, often in relation to groups that claim a majority identity that is allegedly under threat from Islam and Muslims.
- Control – Authoritarian and democratic regulations, systems, and processes that affect the mobility, security, and dignity of Muslims.
- Movement – A fundamental aspect of civil society or social movements that seek to advance a private agenda, influence policy, or obtain political power.
- Discourse – The construction of knowledge about Islam and Muslims. (Ganesh et al, 2024: 899)

These modalities are undoubtedly an interesting and useful framework from which to understand how Islamophobia operates, as practices of group-making, control, movement, and discourse interact to shape its global flow and spread. However, my concern with this is that it downplays the significance of racialization as being only one of five modalities. The authors note that they situate 'racialization as one aspect among others to better compare and understand Islamophobia as it manifests in particular contexts' (Ganesh et al, 2024: 898). This framework, then, appears to offer a relatively equal weighting to each of the five modalities. I would contend that all these modalities are racialized, and thus racialization is arguably more significant than – and indeed permeates – the others, and there are perhaps some dangers in downplaying its significance and seeing it as only one of a set of flows in operation.

Orientalism, empire, ethnonationalism, and the othering of Muslims and Islam

Additional factors shaping the nature of contemporary Islamophobia are those associated with a broad set of intersecting issues relating to Orientalism, imperialism, and ethnonationalism (Sayyid, 2003; Zine, 2022a; Beydoun, 2023), which, likewise, intersect with the processes of racialization. It is important to note that these different factors do not operate in isolation but inform and reinforce each other. For example, processes and practices of racialization tend to be informed by discourses of Orientalism. Said's (1978) influential work has contributed to our understanding of Orientalism as a process in which a distinction is made between the Orient (including contexts such as Asia and the Middle East) and the Occident (the West) and where such assumptions are used as a form of control and domination. This promotes a Western and European-centric view of the world and associates the Arab world with being inferior, irrational, violent, primitive, and lacking in enlightenment. Beydoun (2018) refers to the re-use of Orientalist discourses in stereotypes about Muslims:

> These tropes are embedded within popular representations of Muslims, such as news coverage or depictions in film. But more saliently, they are embedded within the institutional memory of government agencies, including the judiciary, the legislature, and the executive branch – most notably, in the Department of Homeland Security and anti-terror law enforcement during the protracted war on terror. (Beydoun, 2018: 37)

Interconnected with these Orientalist ideas, we often find that Islamophobia is also strongly rooted in empire (Kumar, 2017; Kundnani, 2017). Kumar (2021: 7) notes that 'Empire creates the conditions for anti-Muslim racism, and Islamophobia sustains empire' and, as Kundnani (2017) reminds us, violence is always needed to sustain an empire and the violences enacted by those holding power always take on a racial character. He observes how US foreign policy often identifies the Middle East as the most problematic world region, and this is often associated with concerns about a threat associated with Islam. Such discourses of empire feed through into people's everyday lives – often in subtle ways that may go unnoticed by many – and work to embolden and sustain Islamophobia.

In addition to Orientalism and empire, some accounts of Islamophobia are strongly shaped by ethnonationalism. This is a process in which ethnicity and ethnic group membership are regarded as key components of national belonging and used to justify exclusion, violence, and aggression against Muslims. Perhaps one of the best-known examples of this can be seen in the events in Bosnia and Herzegovina in the late 1980s: Karcic (2023) discusses how it became commonplace to represent Slavic Muslims as betraying Orthodox Christianity and to see them as a lesser race with weak genes. He then recounts:

> During 1992–95, an international armed conflict and genocide (the aim of which was establishing a Greater Serbia and Greater Croatia which meant dividing Bosnia and Herzegovina and getting rid of its Muslim population) caused the deaths of at least 100,000 people, 30,000 enforced disappearances, and the rape of 30,000 women and girls. The vast majority of the victims were Bosniaks, whose remains were buried in hundreds of hidden mass graves throughout the country. In addition to this, an estimated 600 mosques and a variety of Islamic religious objects were deliberately destroyed by the Bosnian Serb Army and the Croatian Defence Council. (Karcic, 2023: 114)

Although the 1995 Dayton Peace Agreement brought an end to the war, 'entrenching results of genocide, and cementing the divide in the country' (Karcic, 2023: 115), a sense of interfaith understanding and appreciation remains fragile.

Other examples of ethnonationalism include the situations in India and in China. In the former, a route to citizenship was made available to some religious minorities who were fleeing persecution (such as Hindus, Sikhs, Buddhists, Jains, and Christians), but this was not offered to Muslims, reinforcing an 'ethnonationalist vision of India as a Hindu nation' (Koch and Vora, 2020: 1). I discuss the situation in China in more detail in Chapter 4 but note here that the promotion of a '"Han-centric" ethnonationalism has always been an important threat in Chinese identity narratives' (Koch and Vora, 2020: 1).

A further example of ethnonationalist thinking can be found in the widespread rumour at the time of Obama being elected as US president that suggested he was a Muslim (Aziz and Esposito, 2024; Selod, 2024). Selod (2024: 67) refers to this 'birther movement' as relying on a basic assumption that 'President Obama was not born in the United States but in Kenya' and therefore is 'not an American citizen and ineligible to be president'.

So, Islamophobia is anti-Muslim racism and relies on racialization processes, but, added to this, it is also often shaped by Orientalism, empire, and/or ethnonationalism. Although racialization is dominant here, these issues all operate to promote a view of Muslims as culturally homogeneous and the Muslim community as devoid of any diversity or internal variation.

Forms of Islamophobia: hate crime, stigma, discrimination, and absences

I often hear people directly associate everyday Islamophobia with hate crime as if they are one and the same. Indeed, I find myself in regular conversations with people in which the assumption is that I am a researcher of hate crime because I am studying Islamophobia. Iris Marion Young's (1990) five faces of oppression – exploitation, marginalization, powerlessness, cultural imperialism, and violence – is a useful framework to consider here in terms of how a specific group might be marginalized and oppressed in different ways and through different mechanisms. This presents specific challenges to accurately accounting for Islamophobia, as there is no consistent way of collecting data on such incidents of 'hate crime' and, although some may be recorded and fall within legal definitions of hate crime, many are not fully reported, or fall outside of this definition, and so do not appear in the 'official' statistics. As Campbell (2013: 21) usefully reminds us, there are 'a range of events and practices which are troublesome, unconventional or mischievous, but which are not necessarily unlawful'. She employs the term 'transgression' here to refer to these, and much of which I have discussed earlier could fall within this. So, while some incidents of everyday Islamophobia involve hate crimes that fall within the official definition of the criminological, other incidents do not and are more closely aligned with either stigmatization or discrimination, or a combination of both these as exclusionary transgressions.

Awan and Zempi (2020a) note that hate crime is a broad term that is used to describe an incident or series of targeted incidents generated by a hate or hostility towards specific identities of an individual or group, although people may be targeted for several reasons and can be a target because of their association with Islam or with Muslims even if they do not follow the Islamic religion. Definitions of hate crime vary from country to country, so it is difficult to provide a precise outline here, but it is important to note that some cases of everyday Islamophobia involve forms of hate crime or hate-related violence against Muslims or those perceived to be Muslims. These can include terrorist attacks, damage, and vandalism of mosques and religious buildings, or abusive or threating behaviour such as physical assault.

A lot of everyday Islamophobia is about stigmatization, which Tyler (2020: 17) conceptualizes as 'a practice that, while experienced intimately through stigmatising looks, comments, slights, remarks made face-to-face or digitally mediated encounters, is always enmeshed within wider capitalist structures of expropriation, domination, discipline and social control'. These stigmatizing looks are all forms of microaggressions that send a clear message – albeit brief, fleeting, and casual – that Muslims are out of place. So, stigma is about 'the degrading marks that are affixed to particular bodies, people, conditions and places within humiliating social interactions' (Tyler, 2020: 8) and an important issue here is the shame that is generated by stigma and the ways in which this 'corrodes well-being and damages your sense of self' (Tyler, 2020: 9). Appreciating stigma as a psycho-political phenomenon positions it as an enactment of power that is not only written on people's bodies but gets under the skin and enters people's psycho-social sense of wellbeing. Shaheed (2021: 2) notes that in a climate of 'exclusion, fear and distrust, Muslims report that they often feel stigma, shame and a sense that they belong to "suspect communities" that are being forced to bear collective responsibility for the actions of a small minority'. Here we can see that stigma is not only a personal, embodied experience but connects to broader experiences of community and politics as stigma interweaves with power and the political. Stigmatizing Muslims – or those perceived to be Muslim – is often about specific individual actions that stereotype or scapegoat people. As Zine observes:

> [I]ndividual actions are the most prominent and visible phenomena in the Islamophobia dynamic. ... There are ubiquitous ideologies and tropes that serve to demonize and vilify Muslims and Islam. These include stereotypes that Muslims are terrorists ... who want to install creeping sharia laws that will undermine Western society and civilization. Other stereotypes relegate Muslim women to being backward and oppressed, without agency or freedom. (Zine, 2022a: 15)

A notable way of stigmatizing Muslims is to reinforce the assumption that they do not matter, or that they do not matter as much as other people (Aziz and Esposito, 2024; Warsi, 2024). Alternatively, stigmatization can work by positioning Muslims as scapegoats for social and political problems and challenges, rather than seeing these as connected to broader historical and political decisions.

In addition to stigmatization – but often working in close operation with it – everyday Islamophobia can be experienced through discrimination.

This might include direct or indirect discrimination or experiences of harassment or victimization. Many of these rely on the active employment of stigma but tip into being discriminatory.

> By way of illustration, in an EU wide survey, about four in ten Muslims (39%) reported experiences of discrimination, while one in five indicated that religion was the primary motivation. For example, persons with names suggesting that they may be Muslims were widely reported to encounter difficulties in recruitment processes, including being refused jobs due to being identified as Muslim. The lack, or reduced prospects, of employment may not only result in economic exclusion but may also make Muslims, in particular young Muslims, more vulnerable, potentially isolating them from society. At a community level, in recent decades, legislative measures have been passed in various national and sub-national contexts that include restrictions on the wearing of religious dress, the construction of mosques, minarets, and halal food production and access to citizenship, some of which were deemed as discriminatory. (European Commission against Racism and Intolerance, 2022: 17)

So, there are different ways in which Islamophobia operates as stigmatizing, as discriminatory, and as hate crime – or a combination of these – and it is useful to be alert to the different types and forms of Islamophobia in operation and not simply to assume that all forms of Islamophobia are necessarily criminal.

I have become increasingly sensitized through my research on Islamophobia to the different forms it might take from the more explicit and aggressive forms of anti-Muslim hate crimes through to forms of Islamophobia that are a lot more subtle and include a range of everyday indignities such as awkward looks and glances or disapproving stares. However, I also think it is important to be attentive to absence as a key feature of Islamophobia. Absence is often associated with a denial of space or participation, and it demarcates who can and cannot belong. Moreover, although absence tends to be seen to be the opposite of presence, often these are relational and each informs the other (Jones et al, 2012). By absence, I am also talking about the ways in which an issue of Islamophobia or anti-Muslim racism might not be referred to at all in a discussion about a whole range of other equalities issues or in which the topic might not surface, because of, for example, assumptions that it is not an issue, given the overwhelming whiteness of the local community. This is part and parcel of the idea that Muslims do not matter (Aziz and Esposito, 2024; Warsi, 2024) and a belief system in which issues of Islamophobia are not recognized, identified, or named. For example, it is noteworthy that Islamophobia rarely features in narratives resisting the war on Gaza, at the time of writing, yet the numbers of Muslims killed or injured in the genocide continue to grow, and the livelihoods of over two million people – the vast majority Muslim – are under threat.

In a sense, then, Islamophobia can be pushed under the carpet, not talked about, ignored, overlooked, and, yet, in the process of not considering it, not referring to it, and not giving it space, it is rendered invalid and not worthy of contemplation. Sometimes this is due to an anxiety about raising questions about Islamophobia, given the presumed sensitivity of discussing such as a controversial topic. However, this absence or silencing is often an Islamophobic act, whether or not carried out intentionally. Ahmed notes that

> Sometimes silence can be a tool of oppression: when you are silenced, whether by explicit force or by persuasion, it is not simply that you do not speak but that you are barred from participation in a conversation which nevertheless involves you. Sometimes silence is a strategic response to oppression; one that allows subjects to persist in their own way; one that acknowledges that, under certain circumstances, speech might not be empowering, let alone sensible. (Ahmed, 2010: xvi)

Silence can be a political act to avoid participating in a discussion that you do not agree with or with people you do not trust. Silencing can also be a powerful outcome of problematic counterterrorism policies (such as counterterrorism policies and strategies such as Prevent in the UK), which I discuss in more detail in Chapter 4.

Categories of Islamophobia

In defining what Islamophobia is, many suggest different categories of Islamophobia or point to the form or mode of operation it takes (see Table 2.1). For Manzoor-Khan (2022: 2), Islamophobia 'functions through processes of imperialist occupation, theft of resources and dislocation of people; procedures of coercive and brutal policing and caging; and measures of co-option, social-engineering and ideological control'. Zine (2022a: 14) clarifies that Islamophobia is part of a system of oppression. She defines Islamophobia as 'a fear and hatred of Islam and Muslims (and those perceived to be Muslims) that translate into individual actions and ideological and systemic forms of oppression that support the logic and rationale of specific power relations'. I now set out some of the different categories of Islamophobia and, although I set these out separately, there is often overlap and interconnection between these different categories, as they rarely operate in isolation and are frequently informed by one another.

Some scholarship on Islamophobia focuses on the *historical* aspects of its development, connecting it to problematic histories associated with, for example, Orientalism, empire, and ethnonationalism (for example, Sayyid,

2003; Kumar, 2017; Kundnani, 2017). Scholarship of historical Islamophobia involves charting the genealogy of Islamophobia and the forces that have shaped its emergence as a social and political phenomenon. It includes work that chronicles the development of Islamophobia over time to the present day, mapping the factors that have shaped, moulded, and formed what we see in the contemporary period. Many of these histories are long, complex, and multifaceted, shaped by a diversity of factors such as histories of colonialism, war, conflict, and migration, to name only a few.

Another important category of Islamophobia focuses on its *structural* and *institutional* factors. Beydoun (2018: 28) defines Islamophobia as 'the presumption that Islam is inherently violent, alien, and unassimilable, a presumption driven by the belief that expressions of Muslim identity correlate with a propensity for terrorism'. He sees it as encompassing three different components: 'private Islamophobia, structural Islamophobia, and Islamophobia as a dialectic between private actors and state actors', which he refers to as 'dialectical Islamophobia' (Beydoun, 2017: 446). Private Islamophobia is not associated with the state. Structural Islamophobia 'is the fear and suspicion of Muslims on the part of government institutions and actors ... through the enacting and advancement of laws, policy, and programming built upon the presumption that Muslim identity is associated with a national security threat' (Beydoun, 2018: 36). He sees this form of Islamophobia as being tied up with historical and contemporary state-enacted policies and practices targeting Muslims and Islam, such as the so-called war on terror. Significantly, Beydoun points out that a focus on structural Islamophobia is one of the most neglected areas of inquiry: 'People have no idea that the state is actually partaking in Islamophobic activity – by way of the programs and policies it advances because legal scholars and the media seldom, if ever, frame it as such' (Beydoun, 2017: 449). The third type of Islamophobia that Beydoun outlines is dialectical Islamophobia, which, he notes,

> focuses on the synergy between private actors on the ground and the state. What responsibility do these policies, these programs, and these laws have on endorsing tropes and stereotypes held by people on the ground? They shape them, in some respects, reshape them, and, during times of crisis, embolden the kind of hate and anti-Muslim violence we see unfolding specifically after times of crisis. (Beydoun, 2017: 451–452)

Similarly, Massoumi et al (2017a: 3) make the useful point that Islamophobia is not simply 'a product of abstract discursive or ideological processes, but of concrete social action undertaken in the pursuit of certain interests'. They emphasize the need to focus on the institutional aspects of it – including institutions and policies – rather than necessarily only paying attention to the construction and contestation of Muslim identities. They point to the significant role of 'specific agents and institutions implicated in racist practices and in the production of Islamophobic ideas, policies and structures' and note that 'Islamophobia is a form of "structural racism"' (Massoumi et al, 2017a: 8). In advancing an account of Islamophobia that sees it as a structural phenomenon, they outline the five pillars of Islamophobia, which are 'specific social actors (pillars) that produce the ideas and practices that result in disadvantage for Muslims' (Massoumi et al, 2017a: 4). The state – and the counterterrorism apparatus that is part of this – is the main pillar. The other four pillars of Islamophobia include the far right, the neoconservative movement, the transnational Zionist movement, and an assortment of liberal groups, including the pro-war and new atheist movements.

Islamophobia presents itself in many forms and in many ways, which is why it can sometimes be harder to detect, yet at other times can be blatantly obvious. Another form of Islamophobia has a more *intellectual* aspect to it and tends to be exhibited by public intellectuals or political think tanks that brand themselves as 'progressive'. Mondon and Winter (2019) usefully distinguish between what they call 'illiberal' and 'liberal' Islamophobia. The former is the obvious type of Islamophobia that is easy to spot and is generally quite explicit and therefore easy to counter; however, liberal Islamophobia is frequently dressed up as being progressive and often distances itself completely from 'traditional racism and hate' and instead 'pretends to focus only on "religion", "culture" and/or values, in relation to democratic rights and tolerance as values inherent to Western societies, most notably free speech, women's rights and LGBT rights' (Mondon and Winter, 2019: 63). In a sense, then, these both constitute Islamophobia and are two sides of the same coin but often they present themselves very differently.

Interpersonal Islamophobia is Islamophobia that takes place between two or more people. This is the form of Islamophobia that is typically associated with everyday Islamophobia. It includes most of what Beydoun (2017) refers to as 'private Islamophobia' and which he defines as 'the fear, suspicion, and violent targeting of Muslims by private actors' (Beydoun, 2018: 32). Interpersonal Islamophobia involves a range of individual actions like verbal abuse, violence, and aggression, as well as other forms of interpersonal indignities such as tutting, sighing, glaring, staring, or glancing in an unpleasant way, directed towards someone who is Muslim or is perceived to be Muslim. This can happen in diverse places, such as on public transport, on the way to work, in the school playground, or at a restaurant.

To add yet further complexity to the picture, such is the strength of Islamophobia that there is also some evidence of Muslims internalizing it, as Hilal points out:

> Internalized Islamophobia refers to the phenomenon of Muslims absorbing dominant narratives and tropes about Islam and Muslims that suggest that they – the religion and its followers – are inherently violent and terroristic, uncivilized, backwards, repressive, uniquely patriarchal and oppressive of women, and opposed to normative democratic ideals. Manifestations of internalized Islamophobia include uncritical acceptance of these and other tropes and advocating for particularized interventions that address Muslims' exceptionally problematic behavior. Internalized Islamophobia is also expressed through efforts to overcompensate for and condemn acts of violence committed by Muslims on the basis of collective responsibility, whilst at the same time denying, minimizing, and otherwise erasing Muslim victimhood. (Hilal, 2021: xix)

She usefully notes that one way that this can manifest is through Muslims perpetuating laws and frameworks that support this system and thereby encouraging the marginalization and exclusion of Muslims. They are therefore explicitly Islamophobic and provide a platform for Islamophobia to flourish.

Another important category here is what I refer to as *representational Islamophobia*. Included within this are the ways that Islam and Muslims are depicted in popular media and culture, such as literature and film. It includes issues such as the problematic representation of Muslims and Islam discussed in newspaper articles and the imagery that sits alongside such pieces, the ways that Islam and Muslims are represented in television programmes, on televised news programmes or documentaries, and on the radio and other related platforms. It also includes the representation of Islamophobia in artwork, drawings, comics, animations, or other forms of visual media (for example, Gottschalk and Greenberg, 2019).

Intersectional Islamophobia is about how the form, nature, and tone of Islamophobia may change as racialized Muslim identities intersect with other identities or markers of social and cultural difference, such as those associated with gender, sexuality, ethnicity, migration status, or disability (for example, Rahman, 2010). Crenshaw (1989) points out that the common approaches to discrimination usually focus on single categories – such as racism and sexism – resulting in a lack of consideration being given to the complex ways in which black women are marginalized, as simply adding racism and sexism together is inadequate. Since Crenshaw's (1989, 1991) early work, alongside the black feminist activist work that partly informed the development of the concept (Combahee River Collective, 1983), intersectionality has become an increasingly popular way to consider how multiple forms of social oppression interact with each other, often changing in the process (Collins, 2000; Collins and Bilge, 2016). The popularity of the approach of intersectionality is such that there is now a field that Cho et al (2013) call 'intersectionality studies'. However, there are concerns that the widespread employment of intersectionality has led to it being reproduced in ways that are problematic, that misunderstand its social justice origins, that whiten it and disconnect it from the clear focus given to race. As such, I have argued that intersectionality should be used ethically and with care (Hopkins, 2019). Intersectional Islamophobia is evident in important research on the nexus between gender, race, and religion (for example, Karaman and Christian, 2020; El Sayed, 2023) and in work about gendered Islamophobia (see Chapter 8). Moreover, intersectional Islamophobia is not only about everyday gendered Islamophobia, as we know that Islamophobia as a form of oppression intersects and interacts with a diversity of other forms of exclusion, such as those connected to migration status, sexuality, disability, social class, caste, and social context (for example, Easat-Daas, 2021). In Europe, 53 per cent of Muslims report experiencing discrimination based on more than one category of exclusion in the year before the European Union Agency for Fundamental Rights (2024) survey took place.

Islamophobia is also *spatialized* (Najib, 2022) and has a particular set of geographies. For example, it varies across geographical scales – such as the global, national, regional, and local – and is often embedded within and across these rather than only taking place in one context (Najib and Teeple Hopkins, 2020; Finlay and Hopkins, 2024). Debates about Islamophobia often invoke concerns about specific spaces, whether this be about Islam versus the West, anxiety in specific nation-states about the 'integration' of Muslim minorities, concerns about the movement of Muslim refugees across nations and over borders, or fears about the presence of Muslims in the public sphere within specific neighbourhoods of cities or in different forms of employment or in politics or public office.

Overlapping with Islamophobias that are interpersonal, intersectional, and spatialized are *embodied Islamophobias*, which refer to the everyday lived accounts and emotions connected with experiencing, negotiating, resisting, contesting, and subverting Islamophobia. Such an approach draws its inspiration from feminist research and focuses on the ways in which Islamophobia is felt on and in the body and lived out in everyday life (Mansson McGinty, 2020, 2023). This is discussed in more detail in Chapter 8.

What is everyday Islamophobia?

My approach to focusing on everyday Islamophobia in this book is all encompassing of the different types of Islamophobia – or Islamophobias (plural) – outlined in Table 2.1. While it is useful to be sensitive to the different ways in which Islamophobia operates and the different sectors,

Table 2.1: Categories of Islamophobia

Historical	This refers to forms of discrimination and marginalization against Muslims that have happened in the past (even if not labelled as Islamophobia at the time, given the relative recency of the concept) and how these have shaped where we are today, including how the term has developed over time (Allen, 2010; Manzoor-Khan, 2022).
Structural and institutional	This refers to Islamophobia by institutions or organizations, including schools, colleges, and universities, government departments, hospitals, and other such organizations (Massoumi et al, 2017b) including the targeting of Muslims by state or government institutions or by powerful structures and agencies (Beydoun, 2017; Massoumi et al, 2017a; Manzoor-Khan, 2022).
Intellectual and political	This is about Islamophobia enacted by academics and public intellectuals, or through think tanks that purport to use research or intellectual property in their work (Massoumi et al, 2017b; Mondon and Winter, 2020), or by political actors who use their position and power to enact political Islamophobia (Kiwan and Wolfreys, 2023).
Interpersonal	This is Islamophobia between individuals that shapes the nature of interactions and the ideas that people bring with them to these encounters. Beydoun (2018) refers to this Islamophobia between 'private actors' (that is, those not associated with the state).
Internalized	This is about the ways in which Muslims can absorb negative stereotypes and dominant narratives about Islam and Muslims (Hilal, 2021), which in turn become a part of their attitude, values, opinions, and beliefs.
Representational	This is about the visual imagery (such as cartoons, comics, animations, film, and other forms of visual representation or media) or other images and representations used in newspapers or on social media that stigmatize and stereotype Islam and/or Muslims (Gottschalk and Greenberg, 2019).
Intersectional	This refers to Islamophobia in operation with other forms of oppression, such as sexism, ageism, homophobia, and ableism (Ansari and Patel, 2024; Easat-Daas and Zempi, 2024), and includes gendered Islamophobia (Hopkins, 2016; Easat-Daas, 2019) through the reinforcement of racist stereotypes and narratives about Muslim women and/or men (Carland, 2011, 2023a; Allen, 2015; Easat-Daas and Zempi, 2024).
Spatialized	This is about Islamophobia that takes places across and within geographical scales (such as the global, national, urban, and the body) (Najib and Teeple Hopkins, 2020; Najib, 2022). Some research refers to online Islamophobia (Sayyid, 2018) – social media and other internet-based platforms – and is contrasted with offline Islamophobia, which takes place in person (Awan, 2014; Zempi and Awan, 2016).

Table 2.1: Categories of Islamophobia (continued)

Embodied	This is about Islamophobia as a lived and emotional experience that is acted out on specific bodies and felt by individuals (Mansson McGinty, 2020). It overlaps with aspects of interpersonal, intersectional, and spatialized Islamophobia.
Everyday	This focuses on the routine, regular, habitual, and customary operation of Islamophobia and is interwoven with the many diverse categories outlined previously, including the structural and institutional, the intellectual and political, as well as those more personal and embodied forms.

movements, and actors involved in its promotion, I employ everyday Islamophobia as a way of bringing together these different facets to emphasize their everyday, routine, regular, habitual, and customary operation. To be clear, I do not see everyday Islamophobia as some form of *low-level* type of discrimination that is somehow separate from the more powerful and all-encompassing institutional, structural, or global forms of Islamophobia. With Zine (2022a: 13), I am wary of 'reducing Islamophobia to a form of "intolerance" or "hate", as is so often seen, as this constructs it as an interpersonal problem as opposed to a structural and systemic one, since the act of "intolerance" operates within the purview of individuals rather than as a function of the state'. I see everyday Islamophobia as bound up and interwoven with broader institutional, structural, political, and societal forms of Islamophobia and not only about interpersonal encounters, even though this is how it is often felt and experienced. Indeed, one of my key arguments in this book is that people experience everyday Islamophobia through interpersonal encounters in everyday life, and the source of these is the Islamophobia industrial complex that I discuss in more detail in the next chapter, and which includes the institutional and structural Islamophobias promoted by the state or by actors connected to the state.

Inspired by work on everyday racism, my approach to everyday Islamophobia draws upon the important work of Essed (2002: 205) who notes that 'the notion of "everyday" is often used to refer to a familiar world, a world of practical interest, a world of practices with which we are socialized' (Essed, 2002: 205) while also pointing to the fact that 'the concept of everyday racism defies the view that racism is either an individual problem or an institutional problem' (Essed, 2002: 205). What is clear about everyday racism is also clear about everyday Islamophobia.

> Personal accounts of lived experience prove most illuminating in telling what everyday racism is about: injustices recurring so often that they are almost taken for granted, nagging, annoying, debilitating, seemingly

small, injustices one comes to expect. The concept of everyday racism related day-to-day experiences of racial discrimination to the macrostructural context of group inequalities represented within and between nations as racial and ethnic hierarchies of competence, culture, and human progress. (Essed, 2002: 203)

So although everyday racism typically focuses on the mundane rather than on extreme incidents or occurrences, I see a hard-line separation between these as being problematic because they fold into and inform each other. As Essed (2002: 205) observes: 'racism is ideologically mediated through actual practices in all these institutions. This means that the taken-for-granted feeling that one's own group comes first, the idea that people of a different racial or ethnic background are less competent, less civilized, a cultural threat, or less intelligent operates (latently)'. So, although everyday Islamophobia is grounded in the everyday, routine and commonplace, it cannot be separated from – or regarded as less important or somehow more insignificant than – other forms of Islamophobia outlined earlier. Appreciating the everyday requires an appreciation of the structural issues too (Dunn and Hopkins, 2016).

Focusing on everyday Islamophobia is challenging as, like everyday racism 'though felt persistently, [it] is often difficult to pinpoint. As a result, these microinjustices become normal, fused into familiar practices, practices taken for granted, attitudes and behaviors sustaining racial injustice' (Essed, 2002: 204). Moreover, everyday Islamophobia is rarely a singular event or act but is a 'multidimensional experience. ... One event triggers memories of other, similar incidents, of the beliefs surrounding the event, or behavioral coping and cognitive responses' (Essed, 2002: 207). Whether they be about the journey to school, experiences in the workplace, eating a meal in a restaurant, or watching television at home, everyday racism and Islamophobia are in operation and being expressed, often in different and diffuse ways.

Having now established what everyday Islamophobia is, in the next chapter I focus on the Islamophobia industrial complex and the multiple stereotypes, conspiracy theories, and reductionist ways of thinking that promote its operation alongside the mainstreaming of right-wing narratives.

3

The Islamophobia Industrial Complex

Now that the complexities of what is meant by everyday Islamophobia have been set out, in this chapter I move towards an understanding of the Islamophobia industrial complex. I see this as the complex web of groups, agencies, organizations, and individuals who are financially and ideologically benefiting from promoting Islamophobia and anti-Muslim hatred. The Islamophobia industrial complex works in a similar way to the 'surveillance industrial complex' (Selod et al, 2024: 20), the 'terror industrial complex' (Rana, 2016), and the 'anti-racism industrial complex' (Andrews, 2023), connecting with understandings of the prison and military industrial complexes (Davis and Shaylor, 2001; Gilmore, 2022; Hafez, 2023b). An industrial complex, as it is used in these examples, develops when finance, business, and trade become enmeshed within specific political, social, and cultural systems – such as those associated with surveillance, or with counterterrorism, or with the promotion of Islamophobia – and generates a set of profits and financial beneficiaries, and often a sense of superiority and power for those involved, regardless of how effective they are. Such complexes aggressively pursue their own interests, irrespective of whether it is morally or ethically appropriate to do so. The Islamophobia industrial complex, then, is the complex layers of resources, funding, and systems in place to promote, sustain, and enhance the spread of everyday Islamophobia, including those who are struggling against it.

In this chapter, I explore some of the issues that provide the foundation to the Islamophobia industrial complex and then build on these further, especially in the two chapters that follow. I consider the role of basic stereotypes of Muslims and Islam and the use of conspiracy theories, alongside mechanisms for circumventing, downplaying, and avoiding Islamophobia. The mainstreaming of Islamophobia then leads me into setting out the key components of the Islamophobia industrial complex.

Simplistic stereotypes about Muslims and Islam

Some of the principal foundations of Islamophobia emanate from a wide-ranging set of simplistic stereotypes about Muslims and Islam that are routinely used, frequently heard, and commonly understood. Afshar (2013) makes the point that there is a strong tendency to lump Muslims together into one group, and to assume that they all agree with each other.

> Muslims are not, however, a homogeneous group. Some Muslims are devout but apolitical; some are political but do not see their politics as being 'Islamic' (indeed, may even be anti-Islamic). Some identify more with a nationality of origin, such as Turkish; others with the nationality of settlement and perhaps citizenship, such as French. Some prioritise funding for mosques, others campaign against discrimination, unemployment or Zionism … the category 'Muslim', then, is as internally diverse as 'Christian' or 'Belgian' or 'middle-class', or any other category helpful in othering our understanding of contemporary Europe. (Modood, 2003: 100)

Although this point about any such category not being homogeneous might be obvious, the strength of some of the stereotypes about Muslims and about Islam is such that ideas about heterogeneity and diversity within the Muslim community fade into the background when these well-trodden and familiar stereotypes are being used. Stereotyping tends to work when we notice a trait or quality in a person or group and then make up the rest of the story about them, based on stereotypes that we carry about with us in our head. However, these ideas we carry — both positive and negative — come from societal ideas and assumptions rather than from the experience of the group being stereotyped (Gottschalk and Greenberg, 2019). Stereotypes about Muslims and Islam often rely on binary thinking, which reinforces ideas of us versus them, and Islam versus the West.

An important set of stereotypes of Islam and Muslims utilizes the idea that Islam and the West are mutually exclusive categories that are incompatible, divergent, and inevitably in conflict with each other. These stereotypes go back a long way and have a remarkable durability. They present Islam and Muslims as a homogeneous block or group that is other, and inferior to the West. The message here is that Islam and Muslims are irrational, primitive, backward, barbaric, intolerant, and alien (Sayyid, 2003; Kundnani, 2007; Dunn and Kamp, 2009). This includes the stereotypes that Islam is associated with 'fundamentalism' (Sayyid, 2003) and that Muslims are 'followers of a uniquely fanatical and anti-modern religion' (Kundnani, 2007: 97). These stereotypes can easily feed into the national political discourse about immigration and citizenship. They promote a binary division between Islam and the West and inform many conspiracy theories and mechanisms for downplaying Islamophobia that I discuss further in this chapter.

Added to these are the stereotypes that focus on the binary thinking associated with segregation, rather than integration. One such stereotype promoted is that Muslims prefer to live in separate communities, to segregate, to ghettoize, and to isolate. This is reinforced through assumptions about Muslims being unwilling to 'integrate', whether this be about learning the main language of the country they are living in, participating in sport or leisure activities, or engaging actively in their local communities outside of the mosque, as discussed in Chapter 6. However, such assumptions are nearly always unclear about exactly what they should be integrating into or with.

While some stereotypes are inflected by national or regional issues, some are enduring and can be found across the world. For example, Cada and Frantova (2019) analysed narratives about Islam and Muslims in the Czech Republic through a discourse analysis of broadcast television, debates, national newspapers, internet blogs, and other sources. They found that there are three common tropes about Islam: first, it is anachronistic and uncivilized; second, it is a violent religion; and third, it is homogeneous and undemocratic. The three most common tropes about Muslims are that Muslims are terrorists, gypsies (parasites), and sexual predators. These tropes feed into, embellish, and interact with stereotypes that resurface in many different places.

Stereotypes about Islam and Muslims are often – if not always – heavily gendered. Muslim women are stereotyped as being oppressed, forced to veil, controlled by their husbands, and the embodiment of a fundamentalist and repressive religion (for example, Dwyer, 1998). The assumption is that they do not work and, indeed, are not allowed to do so, having sole responsibility for the family home. At the same time, 'Muslim young men are increasingly being constructed as militant and aggressive, intrinsically fundamentalist, ultimate others' (Archer, 2001: 81).

Although often very simplistic, some stereotypes work through what Poynting et al (2004: 33) refer to as 'chains of associations'. For example, in the case of Islamophobia in Australia, 'Arab-ness and Islam and Middle Eastern-ness are seen to be the same thing, and are seen to be essentially and pathologically evil, inhuman, violent and criminal' (Poynting et al, 2004: 33). And, as they explore later, stereotypes about Muslims and Islam are often conflated with ideas about specific regions, nations, cultural practices, and migrant groups: 'so Middle Eastern can become conflated with Arab, Arab with Muslim, Muslim with rapist, rapist with gang, gang with terrorist, terrorist with "boat people", "boat people" with barbaric and so are interminable permutations' (Poynting et al, 2004: 49).

Although I have discussed these stereotypes in quite general terms here, as they are racialized they vary to some extent from place to place, depending on specific local, regional, or national issues and politics. In Australia, there is the 'Arab other' (Poynting et al, 2004: 12), which mostly refers to those of Middle Eastern or Arab heritage; in Germany there is the large community of Turkish Muslims (Ehrkamp, 2007); and in the UK, the largest group of Muslims is from the Indian sub-continent. National, regional, and localized stereotypes of these different groups mean that they may be presented slightly differently in different places. And, as we have seen, although some stereotypes have remained constant, others change over time or in response to a major geopolitical event, such as the changes witnessed after 9/11 when Muslim men in particular were quickly constructed as potential terrorists and as a threat to national security.

Conspiracy theories used to promote Islamophobia

Three conspiracy theories, in particular, are becoming increasingly common and widespread in their usage. These are the great replacement, white genocide and Eurabia (see Table 3.1). The outcome of certain events, according to these theories, 'will be the replacement of Western civilizations with Islamic ones, the implementation of Sharia law, and the ultimate genocide of white populations by nonwhite or non-Christian immigrants' (Miller-Idriss, 2020: 13).

Sometimes, these theories can be challenging to spot, as they are often dressed up in very different language or appear amid a statement or sentence that is apparently reasonable but is, in reality, fuelled by such theories. These theories underpin some of the work of the Islamophobia industrial complex, especially those elements of it that support extreme far-right ideologies. Davis (2024: 4) notes that 'conspiracy theories can be understood as a form of displaced political agency and alternative explanatory storytelling in an era

Table 3.1: Conspiracy theories that promote Islamophobia

The great replacement	One of the leading far-right conspiracy theories, focused on the idea that rapid population change will result in the 'great replacement' of white, Christian, Europeans with non-white Muslims
White genocide	A far-right conspiracy theory – more popular in the United States than in Europe – that there is a deliberate and strategic plan to make all white people extinct
Eurabia	One of the earliest conspiracy theories and a key source for the great replacement theory, this far-right dogma focuses on the idea that Europe will be taken over by Muslims and concentrates on concerns about mass immigration and high birth rates

of scientific, political, social, and cultural uncertainty. Conspiracy theories ... are also available as counter-hegemonic weapons that can be used to undermine dominant cultural and political norms'. These three conspiracy theories differ from each other, but they share an obsession with rapid demographic change and the position of white people as the key victims. Miller-Idriss (2020: 9) refers to what she calls 'existential demographic threats and dystopian conspiracy theories' or 'dystopian fantasy theories' that are used by the extreme far right.

Extreme violence is often the foundation of the approach put forward by those who are guided by these theories, and the extreme far right seeking to secure white domination and acceleration is often part of this, as they promote this violence. For example, these three theories were employed by the gunman who murdered 51 worshippers in Christchurch, New Zealand, in March 2019. Davis (2024: 8) points out that the violence involved in these theories is part of their method, 'which is connected to strategies of biopolitical control and the promotion of race-based forms of governmentality'.

The 'great replacement' theory (Community Policy Forum, 2024; Mohammed, 2024; Tazamal, 2024) is one of the leading far-right conspiracy theories of demographic change. 'It argues that there is an intentional, global plan orchestrated by national and global elites to replace white, Christian, European populations with non-white, non-Christian ones' (Miller-Idriss, 2020: 9). It is commonly employed by far-right groups and features in many countries. Much of the original work on this theory focused on the French context (Hancock and Mobillion, 2019; Aziz and Esposito, 2024; Davis, 2024) and that of other European countries. 'The anti-Muslim propaganda and conspiracy theories that eventually merged into the great-replacement narrative were in many cases inadvertently aided by counter-terrorism policies that muddied the distinction between Islamist terrorism and Islam' (Miller-Idriss, 2021: 61). Policies that promote protecting national security and standing up against terror often work to reinforce the idea that nations are under threat from an 'other' or at risk of being taken over by other ethnic and/or religious (read Muslim) groups.

The white genocide conspiracy theory is often used alongside the great replacement theory and is more popular in the United States (Davis, 2024). Miller-Idriss (2020) connects this with the American neo-Nazi, David Lane:

> Lane's famous '14 words' – 'We must secure the existence of our people and a future for white children' – is a call to defend whites against genocide, and the term, or even just the number fourteen, became a global mantra for white supremacists and pan-Aryans, frequently paired with the number eighty-eight (for the eighth letter of the alphabet 'H', making 'HH' or Heil Hitler. (Miller-Idriss, 2020: 10)

Further, she links the theory to several mass-murders committed in the United States:

> Before he allegedly murdered twenty-two people in an El Paso Walmart, a Texas man posted a document online that explicitly referenced the Christchurch shooting and referred to a 'Hispanic invasion of Texas'. The terrorist who allegedly murdered thirteen people in a Pittsburgh synagogue in 2018 was motivated by white-genocide theories suggesting Jews were orchestrating the resettlement of refugees in order to create a multicultural society that would eventually eradicate whites. (Miller-Idriss, 2020: 12)

The third conspiracy theory, the concept of Eurabia, focuses on the idea that

> Muslims are deliberately working to replace white Europeans through immigration and high birthrates to broaden the territory of the Caliphate ... this will create a space in which white Europeans are subject to Sharia law and Islamic rule, forced to convert to Islam or surrender into subservient roles. The end result, described in Eurabia, is a Europe that has been converted from a white, Christian civilization to an Islamic one. (Miller-Idriss, 2020: 10)

This pre-dates the great replacement and is indeed partly where that theory comes from (Davis, 2024). Eurabia was discussed in Breivik's manifesto, which cited a German author (Hafez, 2024b), and it appeared in a 2019 advertising campaign for Germany's Alternative for Germany (AfD) party. Bangstad (2013) discusses the idea of Eurabia as an explicitly Islamophobic idea, introduced into Norway through television and by some politicians, which has essentially led to it receiving far wider coverage than it would otherwise receive. Larsson (2012) notes that it is not only far-right terrorists who support Eurabia theories and points to those such as Samuel Huntingdon and Bernard Lewis, who I discuss later, promoting concerns about the growing numbers of Muslims in Europe. Larsson (2012) undertook an analysis of census data and notes that the claims made in some of the literature about Eurabia vastly overstate the number of Muslims in Europe: it is often claimed that there are 40–50 million Muslims when the census data suggests it is closer to five million (based on available data from 2001 until 2012 when his article was published).

These three conspiracy theories are not distinct from each other and indeed they often inform each other and are used together or in pairs, depending on the user.

> Together, white genocide, Eurabia, and now the overarching theory of the great replacement have helped foster transnational inspiration and

a sense of shared mission among the global far right. These conspiracy theories represent ideas that have been core to white-supremacist beliefs for decades. They place blame on ethnic and racial minorities for the degradation of society, coupled with the global elite manipulation and intentional orchestration. (Miller-Idriss, 2020: 12)

Miller-Idriss (2020) notes with concern that white-supremacist extremism is increasing in the United States, and a preference is being demonstrated for violent action on behalf of the extreme far right. 'In recent years, right-wing radicals in the United States and Europe have made it clear that they are willing and able to embrace the tactics of terrorism; they have become, in some ways, a mirror image of the jihadis whom they despise' (Miller-Idriss, 2021: 56).

In 2020, authorities arrested nearly three times as many white supremacists as they did in 2017, and there was nearly a doubling of the numbers counted of flyers, posters, banners, and stickers shared, with similar trends being found in the UK and Germany. Social media has provided a key platform for the promotion of these conspiracy theories, offering as it does a number of routes for circulating, marketing, and publicizing extreme far-right 'propaganda and disinformation', which has 'forged global connections across groups and movements, and created new ways for extremism to seep into the mainstream' (Miller-Idriss, 2021: 56). As Davis (2024: 16) confirms, these three conspiracy theories utilize the digital world to promote ideas that 'seek to dehumanise and potentially eliminate racialised Others as potential risk objects justifiably subject to violent discipline'.

The global employment of these conspiracy theories is not simply confined to an extremely small group of marginalized and alienated radicals, or isolated 'lone wolves'. Rather, these ideas are increasingly finding their ways into the mainstream through the media, politics, and other fora. In the domain of politics:

In France, the leader of the right-wing National Front, Marine Le Pen, compared groups of Muslims praying on the sidewalks outside mosques to Nazi occupiers. The Dutch far-right leader Geert Wilders described refugees as an 'Islamic invasion'. The British arm of the far-right group Generation Identity linked the fight against multiculturalism to the fifteenth-century efforts of the European forces to retake the Iberian Peninsula from the Muslim rulers who controlled most of it at the time. (Miller-Idriss, 2021: 58)

Many of these far-right political parties have also been making gains in national elections in many European countries 'often by giving even the most vapid extremist ideas the veneer of respectability by draping them in the trappings of intellectualism – an approach perfected by the AfD (which was nicknamed "the professor's party") and by "alt-right" figures in the United States such as Richard Spencer' (Miller-Idriss, 2021: 60–61; see also Hafez, 2024a). In the UK, we see this in the recent gains in the 2024 general election in which Reform UK gained 14 per cent of the national vote (showing it as the third most popular party after Labour and Conservative in terms of percentage share of the vote) and had five MPs elected, including the party leader, Nigel Farage.

Mechanisms for circumventing, downplaying, and avoiding Islamophobia

In addition to these conspiracy theories, there are many other mechanisms often employed to deny, avoid, sidestep, or circumvent Islamophobia. These mechanisms are widely critiqued but frequently employed in the promotion and consolidation of Islamophobia. A key mechanism for circumventing Islamophobia – or for downplaying its role and significance – is the use of deracialization. This generally refers to the ways in which issues of race and racism are absent in public policy, which essentially communicates both a lack of significance being given to matters of race and a strong preference towards not addressing racism (Smith, 2024a). This can be seen in policies that claim to be about race equality but make little or no mention of racism, or indeed, of Islamophobia. Many policies can both obscure and find ways around directly addressing racism and Islamophobia, by not naming them, for example, or by only making observations about racism or Islamophobia, rather than seeking to challenge, overturn, or counter them. Those who seek to decouple racism from Islamophobia are often engaging in a process of deracialization that operates to downplay its significance and avoid addressing it.

A second approach that is sometimes evident in cases of Islamophobia being promoted is what has been called 'racist nativism'. Lippard (2011) notes that nativism tends to rely on nationalistic ideas that separate out native people from non-native people, in other words, 'foreigners'. Nativism often rears its head during periods of crisis, such as through anti-immigrant discourses that represent foreigners as a threat to the economy or to cultural heritage, for example. Nativist approaches view migrants as a threat to the moral order of society, a risk to the cultural heritage of the nation, and to the economy, and some even suggest that immigrants present an environmental threat (Lippard, 2011). Smith notes that racist nativism recognizes

> the simultaneous racialisation of immigrants (where one's immigration status is ascribed a place in a racial hierarchy based on assumed biological or cultural differences and evaluated against the presumed superiority

of whiteness) and nativist assumptions of race/ethnicity (where non-whites are designated as non-natives). In this relationship, immigrants are constructed as a threat to the existing native state, discourses which simultaneously work to position those who are perceived as non-white, wherever they were born, as non-native, or 'the outsider within', and hence also a threat. (Smith, 2021: 64)

Smith (2024b) found widespread usage of racist nativism in educational policy documents in the UK, including statements that associate the values of being Muslim with being in opposition to those held by non-Muslims. These racist nativist discourses were informed by the promotion of so-called 'fundamental British values', which have their source in counterterrorism policy.

Similar to racist nativism, another approach is the widely discredited 'clash of civilizations' thesis. Bazian (2018) discusses Lewis' clash of civilizations, popularized through the work of Huntingdon, which argued that the main source of conflict will focus on cultural and religious issues (rather than economic or ideological concerns): 'The thesis translates Islamophobia into a foreign policy paradigm and re-orients Western states' policies towards confronting the Islamic-Chinese alliance. Islamophobia becomes the tool needed for birthing the new world order' (Bazian, 2018: 6).

Bazian sees an approach like this as contributing to simplistic divides such as those that promote an 'us versus them', 'West versus Islam' typology, when the world is far more complex than a simple division like this. It also reinforces the idea that Islam is not compatible with the West.

> 'The Clash' becomes a reductionist and an irrational analysis of the causes of conflicts in the world and lead 'experts' and 'think-tanks' inhabitants to call for mining Islamic textual sources and examining Muslim cultural norms to understand 'why they hate us' and the best approach to counter them. 'The Clash of Civilizations' is Islamophobia writ large and acts as the blueprint that informs and shapes discourses around Islam and Muslims. (Bazian, 2018: 7)

This approach has been used by politicians such as Berlusconi in Italy, Le Pen in France, Fortuyn in the Netherlands (Marranci, 2004), and by politicians and journalists in Australia (Poynting et al, 2004), and it has framed debates in international relations since 9/11 (Cesari, 2019) to reinforce the idea that there is some sort of clash between European Christian culture and that of the Islamic world. Yet, it is also widely critiqued and discredited, as noted by Cesari:

> [A]s abundantly proven by the social sciences, civilizations are not homogenous [sic], monolithic players in world politics with an

inclination to 'clash', but rather consist of pluralistic, divergent, and convergent actors and practices that are constantly evolving ... the 'clash of civilizations' fails to address not only conflict between civilizations but also conflict and differences within civilizations. In particular, evidence does not exist to substantiate Huntington's prediction that countries with similar cultures are coming together, while countries with different cultures are coming apart. (Cesari, 2019: 24)

A fourth approach that is often used in concert with many of these is the concept of moral panic. Cohen defines moral panic in this way:

A condition, episode, person or group of persons emerges to become defined as a threat to societal values and interests; its nature presented in a stylized and stereotypical fashion by the mass media, the moral barricades are manned by editors, bishops, politicians and other right-thinking people; socially accredited experts pronounce their diagnoses and solutions; ways of coping are evolved or (more often) resorted to; the condition then disappears, submerges or deteriorates and becomes more invisible. (Cohen, 1972: 9)

Morgan and Poynting (2012) note that this approach is useful for understanding how Islamophobia operates and shapes social and political discourse. They highlight four key points about the moral panic framework that are useful tools when considering Islamophobia and the place of Muslims in society. First, there is volatility as public concerns about specific issues often boil over and then subside quickly, often in cycles, some that are longer than others. Second, there is hostility when specific folk devils end up being identified and overly scrutinized, set up as enemies of wider society. We see this in the ways that Muslim youth became the 'Ultimate Others' (Phoenix, 1997), the ethnic crime gangs and 'Arab others' (Poynting et al, 2004) the 'folk devils' of the 'Asian gang' (Alexander, 2000) or the 'new folk devils' in educational settings (Shain, 2011). Third, Morgan and Poynting (2012) note that projection occurs when folk devils are then scapegoated for a wide range of social problems, often in a highly moral fashion. We see this in the way that broader social issues such as cultures of sexism or misogyny, gang violence, or civil unrest are projected onto Muslim communities. Fourth, they point to a disproportionality that is often found in the reaction of the state in measures taken to address the perceived problem that is the source of the moral panic. Often the measures are excessive, given the scale of the issue being addressed. Counterterror measures can be a useful example.

Moral panics are associated with 'Bin Laden groups in our suburbs' in Australia (Poynting et al, 2004: 28), as fictitious stories spread after 9/11 about 'terrorist cells in Australia' (Poynting et al, 2004: 29) and as concerns that associated terrorism with Islam were conflated with anxieties about the arrival of 'boats' of asylum seekers. Graffiti on a wall in Brisbane proclaimed, 'We will kill all Arabs ... scum will die', and a 'school bus full of Muslim children in Queensland was pelted with bottles ... amongst a number of more violent attacks, a mosque in Brisbane was torched' (Poynting et al, 2004: 29). The moral panic thesis has been critiqued and revised:

> In the case of global Islamophobia, it is now clear, however, that the sort of folk demonizing that has constructed little Bin Ladens across the globe is still with us ten years after 9/11, and the Islamophobia raging might be a very long splutter indeed. To put it another way, this is a case where moral panic has long since deteriorated and become more visible, engendering cycle after cycle of panic, of a variety of scope and localities. (Morgan and Poynting, 2012: 4)

Increasing mainstreaming of Islamophobia

Many of the issues discussed previously can easily be dismissed as being exhibited or practised only by a tiny proportion of extremely right-wing individuals or a similarly small 'uneducated' population. A key example of how this typically operates is that individuals committing highly controversial acts of Islamophobia might be classified as a 'lone wolf' (singular), or the acts as 'fringe incidents' (Miller-Idriss, 2021: 59) or carried out by an eccentric individual deemed to be suffering from poor mental health. Essentially, the issue becomes highly individualized rather than seen as part of a broader pattern, trend, or movement. For example, the incident in Norway in 2011 that I have discussed is referred to in this way:

> [A] far-right extremist named Anders Behring Breivik murdered 77 people, mostly teenagers attending a Labor Party summer camp outside Oslo. Breivik had composed a 1,500-page manifesto in which he railed against Islam, warned about the coming of Eurabia, and cited U.S. anti-Muslim activists nearly 200 times. His assault received a high degree of media attention but was often presented as an anomaly, and Breivik himself was sometimes portrayed as a mentally unhinged mass murderer rather than as a terrorist, even though his violence was explicitly political. (Miller-Idriss, 2021: 59)

Despite Breivik's manifesto relying upon conspiracy theories that he had been engaging with and other materials generated by key members of the transnational Islamophobia network that I discuss in Chapter 5, there is a tendency, then, to cast him as a mentally unstable lone wolf.

Rather than occupying highly marginal positions, what we have been witnessing is an increasing mainstreaming of Islamophobia. Miller-Idriss (2021: 56) points out that the far right is a very diverse group and includes those such as 'white supremacists, neo-Nazis, conspiracy theorists, [and] "Western chauvinist" groups such as the Proud Boys' (Miller-Idriss, 2021: 56). She cautions that conspiracy theories such as those outlined, and employed by Breivik, are not confined to the narrow context of far-right activism but can be found in contexts such as FBI training materials. 'Ten years after 9/11, materials used by the FBI for training about Islamophobia described Muslims as terrorist sympathizers whose charitable donations were a "funding mechanism for combat"' (Miller-Idriss, 2021: 61).

Far-right ideas are increasingly featuring in mainstream politics (Mondon and Winter, 2020). This is seen in the election of Donald Trump both in 2016 and 2024, the Brexit vote and Marine Le Pen reaching the second round of the French presidential election, with 30 per cent of the vote (Tazamal, 2024). Moreover, the Lega in Italy and Freedom Party of Austria both managed to enter into coalitions through strong electoral performances. Likewise, far-right political parties have gained representation in 'more than three dozen national parliaments and in the European Parliament' (Miller-Idriss, 2021: 54). Many of the conspiracy theories and mechanisms for circumventing Islamophobia outlined earlier appear in the narratives espoused by politicians, as do stereotypes about Muslims and Islam.

Far-right political parties are always likely to remain marginal if the system as a whole is not welcoming to them. However, what we have seen recently is that the concerns traditionally confined to the far right have increasingly become the narrative of more mainstream political parties. For example, in the UK, immigration was a central theme for David Cameron and the Brexit campaign, and 'UKIP, and Nigel Farage in particular, were allowed to play a particularly disproportionate role in the mainstreaming of racism in the UK, and especially during the EU referendum campaign itself' (Mondon and Winter, 2020: 141; see also Tazamal, 2024). Mondon and Winter (2024) consider some of the more recent issues of the 2024 election in the UK and note the way in which the focus on immigration relied a lot on racialized discourses about who belongs and who is welcome. They point to the key role played by political and media elites in helping to profile this, by manufacturing exaggerated support for such issues. For example, Rishi Sunak's campaign in the 2024 UK general election positioned him standing at a podium with the words 'Stop the boats' as the key motto of the Conservative Party. This worked to place concerns of immigration as the central and primary issue for the election rather than a host of other key social concerns such as health, employment, or education.

Informed by these political issues, an important factor that has contributed to the mainstreaming of far-right ideas are responses to the events of 9/11 and how they were handled – particularly through the war on terror discourse and the introduction of counterterrorism measures, many of which promote the racial profiling of people who may be perceived as Muslim (Aziz and Esposito, 2024; Selod et al, 2024). This has worked to reinforce many of the stereotypes about Muslims and Islam that I have mentioned but has been emboldened by a hard-line focus on all Muslims as potential terrorists. These ideas are so widely held that they are easily utilized by the far right to platform and share Islamophobia. For example, in the Islamophobic riots in the UK in late July and August 2024, which are discussed in more detail in Chapter 6, a group of far-right agitators were stopping cars in Middlesbrough in northern England, apparently allowing those who looked white to drive on and refusing entry to anyone who did not conform to their ideals. I see parallels here with the ways in which Muslims – and those who look Muslim – are routinely questioned at airport security or subject to hostile 'stop and search' incidents by police officers. Essentially, the far right are copying their behaviours and actions, which are mainstream and well understood.

Compounding further the 'normalizing' of Islamophobia is the fact that the establishment has increasingly co-opted different forms of racism and Islamophobia but has done so under the guise of being liberal, tolerant, and advocating freedom of speech. Mondon and Winter (2020) differentiate between what they term 'illiberal' and 'liberal' racism, defining the former as:

> articulations of racism deemed to be in conflict with the post-war liberal order and consensus. They are associated with delegitimised ideas (biological racism, genocide, racist violence, segregation, and so on) claimed to have been defeated by the forces of liberalism during the war, and posited as a challenge to 'our' tolerant, egalitarian liberal societies. When they do appear, they are represented as remnants of the past and as individual aberrations, as opposed to part and parcel of contemporary mainstream society. (Mondon and Winter, 2020: 49)

This type of racism and Islamophobia is often easy to spot. However, Mondon and Winter (2020: 103) point to several examples of this illiberal form of racism being mainstreamed and platformed by liberal individuals and groups. They outline a three-step process: '1. The promotion and platforming of racist, illiberal, extreme equivalences between racist and anti-racist positions; 2. The emboldening of the far right; 3. The legitimization and mainstreaming of far-right ideas and of far right itself' (Mondon and Winter, 2020: 103). The central point here is that the expression of racism and Islamophobia can sometimes lead to the recruitment of those who are liberal and following apparently progressive ideals. And, since the mainstream has largely failed to address racism and Islamophobia, 'it has been possible for the reconstructed far right, with the help of its opportunistic mainstream elite allies, to harness liberal racism to push an increasingly radical agenda' (Mondon and Winter, 2020: 105). This has enabled the mainstreaming of the far right and allowed racism and Islamophobia to gain legitimacy.

In defining liberal racism, Mondon and Winter (2020) challenge the idea that liberalism and racism are necessarily opposed to and separate from each other, and that liberalism is not necessarily the logical way to challenge the far right. They point to the need to understand how liberalism operates, how it is utilized, and how racism can remain part and parcel of liberal agendas.

> [M]ainstream actors with often prestigious positions and access to broad platforms can act as a bridge between the far right and the mainstream, and facilitate the transfer of ideas between liberal and illiberal racisms. Whether they themselves hold far-right views or legitimize them consciously or not is irrelevant; in fact … they often come from varied backgrounds. What matters to us here is how their discourse has played a key role in the denial and perpetuation of racism … it has taken only a small number of savvy public figures to fill the space opened up by poor elite practices in the current (neo)liberal landscape. These loud voices have managed to occupy much of the public space by positioning themselves as rebels, while pushing extremely reactionary and conservative positions predicated on the superiority of the white man. This pitch, with its ability to generate highly marketable polemical confrontation, has proved appealing to media platforms on both the left and right. As the left has failed to counter these strategies decisively, the reactionary right has been allowed to shape much of the agenda, supported in this enterprise by those whose interests are threatened by egalitarian movements, who also happened to control much of the media landscape. (Mondon and Winter, 2020: 81–82)

Mondon and Winter (2020: 82) provide the example of 'a loose coalition of online commentators and public "intellectuals"' who are authors, political commentators, and vloggers, such as people like Sam Harris, Douglas Murray, Carl Benjamin, Christina Hoff, and academics such as Jordan Peterson and Jonathan Haidt. They also point to serious issues in relation to work by, for example, Matthew Goodwin and Eric Kaufmann, who, they say, 'participate in the legitimisation of the ideas central to the far right thus playing a key part in potentially increasing their reach' (Mondon and Winter, 2020: 100).

In this respect, Mondon and Winter (2020) are very clear that it is important not to assume that the mainstream is well intentioned, and that things will simply sort themselves out. They emphasize that it is problematic to accept the idea that these far-right issues are being discussed due to popular demand or because they are necessarily the issues that people are most interested in. A fundamental point of Mondon and Winter's (2020: 107) is that illiberal racism and liberal racism might appear to be in opposition but are, in fact, 'mutually enabling', 'two sides of the same coin', and although supposedly working in opposition to each other are 'indivisible'. They note that

> the resurgence of racism, populism, and the far right is not the result of popular demands, as we are often told, but instead the logical conclusion of the more or less conscious manipulation of the concept of 'the people' to push reactionary ideas in the service of power. This serves to re-enforce existing inequalities and divert us away from real concerns and radical alternatives to the current system. In this move, the far right is used as a decoy, diverting attention away from new political imaginaries: our only choice is between an increasingly resented status quo and the far right. This, in turn, has legitimised the far right as an alternative, strengthening its hand and leading us into a vicious circle. (Mondon and Winter, 2020: 5)

They refer to what they call 'populist hype', which has 'led to the legitimization of far-right ideas and their normalization, as shapers of public discourse have appropriated and repackaged them increasingly brazenly' (Mondon and Winter, 2020: 7).

We see, then, that a set of discursive elites – including the media, academics, and politicians – have played a key role in the mainstreaming of far-right ideas. In addition to this is the growth in coverage of these issues in news reports, documentaries, films, and so on, which 'has contributed to the hyping of far-right ideas, and played a key role in their legitimisation' (Mondon and Winter, 2020: 2). This mainstreaming of right-wing ideas not only distracts us from addressing racism and Islamophobia but works to

> legitimise its cruder expressions by giving them platforms. This has served to place concerns about systemic racism further in the back of the liberal mind, as it focuses instead on the extreme and far right. We argue that liberal democracies have become consumed by a fight for survival against a threat they have themselves nurtured, to divert attention away from their inability to respond to the inequalities and growing number of historical crises fuelled by capitalism and its innate conflict with liberal-democratic ideals of liberty and equality. (Mondon and Winter, 2020: 2)

This not only increasingly mainstreams racism and Islamophobia but emboldens far- right actors and promotes a growth of far-right groups. For example, in 2015 Europe witnessed the increasing popularity of PEGIDA

(Patriotic Europeans against the Islamization of the West), record numbers of hate groups emerged after the election of Barack Obama as US president, and far-right violence became increasing common (Mondon and Winter, 2020; Miller-Idriss, 2021). This normalizing of far-right ideas is a key mechanism within what I refer to as the Islamophobia industrial complex, and the actors and groups involved in mainstreaming play a key role in this, which I say more about in the following section.

The Islamophobia industrial complex

Having discussed some of the principal factors that have helped to generate the spread and promotion of Islamophobia, I now set out the key constituents of the Islamophobia industrial complex, important aspects of which are covered in the two chapters that follow.

Manzoor-Khan (2022: 2) is clear that Islamophobia is historical and structural, the outcome of white supremacy, its promotion of a racial hierarchy, and the influence of global capitalism, all of which have 'generated a story about Muslims as threats, barbarians and misogynists'. Mention of global capitalism is crucial here, as many of the different ways in which everyday Islamophobia operates, and which I discuss in this book, are perpetuated by a profit-making global enterprise with specific beneficiaries. Diverse ethnic and religious minorities – Muslims and other racialized communities – are demonized, excluded, marginalized, abused, tortured, and killed as a result.

The key actors of the Islamophobia industrial complex are outlined in Figure 3.1. The central role is played by the state, leading the global war on terror and the associated counterterrorism apparatus that works across diverse sectors in many contexts to racially profile and exclude Muslims. The state as the principal actor of the Islamophobia industrial complex is also the central player in what Rana (2016) refers to as the 'terror industrial complex', which I alluded to earlier, which includes all the resources, equipment, funding, salaries, and so on needed to maintain the systems and the processes that keep the global war on terror operating. This is not just about the costs of airport security or border control staff, but about how these systems and processes operate in schools, colleges, universities, health, social care and social work, and many other areas of society, and the resources that are needed to keep them active.

This model is similar to the five pillars model proposed by Massoumi et al (2017a), in which the state – and the counterterrorism apparatus that is part of it – operate as the main pillar. Working closely with and supporting the state, is a set of groups that benefit financially from their participation in the Islamophobia industrial complex and make up the other four pillars of Islamophobia. Massoumi et al (2017b) theorize that these pillars are the far

Figure 3.1: The Islamophobia industrial complex

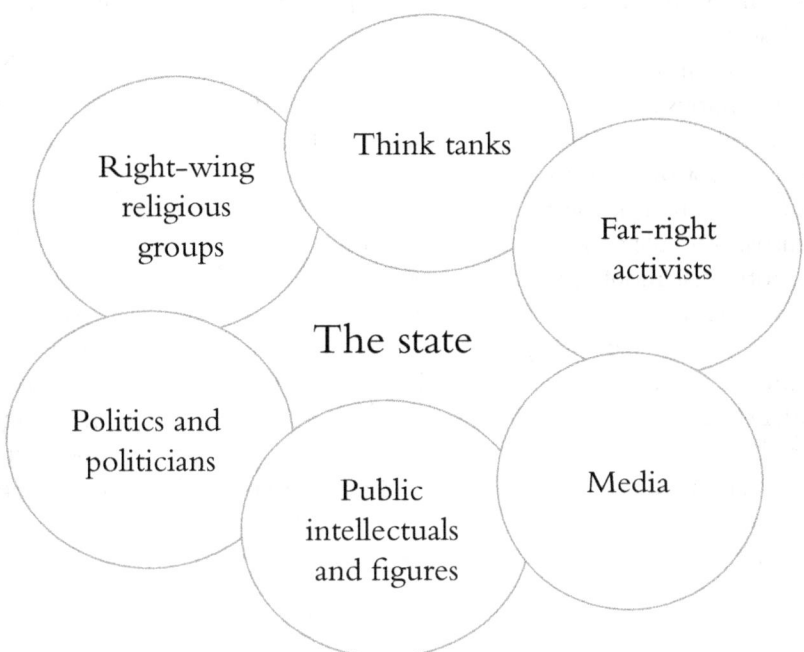

right, the neoconservative movement, the transnational Zionist movement, and an assortment of liberal groups including the pro-war and new atheist movements. This is a useful model that emphasizes the crucial role played by the state and by state actors (for example, Kundnani, 2017), and from which to consider the diversity and interconnectivity of other movements that operate to promote Islamophobia (see also Kumar, 2021).

The model presented in Figure 3.1 extends the idea of the five pillars and identifies the media, think tanks, and politics and politicians as key actors working with the state in perpetuating Islamophobia. I say more about these groups in the next two chapters. To be clear, not all aspects of the media necessarily participate actively in the Islamophobia industrial complex, and there are plenty of politicians and political movements resisting Islamophobia. Likewise, there are many think tanks doing important work to tackle it. However, within each of these three groups there is a significant presence of people, resources, power, and influence that act as important catalysts for driving the Islamophobia industrial complex forward and, ultimately, many benefit from its existence. The different constituents of the Islamophobia industrial complex change over time and are not always the same size or in the same sets of relationships as identified in Figure 3.1. Sometimes, they grow bigger and work more closely with specific sectors than others and, at other times, they are not as influential as other sectors of the industrial complex. The key point here is that these different actors work in collaboration to form the Islamophobia industrial complex and to catalyse everyday Islamophobia.

In addition to these are high-profile groups are far-right activists, right-wing religious groups, intellectuals, and other public figures, often having the advantages of a strong media presence and large online following. It will probably not be surprising to see the far right mentioned here. As I make clear in Chapter 5, the far right is often a key agent in the Islamophobia industrial complex, given the significant financial benefits they receive from promoting Islamophobia. The other two groups may be more surprising, as they frequently present themselves in ways that promote tolerance, respect, and understanding. However, as Beydoun (2018: 31) points out, 'Islamophobia coming from the left (and center) is often more latent and harder to detect than that which emanates from the right, and particularly the far right'. Alongside many of the right-wing religious groups (Massoumi et al, 2017a) are intellectuals and a coterie of public figures who have generated substantial followings in their promotion of Islamophobia, often alongside other forms of hatred, and whom I will discuss further.

4

Global Islamophobia, Nation-States, and Politics

It may seem out of place to have two chapters that focus exclusively on global and national issues in a book about everyday Islamophobia. Such concerns may appear to be distant, disengaged, and remote from people's daily comings and goings in their local communities and from the everyday. Whether they be the policies formed by national or supranational government bodies, or the rhetoric of politicians on an international stage, or military activity played out in places that may be geographically distant or remote, there is often a sense that such issues are not high on the priority list when thinking through accounts and experiences of everyday Islamophobia. However, in this chapter – the first of those two chapters – I argue that the reverse is the case, as global political issues, policy decisions and enforcements by national governments, the rhetoric of political leaders – and a myriad of other factors often framed as 'global' or 'national' – have a profound effect on people's everyday experiences of Islamophobia. Indeed, it is frequently these global and national issues that are the root cause and primary source of everyday interactions and encounters that are intrinsically Islamophobic. Further, it is the national policies and specific strategies of nation-states that often act as a catalyst for the spreading of Islamophobia globally.

Morgan and Poynting (2012) observe the moral panic associated with the presence of Muslims and the distinctive transnational characteristics that have come to shape contemporary Islamophobia. Similarly, Hafez (2020) reflects on Islamophobia as part of a global system that promotes white privilege and global capitalism, while extending its reach into new territories. In a sense, then, Islamophobia operates through proximate geopolitics, as matters of national and global politics, international relations, and territory – frequently constructed as remote issues – are instead positioned close by. Matters normally confined to the domain of international politics, to transnational decision-making processes, or to influential political leaders, have a closeness and nearness to them. There is a propinquity and a proximity in these interactions.

Katz (2007: 350) employs the idea of 'banal terrorism', which 'produces a sense of terror and fear in a drivelly and everyday way'. She explains that there are several common-sense everyday ways in which constructions and assumptions about terrorism and terrorists are utilized — especially during moments of crisis — to justify the erosion of civil liberties or, indeed, the ongoing war on terror: 'The common sense is predictably racist and also ignorant. It conflates Islam and Arab to embrace all brown men no matter what their national origins or religious beliefs. The working profile largely ignores women and excludes the angry white men of the Oklahoma City bombing as types' (Katz, 2007: 351). This is not only about national security being performed in local, everyday contexts, whether through security guards on buildings or stickers on car windows, but also about the process through which people adopt various acts as common sense, as they go about their daily lives. This all works to reinforce an 'us versus them' discourse and promotes a form of hysteria and paranoia related to the idea of moral panic mentioned earlier.

One of the most obvious ways in which we have seen this happen has been in response to the events of 9/11 and the widespread impacts that those events had for Muslims across the world. As much research has documented, Muslims have been subject to increasing hostility since 9/11, including experiencing racist abuse and attacks and stereotyping in the media (Hopkins, 2007; Sirin and Fine, 2008; Peek, 2011; Walklate and Mythen, 2015). Although the problem of Islamophobia was around long before 9/11, it was the events that day and the response of many nations that have catalysed and perpetuated the everyday Islamophobia that is so familiar today and to which the global war on terror was one response (Ganesh et al, 2024). Across the globe, including in Australia and New Zealand, in European countries and in North American contexts very far away from New York and Washington, there is clear evidence that marginalization and exclusion of Muslims increased following the events of 9/11. Marranci (2005) notes that before 9/11 Muslims in Northern Ireland were seen as 'immigrants' or 'Pakistanis', but they quickly turned into 'bin Laden' as they were reimagined as a Muslim threat. Young Muslims in Britain, in the aftermath of 9/11 and in the context of riots in Bradford, Burnley, and Oldham that same year, found that Islamophobia and racism gave them an increasing sense of difference in terms of how they understand their lives in Britain (Bagguley and Hussain, 2005). We see this in events such as the *Charlie Hebdo* incident becoming an important vehicle for the sharing of Islamophobia in Australia (Poynting and Briskman, 2017).

Many European countries responded by developing understandings of, and approaches to, radicalization through counterterrorism strategies (Selod et al, 2024) and continue to spend millions on funding such schemes, despite the fact that some of the key threats are coming from the far right rather than from Islamic extremism. The outcomes of this have led scholars such as Massoumi et al (2017a: 8) to suggest that 'we regard the state, and more specifically the sprawling official "counter-terrorism" apparatus, to be absolutely central to the production of contemporary Islamophobia – it is the backbone of anti-Muslim racism'. One example of such a response is the Prevent programme in the UK.

> One program that Prime Minister Tony Blair put into place was called 'Preventing Violent Extremism (PVE), later called 'PREVENT'. This policy aimed at surveilling a British Muslim population, by targeting mosques and individuals that the government thought was susceptible to 'extremism' as a way to prevent the radicalization of Muslims and consequently violence. But PREVENT is deeply problematic because it relies on stereotypical associations of Muslim=radicalization=potential terrorist. The policy was based on these stereotypical assumptions. (Selod et al, 2024: 2–3)

The Prevent strategy was developed in the UK, inspired by initiatives in the Netherlands and then imported into other contexts such as the United States, where it morphed into Countering Violent Extremism (Selod et al, 2024). While these state-sponsored initiatives might seem quite distant or remote from the everyday, they have generated 'unprecedented levels of state-led discrimination and human rights abuses of Muslims internationally' (Selod et al, 2024: 2). We see similar logics at play when we think about the US Department of Homeland Security launching its campaign, 'If you see something, say something' and the slogan and the various materials used to promote it finding their way into train stations, airports, bus shelters, university campuses, shopping areas, and so on (Kumar, 2018). Essentially, such campaigns encourage people to take on the role of the state in monitoring and reporting suspicious activity that they think could be linked to terrorism. Kumar (2018: 157) notes that the print material of campaigns such as this 'constructs ordinary locations and activities such as walking in the park, participating in a marathon, or attending a football game as potentially ominous' and observes that 'everyday spaces are turned into war zones where an attack can be expected at any moment'.

State-sponsored policies and strategies that circulate globally shape how specific bodies become read and responded to. Kumar (2020) uses the idea of 'terrorcraft' to describe the ways in which brown men – and points out that it nearly always *is* men – come to embody and represent terrorism. This racialization is embodied and everyday, even though it is framed as a national policy response to a global challenge. Significantly, Selod et al

(2024: 20) refer to the 'surveillance industrial complex'. An example of this trickle-down process demonstrates how such policies have spread: '[T]he counter-terrorism apparatus has spread from its traditional home in the police and intelligence services, to occupy almost every branch of the state, from schools and universities, to GP surgeries, social care, opticians, libraries and even nurseries' (Massoumi et al, 2017a: 12). This complex apparatus of counterterrorism policies, initiatives, and schemes has generated the 'terror-industrial complex', a concept that Rana (2016) uses to convey the complex sets of equipment, resources, and funding needed to maintain the systems that seek to monitor terrorism.

The key point here is that the state plays a central role in promoting policies, initiatives, and funding strategies that are operationalized in such a way that promotes and encourages everyday Islamophobia. Beydoun (2018: 29) frames 'the state as a potent collaborator that influences and (periodically) drives the acts of individual hatemongers, or Islamophobes, making it complicit in the range of hate crimes and hate incidents targeting Muslim individuals and communities'. However, these policies and approaches are often shared across nations in the name of 'good practice'. Selod et al (2024: 20), for example, argue that 'global racialization' as a term explains how 'security and surveillance practices rely on the construction of Muslims as a threat to national security'.

In this chapter, I consider ways in which Islamophobia operates globally and nationally through the promotion of policies and initiatives introduced and endorsed by specific governments:

> Global manifestations of Islamophobia are growing and include Buddhist Islamophobia in Myanmar against the Rohingya, Islamophobia in China against the Uyghurs, Hindu nationalist Islamophobia in India and Kashmir, and the Islamophobic oppression of Palestinians by the Israeli state ... Islamophobia also exists in Muslim majority countries, where it is embedded in systems of power supported by postcolonial elites and secularization policies and practices. (Zine, 2022a: 17)

In exploring these state-sponsored initiatives that are a response to widespread Islamophobia and the global war on terror, the crucial argument I want to put forward is that these are experienced, encountered, and negotiated as key forms of everyday Islamophobia. In other words, everyday Islamophobia is often catalysed by a complex concoction of the global war on terror and counterterrorism initiatives as a key part of that, many other state policies, the media, and a host of other factors. The Islamophobia industrial complex outlined in the previous chapter is that very concoction, and these state-sponsored and globally interconnected forms of Islamophobia have very real consequences for people's everyday lives. As Katz (2007: 351) notes, 'the material social practices of banal terrorism work at all scales, and their intricate circuitry not only enables them to authorize and reinforce one another, but naturalizes their acceptability and seeming common sense'. This is why I frame this complex as a key component of everyday Islamophobia, rather than simply a remote form of global, supranational, or national policy making. I am talking about the role that political parties, party leaders, and elected politicians play in promoting Islamophobia in the context of the nation-state policies and the perpetuation of global Islamophobia. 'Islamophobia is now more than ever a global phenomenon, and the War on Terror has evolved into an imperial project that advances it across longitudes and latitudes' (Beydoun, 2023: 8).

In considering the promotion and endorsement of Islamophobia by state organizations, I first consider issues of counterterrorism initiatives introduced in response to the war on terror through three examples of Muslims being securitized in Europe. I then turn to Donald Trump's Muslim ban in the United States, to demonstrate the role that Islamophobic politicians play in promoting anti-Muslim hatred. After this, I consider China's employment of the language of the war on terror in its mistreatment of Uyghur Muslims. Finally, I turn again to Europe and focus on France, where the presence of Islamophobia is often downplayed and frequently denied. Even though many of these events happen in other places 'far away', in this chapter I point to the impact that they have 'close by', in everyday negotiations of public space and embodied everyday encounters.

Counterterrorism and everyday Islamophobia

State-sponsored policies targeting Muslims (directly and indirectly) – motivated by global concerns – work to promote hardline everyday Islamophobia, and it is this state-sponsored Islamophobia that Massoumi et al (2017a) identify as one of the five pillars of Islamophobia. Crucially, as I have discussed, they note that this is the most influential pillar of the five. We see this clearly in the global war on terror. It is focused on making a clear division between Muslims who are 'good' and those who are 'bad', yet the process is such that all Muslims are always associated with some level of suspicion (Kundnani, 2023) and it has normalized the securitization of Muslims (Abbas, 2021). Key here is the *impact* of securitization rather than the securitization in and of itself. Muslims have increasingly been subjected to Islamophobia since 9/11, not only through institutionally racist structures but through those that place them in the position of suspect communities through counterterrorism initiatives (Mythen et al, 2009; Walklate and Mythen, 2015).

> War on Terror administrators talk about 'radicalization' as the process by which moderates are gripped by extremist Islam, transforming them,

the theory goes, into violent fanatics. Governments have established vast systems of surveillance to try to identify the would-be extremist Muslim hidden among the moderates. In practice, the classifying of Muslims into these two categories is not a matter of consistent and explicit criteria. Moderate Muslims are defined as those who restrict their religion to the private sphere. But they are also expected to publicly condemn interpretations of Islam that Western governments consider dangerous. Moderate Muslims are supposed to value freedom of speech. But they are considered extremists if they use their freedom of speech to criticize the West. Moderate Muslims are required to publicly condemn the use of violence to achieve political ends. But when the US government uses violence to achieve its political ends, condemnation must give way to consent. Western governments define Muslim extremism as a rejection of liberal values but, in practice, they almost always use the term to label Muslims who oppose their own power. (Kundnani, 2023: 20)

The globally circulating war on terror operates by securitizing those who are deemed to be a problem by castigating them as a threat to the security of the nation. Hussain and Bagguley (2012) refer to Muslims as 'securitized citizens', constructed as they are as a possible threat to security through counterterrorism policies and practices, noting also that there are gendered experiences involved in this:

> Muslims have become 'securitized', becoming increasingly viewed as a security threat by politicians, the media and many non-Muslims. ... The securitization perspective analyses the process by which an issue or group comes to be defined as a security threat so that governmental and societal resources can be mobilized to counter it. (Hussain and Bagguley, 2012: 716)

Moreover, 'the securitization of Muslims is reflected in the widespread questioning by politicians and in the media of whether Muslims can be integrated into European society' (Hussain and Bagguley, 2012: 717). The problem here is that, once a specific issue is securitized, it then becomes common sense to see this issue as a threat and almost impossible to refer to it without the security threat being implied in the process. Hussain and Bagguley (2012) suggest that the process of securitization can helpfully be compared to the moral panic discussed earlier. To demonstrate how this operates, I consider examples of lived experiences of everyday Islamophobia from the UK, Austria and the United States. In all three examples, those who suffer are researchers or students, some of whom are studying the issues that are the topic of this book.

Rizwaan Sabir was researching Al-Qaeda for his master's dissertation in politics at the University of Nottingham in the UK and was planning for a forthcoming PhD study. He had a daily routine of travelling to university to study in the graduate centre and chatting to his fellow students about politics over coffee. He felt increasingly motivated to study politics at university, as his interest in such issues had been sparked by the events of 9/11 and what he calls an 'awakening' to the ways in which the category of the 'Muslim' was becoming increasingly politicized. One day, while searching for source material for his dissertation, he happened upon an *Al-Qaeda Training Manual* on the US Department of Justice website. This freely available document could be downloaded by anyone who came across it, and the full version of it is available from several bookshops and websites. Sabir often shared articles and reports of interest with his friend, Hicham Yezza, who was employed by the university, and so he sent a copy of this report to Hicham. Unbeknown to Sabir, one of Yezza's colleagues noticed this report on his computer and reported it to the authorities without consulting either Sabir or Yezza.

Sabir was arrested under Section 58 of the UK Terrorism Act 2000 but was baffled as to why, given that he lived a quiet life and focused on progressing with his studies. He soon discovered that this was all part of Operation Minerva, and he was held in police custody for seven days before being released without charge, but with no apology. For a long time after his release, Sabir continued to be monitored by the authorities and to be a 'subject of interest' to the police. He outlines how his arrest and treatment by the police led to his wider family being treated with suspicion and to a decline in his mental health and wellbeing. His experiences of everyday Islamophobia included frequent incidents of being pulled over by the police, and one when he was questioned by the police while sitting in his car with a friend outside his family home. He also experienced being questioned by airport security staff while travelling for conferences or to present at events at which he was an invited speaker.

His experiences speak powerfully of the impact that counterterrorism policies motivated by the war on terror – such as Prevent – have in promoting the monitoring, regulation, and surveillance of Muslims (see also Jones, 2022). Sabir was studying at a UK university, which – as Massoumi et al (2017a) note – is an institution that is legally compelled to comply with the Prevent duty in reporting anyone who they believe could be potentially engaging in extremist activities. He powerfully documents his experiences in his book, *The Suspect* (Sabir, 2022), and discusses the mental health consequences of his arrest and monitoring. These experiences of everyday Islamophobia led to much of his everyday life being transformed. The university where he was able to feel supported and intellectually curious was transformed into a context in which Sabir was unwillingly embroiled in the counterterrorism and surveillance apparatus of the state. Someone who lived a generally healthy life found that his mental health declined as he struggled to sleep, disturbed by a decreasing feeling of trust for those closest to him and increasing feelings of paranoia that he was being watched and monitored. He considered sleeping rough in his car so that he could be constantly on the move and know if he was being followed. And on one occasion – in the middle of a mental breakdown – he drove 1,200 miles across Europe to avoid being with a family member whom he suspected of working for intelligence services. As he notes, 'Once you are marked as a "subject of interest", it becomes difficult to become uninteresting' (Sabir, 2022: 59). Although he was awarded an out-of-court settlement of £20,000 in damages, this did little to stop his frequent encounters with the regulation, monitoring, and surveillance of the state. Moreover, the effects of this became a medicalized issue when he was prescribed sleeping pills by a psychiatric nurse, which he sees as symbolic of the state's attempt to 'put him to sleep'.

Moving across to mainland Europe, Austria is the focus of the second example. Farid Hafez is a respected political scientist who was employed at the University of Salzburg as an associate professor and, since 2015, he has co-authored (with Enes Bayrakli) the annual *European Islamophobia Report*. The 2022 report (Bayrakli and Hafez, 2023) sets out 23 chapters about Islamophobia across Europe and includes chapters that focus on Finland, Spain, Bosnia and Herzegovnia, Ireland, and Malta, to name only a few. The most recent report, of 2023, includes 28 national reports and an introduction (Bayrakli and Hafez, 2024). On 9 November 2020, Hafez reflects:

> It was the early hours of the morning in Vienna, Austria. As my (Farid's) wife awoke, she noticed some strange movements outside the bedroom window of our second-floor apartment. We peered out into the street and noticed heavily armed men in tactical gear standing below. To us, they appeared as soldiers ready for battle in a war zone. It was then that we began to notice the infrared dots speckled over our upper bodies. The terrifying glow of these red beams was accompanied by violent screaming, commanding us to put up our hands. All of a sudden, armed men burst into our bedroom, pointing large artillery weapons at us. My mind could not fully grasp what was happening. For a moment, I began to believe we had somehow been transported to some faraway war-torn nation in our sleep. Still unable to grasp the severity of the situation, I began to plead with these armed state henchmen to not disturb our children, as they were still soundly sleeping in their rooms, seemingly a world away from the chaos ensuing on the other side of their door. The men had callously burst into the next rooms pointing their guns and flashlights at our children, whose only crime was to

have a father who was an outspoken scholar and critic of draconian state measures that have targeted minority communities in Europe, particularly Muslims. (Bakali and Hafez, 2022: 1)

Hafez was one of 70 targets of Operation Luxor, an extensive police operation that involved just under 1,000 officers raiding the homes of those from whom they felt it was necessary to 'cut off the roots of political Islam' (Bridge Initiative, 2024). This operation was part of the same initiative that promoted other forms of state-sponsored Islamophobia such as the 2015 Islam Act and attempts to ban the wearing of the hijab in schools (Hafez, 2023b). These raids were later deemed unlawful by the Austrian courts, yet the damage had already been done to Hafez and his family, and in the promotion of everyday Islamophobia in Austrian society. Hafez's children now struggle to sleep, alert to any noises they hear that could be the police visiting again. His family was treated for post-traumatic stress disorder. Hafez was born and grew up in Austria and was educated at the University of Vienna, yet this did not seem to matter when he was identified as a target of this Islamophobic initiative. Hafez (2023a) documents the emergence of the use of 'political Islam', a phrase used in European countries such as Austria, Germany, and France, pointing to this as an extension of the narratives on preventing violent extremism.

In the third example, the focus is on the United States and the experiences of a Somalian refugee who resettled in Minneapolis. Beydoun (2018) recounts the experiences of Ahmed, the son of Somalian refugees, who created a new life for himself and his family in Little Mogadishu in Minneapolis, Minnesota. We learn that he was studying biology at his local college, regularly attending his local mosque, and following his parents' suggestions of sending money back home from his earnings from his part-time job. He is a committed fan of Minnesota Timberwolves, and his social media account is full of posts about the ups and downs of the team's performances, along with occasional posts about life back in Somalia. In 2014, during Ramadan, Ahmed was spending more time at the mosque as he more fully embraced his faith and, at the end of Ramadan that year, he kept a beard to signify his commitment to his faith. However,

[t]o the Minneapolis police department and the DHS agents it collaborated with, Ahmed's spiritual growth signalled a risk and prompted suspicion. His name had made its way onto the list of 'subjects of interest' – all of whom were Muslim men, whether Somali, Arab, black, or white – tallied by Minneapolis police officers as suspects of 'being radicalised' by Al-Shabab, ISIS, or other Islamic transnational terror networks. Ahmed's spiritual growth and placement on the suspect list all happened in less than a year. (Beydoun, 2018: 129)

Yet, Ahmed had no idea at all that he was of any interest to the police until, one weekend, two police officers visited his family home to question him. It transpired that the police were working with a student from Ahmed's school, who was keeping an eye on him and reporting any points of potential interest to the police. The added irony here is that, in return, this student was receiving reduced probation time for their involvement in criminal activities. As Beydoun (2018: 129) points out, 'Ahmed has done no wrong, he had no prior convictions, no criminal record at all, and yet he was deemed a subject of special interest – a prospective radical on account of his nationality, neighborhood, and especially, his spiritual evolution from secular to devout Muslim'.

The grim irony across each of these three accounts is that the counterterrorism initiatives promoted on the back of the global war on terror are supposed to prevent the likelihood of violence, terrorism, or other forms of unrest. Yet, in each case, these initiatives have enacted state-supported violence and profoundly disrupted the everyday lives of those targeted by these policies, including wider networks of family, friends, and acquaintances. As Manzoor-Khan (2022: 30) notes, 'the War on Terror not only failed to end violence, but actively produced more. ... In fact, the War on Terror has created endless streams of profit through murder, dispossession and exploitation'.

Trump's Muslim ban

US President Barack Obama asked the country for tolerance towards Muslims in his speech after the terrorist attacks on 2 December 2015 in San Bernardino, California (Tesler, 2018), when a married couple, Syed Rizwan Farook and Tashfeen Malik, killed 14 people and injured more than 20 at a social welfare centre. They were later killed by the police in a shootout (Kabir, 2023). However, Obama's request did not reach far, as those who disliked Muslims did not favour him. Indeed, attitudes towards Muslims among the US electorate were a strong predictor of vote choice in both the 2008 and 2012 elections. A 'strong link between anti-Muslim sentiments and opposition to Obama helped Islamophobia emerge as a significant predictor of party identification for the first time ever during his presidency' (Tesler, 2018: 153; see also Aziz and Esposito, 2024). This provided Donald Trump with an ideal platform from which to raise questions about the apparent legitimacy of Obama's citizenship and religious identity. The day after the San Bernardino incident, Trump proposed 'a complete and total shutdown of Muslims entering the United States' (Tesler, 2018: 154).

> President Trump promised a more hardline domestic surveillance program, which he called Countering Islamic Violence; a registry to

keep track of Muslim immigrants within the United States; legislation that would bludgeon the civic and advocacy programs of Muslim American organizations; and other measures that would threaten Muslim immigrants, citizens, and institutions. (Beydoun, 2018: 9)

So, what was already called Countering Violent Extremism turned into Countering Islamic Violence under Trump (Beydoun, 2018; Hilal, 2021), providing clear evidence of the explicit Islamophobia he exhibited. However, while Trump's rhetoric motivated the most Islamophobic components of his party, others challenged his approach, arguing that it conflicted with an inclusive American identity. Yet, Beydoun notes:

> Seven days into his presidency, Trump delivered on the promise he first made on the campaign trail on December 7, 2015 enacting a travel ban that restricted the entry of nationals from seven Muslim-majority nations. ... To me, the Muslim ban was not merely a distant policy signed into law in a distant city; it was personal in a myriad of ways. First, I am a Muslim American, and second, I had close friends from several of the restricted nations and had visited several of those nations. (Beydoun, 2018: 8)

Many American Muslims will have felt similar feelings to those expressed here, as Trump enacted a direct attack on their religious faith and a targeted set of restrictions on those travelling to and from specific countries. This Muslim ban was the first policy that Trump – the leader that Beydoun (2018: 8) calls the 'Islamophobia President' – introduced that targeted Muslims. Alarmingly, Pew Research found that 76 per cent of white evangelicals in the United States supported this travel ban (Uddin, 2024).

The first Muslim ban became law on 27 January 2017 and restricted those travelling from seven countries – Iran, Iraq, Libya, Somalia, Sudan, Syria, and Yemen – from entering the United States and banned refugees from Syria indefinitely. Of the seven countries that Trump banned travel from, three (Libya, Somalia, and Sudan) are in Africa and the remaining four in the Middle East, thus representing a combination of Islamophobia and anti-black racism (Beydoun, 2018).

> Remember that this ban, although intended to prohibit the entry of visa holders from these states, also led to the denial of entry of green card holders. So, there were a couple of days where this ban detrimentally impacted lawful permanent residents and green card holders. And then, remember that there was a serious challenge to this ban on grounds that it violated the Establishment Clause by specifically targeting Muslim countries. The resulting debate was whether it could really

> be called a Muslim ban or not. The seven states that were listed in the ban were predominantly Muslim majority countries. The initial order had an exception for individuals, from these countries, who could persuade the United States that they were, in fact, not Muslim. (Beydoun, 2017: 454)

Here, then, we see a form of state-sponsored Islamophobia that has a transnational reach, with the arrogance of Trump seeking enhanced border controls and, in a sense, power over international travel and airspace.

Trump's Muslim ban was not an isolated example of his Islamophobia. Waikar (2018) undertook a detailed analysis of 20 speeches made by Trump and concluded that he clearly sees the source of terrorism being radical Islam. Furthermore, he dramatizes this as a global threat and then uses Muslim refugees and immigrants as being emblematic of this. His immigration policies clearly conflate Muslim refugees with radical Islam, portraying them as two sides of the same coin.

> Rather than appealing to the Supreme Court after the Ninth Circuit issued a national stay on the first ban, Trump re-sketched the travel ban and came up with the second iteration – which is more clever in the way it is framed. The second ban focuses less on religious identification, and more on national identification. One major reform, with the second iteration, is a description of the six states. (Beydoun, 2017: 454)

Iraq was removed from the initial list of seven states, and an outline of the threats posed by each state was set out in an attempt to 'circumvent or weaken the Establishment Clause challenges against the order' (Beydoun, 2017: 454). Trump was clearly determined to implement his Islamophobic policy, irrespective of any constraints presented to him. However, a restraining order was also placed on the second ban.

The details of Trump's policies that ban Muslims demonstrate the ways in which he draws upon Islamophobic stereotypes that are also patriarchal, sexist, and highly gendered. The negative rhetoric around these issues relies on and reproduces

> deeply gendered stereotypes about Muslims and Islam by depicting all Muslim men as potential terrorists, Muslim women as helpless victims of oppression, and Islam as inherently tyrannical, violent, and patriarchal. The reference to honor killings in the first EO is a prime example of how anti-Muslim thinking manipulates gendered (mis)conceptions. The EO appropriates violence against Muslim women by Muslim men to justify the targeting of all Muslims (men, women, children, elderly, young) as security threats and condones

their collective punishment, echoing once again the historical enlisting of women's suffering in the service of Western imperial projects and military invasions. (Gökariksel, 2017: 469)

Although Trump's Muslim ban was repealed by US President Joe Biden in spring 2021 (Schenk et al, 2022), the consequences of his approach have been – and crucially, continue to be – deeply felt in everyday life for many. A national policy targeting travel from other specific nations across the globe has direct consequences for people living their everyday lives as they travel to and from work, take their children to school, or engage with the news media. Hassan (2017: 187) argues that 'Trump's Orientalism, Islamophobia and the securitisation of Islam have come to define Trump's approach to the MENA (Middle East and North Africa) more than any strategic rationale. In particular, this has manifested in the identity construction of "Muslims" and "Arabs" as an existential threat'. Furthermore, Beydoun (2018: 205) notes that 'the decision to act as non-Muslim as possible is an emergent phenomenon in Trump's America'. While these policies 'wrought mayhem in American airports, [and] broke up families' (Beydoun, 2018: 176), the anxiety of travelling through airports and concerns about family separation continue to be regular experiences for Muslims or those who may be mistaken for being Muslim.

> Even as the US courts have challenged and issued stays on the EOs, their effects continue to reverberate across public debates, in the streets, and at border checkpoints. They negatively affect all Muslims and those who look like Muslims, as well as the relations between the United States and the Middle East. While Muslims have been subjected to surveillance, discriminatory practices, and hate crimes in the United States for decades, violence targeting Muslims and those who look Muslim has increased since the presidential campaign. Muslim women who wear the headscarf have become easy targets for attacks because of their publicly visible religious alignment. (Gökariksel, 2017: 470; see also Gökariksel and Smith, 2017)

It is important to emphasize that Trump does not stand alone as a US president who promotes Islamophobia and anti-Muslim hatred. For example, Kumar (2010) documents how US presidents such as George H.W. Bush, Bill Clinton, and George W. Bush drew upon a 'clash of civilizations' discourse to reinforce five sets of problematic stereotypes of Islam and Muslims. These include the assumption that Islam is a monolithic and homogeneous religion, that it is sexist and patriarchal, that Muslims are not capable of rational or scientific thinking, that Islam is violent, and that while the West supports democracy, Islam promotes terrorism. So, in many ways, Trump was continuing the trend of those who served before him, and 'the election of Trump restored the fears Muslim Americans had after 9/11. Muslim Americans faced scapegoating, rising hostility, hate crimes and, most strikingly, an executive branch that subscribed to the worldview that the US was at war with Islam' (Beydoun, 2018: 179). Lajevardi (2020) observes how the introduction of Trump's 'Muslim ban' led to an increase in Islamophobia with the cases of Islamophobia being 91 per cent higher in the first quarter of 2017 than the year before, indicating that the policy itself provided a clear platform for the spread of Islamophobia.

China's incarceration of Uyghur Muslims

In a rather different context, another explicit form of state-sponsored, state-sanctioned and nationally promoted Islamophobia is found in the Chinese response to the presence of Uyghur Muslims in the northwest of the country (Caksu, 2020). Uyghurs generally have a Turkic heritage and are traditionally associated with East Turkestan, an area located in northwest China. Uyghurs started to embrace Islam in the 10th century, and it is now the most widely practised religion in the region and embedded within the local culture. The region was invaded in the late 1800s and renamed Xinjiang. Although the Uyghurs twice established independence, the region was invaded again in 1949 by the Chinese Communist Party (Center for Uyghur Studies, 2024).

> The Xinjiang (Uyghur) Autonomous Region (XUAR) reveals China's expansionist, colonial endeavors. Despite national revisionist accounts, history shows that the Chinese state acquired the region by violent conquest. ... With the creation of the XUAR in 1955 after its annexation, the CPC (Chinese Communist Party) promised autonomy to the Uyghurs, assuring the protection of linguistic, cultural, religious, and ethnic rights and freedoms. These promises would not come to full fruition. The communist government considered Islam a competing ideology that undermined allegiance to the PRC (People's Republic of China) and challenged the government's nation-building project. This resulted in state repression of Uyghurs and Islam: individuals who were considered politically deviant and religiously subversive were executed as counter-revolutionaries, while the imams (Muslim religious leaders) were assaulted, mosques were defiled, Islamic taxes were eliminated, lands upon which mosques existed were expropriated, and religious texts were scorched in public. (Shibli, 2021: 156)

So, since this invasion, Uyghur Muslims in the region have had to negotiate restricted freedoms, especially in the practice of their religious faith. As Smith Finley (2021: 352) notes, 'the indigenous Turkic Muslim peoples are viewed as "deviant" and disloyal subjects that must be "corrected" or else eradicated'. Not surprisingly, 'Uyghur separatists have regularly resisted Chinese rule through protest, rebellion, insurgency, and what the government has more recently categorized as terrorism' (Shibli, 2021: 156). There are around 11 million Turkic-speaking Uyghur Muslims, most of whom live in the Xinjiang province, making up more than half of the 20 million Muslims resident in China (Shibli, 2021).

From 2001, the Chinese government increasingly employed the language of the global 'war on terror' (Shibli, 2021; Center for Uyghur Studies, 2023, 2024).

> Islam – often synonymous with extremism, subversion, and difference – and those who visibly practice it have become convenient marks of increased surveillance, socio-political oppression, extrajudicial detention, and even torture/death, all officially under the guise of the elusive war on terror and for the purpose of state security. In China, Islamophobia has effectively been state-sanctioned, legislated, securitized, and widely accepted. (Shibli, 2021: 152)

This led to the regular racial profiling and exclusion of Uyghur Muslims. Shibli (2021) notes that there is not much evidence at all to link local or national issues within the Xinjiang region to concerns about global terrorism and the war on terror, but the Chinese government successfully employed such strategies to target Uyghur Muslims. 'Chinese Islamophobia has been institutionalized through state policy which has enacted structural and slow violence onto a population considered subversive, backward, anti-Chinese, and thus unwanted' (Shibli, 2021: 162).

Selod et al support this, noting that:

> [A]ccording to a *New York Times* article that exposed leaked Chinese documents about the detention of and crackdown on Uyghur Muslims, 'Mr Xi urged the party to emulate aspects of America's "war on terror" after the Sept. 11 attacks' in response to a violent attack committed by a Uyghur Muslim. (Selod et al, 2024: 26)

Shilbi (2021: 162) observes that:

> The Global War on Terror became an opportune pretense for the continued and intensified system of marginalization and violent subjugation: disguised as a legitimate response to the alleged global threat embodied by Uyghurs whose identities necessarily equate desires for greater autonomy and separatism by any means. ... Legitimate security concerns were hijacked by the state for the nefarious purpose

of ostracizing an ethno-religious group that presented an inconvenient problem to official narratives. (Shibli, 2021: 162)

The specific approach that has been employed in Xinjiang is essentially a form of securitization focused on Islam: in practice, 'the definition of a "religious extremist" – and potential terrorist, since "extremism" is deemed the ideational basis of terrorism – has come to mean anyone participating in any Islamic practice, however peaceful' (Smith Finley, 2019: 11).

One tactic adopted in this context often relied on local officials being sent out and 'tasked with reporting on "extremist" behaviours, including a range of innocuous everyday Islamic practices such as fasting during Ramadan, sporting a long beard, avoiding alcohol, or possessing Qu'rans' (Smith Finley, 2019: 4). The information was then used to rank the trustworthiness of individuals, including points relating to their ethnic group, family migration history, visits to overseas countries, and their religious knowledge and practices. Some were assessed via their children through school visits, during which children were questioned about the religiosity of their parents or their participation in faith-based activities (Smith Finley, 2019). In addition to the employment of local officials,

> religious and residential committees have been set up whereby locals are required to report on any activities which contain Islamic religious customs, including funerals, weddings, and circumcision. ... There are also comprehensive lists of prohibited religious practices which target Muslims. One such list, titled the 'Manual for Ethic and Religious Work' in a Urumqi town, has cited the following practices as illegal: proselytization, encouraging participation in religious activities, adorning or aesthetically improving spaces for religious activities without proper permits, studying religion outside of state-sanctioned organizations, studying religion abroad, and printing unsanctioned religious texts without authorization. (Shibli, 2021: 159)

One specific strategy employed in response to anyone considered to present a possible risk according to officials is that they could be considered to be eligible for internment. For example, in March 2017, 'the Xinjiang Uyghur Autonomous Region (XUAR) Regulations on De-Extremification' were published (Smith Finley, 2021: 351). These regulations promoted the development of 'transformation through education' camps:

> This phase has seen political re-education involving coercive Sinicization, deaths in the camps through malnutrition, unsanitary conditions, withheld medical care, and violence (beatings); rape of male and female prisoners; and since the end of 2018, transfers of the

most recalcitrant prisoners – usually young, religious males – to high-security prisons in Xinjiang or inner China. (Smith Finley, 2021: 351)

As of December 2018, it was estimated that there was something in the range of 800,000 to two million Uyghur and Turkic Muslims interned in re-education camps in the region (Smith Finley, 2019). The criteria for 'extremist religious practices' that could lead to someone being seen as deserving of internment include:

> [G]rowing a beard (especially a long one); praying regularly; inviting too many people to one's wedding; giving children names of Islamic origin; appearing too religious (e.g., wearing veils, headscarves, or long clothes in Muslim style); reciting an Islamic verse at a funeral; washing bodies according to Islamic custom; holding strong religious views; allowing others to preach religion; teaching the Qur'an to one's children; asking an imam to name one's children; attending the mosque regularly; studying or teaching 'unauthorized' forms of Islam; praying at a mosque other than on a Friday (the traditional day of prayer in the Central Asia region); attending Friday prayers outside of one's own village; making the pilgrimage to Mecca. (Smith Finley, 2019: 5)

The scale of this initiative should not be underestimated. Smith Finley (2021: 348) points out that the region of Xinjiang has seen the 'largest forced incarceration of an ethno-religious minority anywhere in the world since the Second World War: upwards of one million Uyghurs and other Turkic Muslims have been forced into internment camps for "re-education" and "thought transformation", or into high-security prisons, or situations of forced labour'.

State-sponsored and promoted forms of Islamophobia often spill over into other aspects of everyday life, as Uyghur and Turkic Muslims find themselves being subject to Islamophobia from state and non-state actors. Some of the specific forms of Islamophobia include birth control measures being forced upon women; Muslims being asked to 'renounce their mother tongue and Islam' (Smith Finley, 2019: 2); women wearing a hijab or men with beards being made a mockery of and not allowed to enter hospitals; Muslims being refused employment (Center for Uyghur Studies, 2023); participation in the pilgrimage to Mecca not being permitted; and fasting during Ramadan forbidden. There is also reference to Qurans being burnt, mosques and cemeteries being destroyed, and the Arabic language being banned (Center for Uyghur Studies, 2023). Furthermore, China has tried to water down any claims that Ughyur Muslims have to the Xinjiang region by encouraging those of Han Chinese ethnicity (the largest ethnic group in China) to migrate to the region, which in turn has led to social and economic inequalities in the region (Smith Finley, 2019).

Shibli (2021: 162) points out that China's treatment of Uyghur Muslims has been met with 'little more than silence from the international community', highlighting the role that silencing and absence can play despite being 'laced with clear manifestations of Islamophobia' (Shibli, 2021: 156). Furthermore, Younis (2024) observes that the Chinese imagery of extremism associates it with infection, disease, or drug abuse, suggesting that there are concerns about the transmission of Islam and that it requires some form of treatment.

This is not an isolated example. Selod et al (2024: 4) indicate similar discourses in operation: 'Uyghur Muslims, Indian Muslims, American Muslims, and British Muslims are all framed as misogynists, violent, irrational, and a population that should be watched, monitored, deported, or even detained.'

The denial of Islamophobia in France

In 2022, the far right in France saw its best-ever election result. Marine Le Pen secured 13 million votes in the second round of the presidential election, and the two far-right candidates – Marine Le Pen and Eric Zemmour – together secured almost a third of first-round votes. Le Pen pledged to remove basic rights for foreigners, and Zemmour drew heavily on the great replacement theory (Kiwan and Wolfreys, 2023), discussed in Chapter 2.

Given this context, we might think that Islamophobia would be taken seriously in France. However, the approach to it is dominated by a culture of denial, which only serves to exacerbate the unavailability of certain rights to Muslims (Hajjat and Mohammed, 2023; Bayrakli and Hafez, 2024; Mohammed, 2024). Indeed, there is outright denial of any suggestions of racialization, as 'race' is not recognized, and Hancock (2015) observes that the denying of difference is seen as progressive. France has long prided itself on being 'colour-blind', and there is a strong resistance demonstrated by many to the collection of any data about issues of ethnicity or racial group, which instead results in factors such as 'spatial otherness, or implied foreign-ness' becoming the most acceptable way to discuss ethnic or racial differences (Hancock, 2015: 1030).

The French government banned the wearing of the full veil in public spaces in 2004. In 2011, the government launched a campaign, '*La République se vit à visage découvert*', which Hancock (2015) explains roughly translates into English as 'the Republic is lived with an uncovered face'. This was represented by the classical bust of Marianne who has been the female symbol of the French republic for over 200 years. Hancock (2015) further documents the strategies employed in the government's promotion of different categories of citizenship associated with forms of female dress. Further, in her analysis of the sessions of the parliamentary commission that discussed the issue of the veil, Hancock (2015: 1031) detected that the implication was that 'wearing the full-face veil is not so much a personal choice of dress as a major geopolitical threat and the beginning of an "invasion"'.

One of the important ways in which this plays out in everyday life for French Muslims is through what Hancock sees as the selective employment of *laïcité*, or secularism, against Muslims in France and through what Kiwan (2023: 143) refers to as the 'political weaponization of *laïcité* in French electoral politics'. *Laïcité* is seen to be key to the achievement of *liberté, égalité, fraternité*. First, it secures freedom of conscience (liberty); second, it focuses on the strict separation of state and religion, thus enabling equal treatment (equality); and, third, it ensures that no one religion is favoured over another (fraternity). However, the way it has been weaponized, hijacked by the far right (Kiwan, 2023: 149), and radicalized (Wolfreys, 2023) is such that there is now a hypersensitivity to any gestures or acts that might be considered to be contravening it. This has included concerns about supermarkets that do not stock pork or alcohol and the use of apparently fake doctors' notes so Muslim schoolgirls can be excused from swimming lessons.

> The escalation of Islamophobic reaction in contemporary France derives in part from the disarray of state actors caught up in a crisis of political representation. Some of the tools deployed to navigate this crisis are being reshaped in the process. First among these is laïcité. Ostensibly a modality, a mechanism for the arbitration of public life, its significance is increasingly emphasised as a value, appended to liberté, égalité, fraternité as a defining feature of Frenchness. The result has been a convergence of France's Republican model of citizenship, based around identification with political ideals, with what might appear to be a diametrically opposed ethno-culturalist outlook that sees shared affinities or heritage as fundamental to a harmonious society. (Wolfreys, 2023: 173)

In 2020, the French authorities closed two Muslim charities, BarakaCity and Collective against Islamophobia, alleging that they were engaged in provoking terrorism (Shaheed, 2021). And on 24 September 2021, the French Council of State confirmed the dissolution of the CCIF (Collectif contre l'Islamophobie en France), which was the leading organization working to monitor and challenge Islamophobia in France (Najib, 2021; Bechrouri, 2023). It was established in 2003 and was widely respected as an effective anti-racist organization among the local and national community. Beyond France, the organization was also well respected within Europe and by the United Nations. Bechrouri (2023) confirms that the process to close this organization can be traced back about a year when Macron announced plans to address Islamist separatism.

> Denial of Islamophobia took a more aggressive turn under Macron. The Collectif Contre l'Islamophobie en France (CCIF) played an important role in collecting data on Islamophobic acts, investigating them and providing legal support to those facing discrimination. In a move that Amnesty International warned might threaten freedom of association, the government simply dissolved it. (Kiwan and Wolfreys, 2023: 141)

Wolfreys (2023) explores other ways in which Muslims have been discriminated against and marginalized in France, especially under the leadership of Emmanuel Macron. These include the denial of opportunities to open Muslim schools and the development of a charter that means that imams must agree that the state is not responsible for anything deemed to be anti-Muslim.

Hajjat (2021: 622) is clear that 'France is a textbook case of Islamophobia' as a 'social phenomenon' cross-cutting various aspects of society, including politics, administrative processes, legal systems, economics, media, and institutions of education. Hajjat and Mohamed (2023: 3) claim that 'Islam has been a "problem" in France for decades', and they point out that France is one of the least responsive countries in Europe in addressing Islamophobia (Hajjat and Mohammed, 2023). Islamophobic acts in France increased 12-fold between 2005 and 2019. Moreover, the obstacles encountered in the labour market by Muslim men in France compared to Catholic men are six times greater than those for African American men in the United States compared to white men (Hajjat and Mohammed, 2023).

The extension of denial reaches into the terrain of universities and other educational institutions. For example, government ministers have promoted the idea that activist academics were disrupting research by focusing on issues such as Islamophobia. The Centre national de la recherche scientifique, one of the leading research institutions in France, was called upon to conduct an inquiry, and its findings were dismissive of the topic, rejected the term, and condemned fields such as postcolonial studies, intersectional research, and studies about race. In 2017, an annual conference focusing on Islamophobia that was due to take place in Lyon was cancelled following internal and external pressure, including from the far right (Hajjat, 2021; Najib, 2022). Najib (2022: 3) observes that 'it has become increasingly clear that in France there are significant reactionary forces on the march to eliminate certain themes, in particular the study of Islamophobia, and systematically to question the skills, contribution, and quality of research by racialized and Muslim researchers'. Najib (2022) suggests that the French academic system is such that there is a focus on objectivity and neutrality in research and that French academia wants to steer clear of activism and politics and not include researchers working on topics such as Islamophobia. Perhaps not surprisingly against this background, in 2015, 98 per cent of reported incidents of anti-Muslim hatred in France took place in institutional and professional contexts, and 64 per cent occurred in schools, town halls, or hospitals (Najib and Hopkins, 2020), rather than being associated with public spaces (see Chapter 6).

Crucially, this widespread culture of denial of Islamophobia has serious consequences for Muslims' navigation of everyday life in France. On the one hand, they find themselves in an increasingly hostile context, where incidents of Islamophobia are becoming more frequent, and the state is utilizing a radicalized version of *laïcité* to police, control, and manage Muslim citizens and their relationships with others (Najib, 2024). At the same time, and as a result of this culture, they find the very legitimacy of Islamophobia as a concept being rejected. As we have seen before, these state-sponsored forms of Islamophobia are not confined to the spaces of government but have very real consequences for the ways in which Muslims in France are able to live their everyday lives, choose what they wear, practise their religion, and engage in work or leisure.

Islamophobic politicians

A key mechanism through which Islamophobia is promoted at the global and national level is through the narratives of Islamophobic politicians. The *European Islamophobia Report* (Bayrakli and Hafez, 2024) devotes more than six pages to setting out examples of Islamophobia exhibited by politicians in Europe in the last year. As discussed earlier, far-right politicians are increasingly finding that they can win seats in elections and, even if they are not members of the winning party, their gains are such that they can still wield significant influence and potentially enter coalitions. In being elected, they are given a platform through which to share their Islamophobic views. Furthermore, given the mainstreaming of these issues, as discussed in Chapter 3, right-wing ideas have increasingly found their way into mainstream politics and are routinely espoused by political parties that are regarded as more centrally positioned or even left-wing on the political spectrum. While Islamophobic views are expected from the likes of Marine Le Pen in France, Pauline Hanson in Australia, Nigel Farage in the UK, or Geert Wilders in the Netherlands, we find that increasingly politicians who occupy broadly mainstream positions – and can therefore win elections and end up in power – are sharing these ideas. We see examples of powerful politicians, such as Emmanuel Macron in France, espousing Islamophobic opinions, and their words, actions, policies, and overall approach can have a remarkable effect in the promotion of Islamophobia.

In August 2018, Boris Johnson – when still a backbench MP in the UK and a year before being elected as prime minister – published a piece in the *Daily Telegraph* newspaper. Boasting about a recent visit to Copenhagen, he discussed Danes exercising early in the morning and their culture of cycling and expressed his apparent surprise that Denmark had imposed a ban on the niqab and burka. He then launched into an explicit Islamophobic rant, saying, 'If you tell me that the burka is oppressive, then I am with you. If you say that it is weird and bullying to expect women to cover their faces, then I totally agree.' He continued, 'I would go further and say that it is absolutely ridiculous that people should choose to go around looking like letter boxes.' He cautioned his concern that Muslim women look like 'bank robbers' and described the burka and niqab as 'odd bits of headgear' (Johnson, 2018: 14). In the week following this, TellMAMA (2019) reported a 375 per cent increase in anti-Muslim attacks in the UK, the majority of which were directed at visibly Muslim women. Over the next three weeks, 42 per cent of street-based incidents either referenced Boris Johnson or used language taken from his article.

While the influence of Johnson's Islamophobic comments was mostly felt in the UK, many politicians have an international influence through their engagements with political leaders in other countries or through transnational communication. Geert Wilders is an explicitly Islamophobic Dutch politician who has been the leader of the Party for Freedom since 2006. As Lean (2012: 173) observes, he is 'charismatic, eloquent, and fervently dedicated to stirring up hatred of Islam', and often says that Muslims who want to stay in the Netherlands should 'tear out half of the Koran', which he refers to as a 'fascist book that should be banned' (Lean, 2012: 173). Widely known as an Islamophobic figurehead in the Netherlands, Wilders' popularity is such that his party secured sufficient votes to become a key player in the new government that was formed in 2024. Moreover, his influence extends well beyond the Netherlands. Poynting and Briskman (2017) discuss his visit to Melbourne, Australia in 2013, when he started to become more explicitly Islamophobic once he picked up the vibes from the audience.

> His inflammatory language about mosques and halal food ought to have rung alarm bells, but rather than failing the visa "character test" for his propensity to incite racial hatred, he was invited to return in 2015 to speak at the launch of the ALA (Australian Liberty Alliance) political party – a party much like his own in the Netherlands – to further propagate and institutionalize anti-Muslim rhetoric. (Poynting and Briskman, 2017: 144)

Here then, we see a clear example of the transnational impact of right-wing politicians – who are courted as invited speakers – sharing their Islamophobic ideas and motives across the globe.

Another context in which Islamophobia is often able to flourish is at the time of elections, particularly national elections, or those for supranational collectives such as the European Union. These elections provide a platform for right-wing parties to share their Islamophobic ideas through party conferences, leaflets, advertisements, and so on. The discussions of the mainstream political parties are – as noted earlier – increasingly focusing on topics and issues that provide a clear way in for Islamophobic views, even though they may not explicitly be expressed in Islamophobic ways. We see this most clearly in the attention given to the apparent challenges of immigration issues in national elections. In the UK, TellMAMA (2017) reported a 475 per cent increase in episodes of anti-Muslim hatred in the reporting period after the Brexit vote to leave the European Union, and, following the election of Barack Obama as US president, there was a sharp increase in the number of far-right groups (Miller-Idriss, 2021).

Perhaps even more significant in the perpetuation of Islamophobia than the words and actions of Islamophobic politicians are the policies that are introduced by said politicians. Again, this is not just about extreme right-wing parties contributing to policy formation but more mainstream political leaders introducing policies about border controls, anti-terrorism, international geopolitics, and other issues that essentially allow Islamophobia in through the back door. Bowler and Razak (2022) observe that policies such as the 'hostile environment policy' in the UK contribute to a broader culture of intolerance and hate. Although this policy is targeted at creating an environment that is hostile and difficult for those seeking asylum – in the hope that they will not try to migrate to the UK (Benwell et al, 2023) – it has wider reverberations for other racialized groups and provides a strong platform for Islamophobia to flourish.

Everyday Islamophobia and the Islamophobia industrial complex

The key components of the Islamophobia industrial complex covered in this chapter focus on the state: its policies targeting Muslim communities through counterterror measures and its unwillingness to accept the existence of Islamophobia as a problematic social, cultural, and political force. Included here is the domain of politics and the actions of key politicians in the promotion of Islamophobia. My central hypothesis is that these apparently distant geopolitical issues directly impact on the banal, routine, and customary experiences of everyday Islamophobia of Muslims and those who are assumed to be Muslim, who are increasingly seen as a global and national security threat.

5

Transnational Networks and Media

I now turn to explore the very well-funded networks promoting Islamophobia and the role of diverse forms of media, which work together within an intimate, familiar, and very cosy relationship, to enable the Islamophobic processes explored in the previous chapter to take place, often very quickly and with little regulation. The networks I am referring to here are what Lean (2012) calls 'the Islamophobia industry', Kumar (2021: 178) refers to as the 'right-wing Islamophobia network', and Marusek (2017: 186) calls the 'transatlantic Islamophobia network'. It is a key component of the Islamophobia industrial complex, for which Zine (2022a: 24) notes that 'there is a $208 million, small, tightly networked group of donors, organizations, and misinformation experts' that work to promote Islamophobia and anti-Muslim hatred. This transnational network operates much like a 'metastasizing cancer' (Lean, 2012: 14), spreading across the globe, infecting many different places and people in the process.

Providing the ideal set of platforms for these networks to operate from are many different forms of media. 'The media' are not a single homogeneous entity (Poynting et al, 2004) and produce a plethora of outputs, formats, imagery, and text. The obvious examples here include print, broadcast, and social media, but there are also those that may not immediately come to mind such as comics, cartoons, magazines, zines (Titley et al, 2017), and digital war games (Mirrlees and Ibaid, 2021). There is a great diversity to 'the media', and there is much research documenting the ways in which the media promote Islamophobia (Allen, 2005; Saeed, 2007), and references include such vivid descriptions as the 'relentlessly unhinged media' (Poynting and Briskman, 2017: 145).

The UN Special Rapporteur on Freedom of Religion and Belief notes:

> Muslims are generally underrepresented and are often misrepresented in the media. In one study, the European Commission against Racism and Intolerance (ECRI) reported that in over 600,000 news items published in 2016 and 2017 in the Netherlands, the adjectives most

used to describe Muslims were 'radical', 'extremist' and 'terrorist'; in contrast, people from the Netherlands were often described as 'known', 'average' and 'beautiful'. Other studies have shown that media outlets in several countries disproportionately focus on negative angles for news stories involving Muslims such as reporting on their perceived failure to integrate, and more media attention is often paid to terrorist attacks committed by Muslims than to terrorist attacks committed by far right extremists. Indeed, a study commissioned by the Federal Commission against Racism of Switzerland on the quality of media coverage of Swiss Muslims in 18 print media outlets between 2014 to 2017 found that reporting predominantly condemned a lack of will of Muslims to integrate, but only 2 per cent of reporting covered the daily life of Muslims or their successful integration in society. (Shaheed, 2021: 5)

It is within the domain of the media that the modalities of Islamophobia, which Ganesh et al (2024: 898) refer to as discourse – 'the construction of knowledge about Islam and Muslims' – are particularly powerful. I now explore the role of these key actors in the Islamophobia industrial complex – transnational Islamophobia networks, think tanks, and diverse forms of media – and point to the ways in which they often work closely together in a mutually beneficial relationship, which enable them to enhance their power and reach and to benefit financially.

Transnational Islamophobia networks

Zine (2022a, 2022b) emphasizes that an important characteristic of Islamophobia compared to many other forms of oppression and exclusion is that there is an organized industry working to fund, promote, and spread anti-Muslim narratives and hatred (see also Bayrakli and Hafez, 2024). Zine (2022b) notes that this industry that funds it makes Islamophobia a distinctive form of oppression. One of the most influential texts on this topic is Lean's (2017) book, *The Islamophobia Industry*, in which he charts the closely connected networks of right-wing organizations that work to promote anti-Muslim rhetoric in the United States. Especially since 9/11, this industry is very well funded, strongly networked, and carefully coordinated, and is called an industry precisely because it is income-generating. It is the 'product of a tight-knit and interconnected federation of fear merchants. … Bigoted bloggers, racist politicians, fundamentalist religious leaders, Fox News pundits, and religious Zionists, theirs is an industry of hate: the Islamophobia industry' (Lean, 2012: 10).

Although it is, indeed, an industry in many respects, Lean (2012) differentiates the Islamophobia industry from other industries, in that it is very flexible and has various components that are not necessarily controlled by one person or group. Some anti-Muslim groups grow and scale, develop smaller spin-off or splinter groups, but yet are often led by the same individuals or groups of people. One example here is Stop Islamisation of Europe, which is the parent organization of Stop Islamization of America. Close financial ties bind people into such networks so that, to receive a monthly salary, a staff member may be required to take part actively in these networks. Lean (2012) also refers to the industry selling products that are consumed by those who have an interest in promoting anti-Muslim hatred.

Right-wing Zionists and the evangelical Christian community participate in such networks and discourses, and sometimes they even join forces, as seen in the rather surprising collaboration between conservative Christian groups, pro-Israel groups, and part of the Tea Party, to create what has been called the 'teavangelicals', who vocally promoted scares about Sharia law and insisted that it is taking over the United States (Lean, 2012).

Although this might represent a relatively 'small cabal of xenophobes' (Lean, 2012: 14), it is clear that the Islamophobia industry is a

> growing enterprise, one that is knowledgeable about the devastating effects of fear on society and willing to produce and exploit it. They may be a relatively small group, but the scope of their reach and the consequences of their program engender anti-Muslim hate within vulnerable groups of people who, once turned in to such propaganda, join their ranks. (Lean, 2012: 183)

Marusek (2017) has charted the key funders involved in supporting, promoting, and sustaining the Islamophobia industry. She consulted tax filings to do so and found that

> human resources are not the only thing that this network has in common; it also shares funders. Although none of these organisations publish their list of donors, it was possible to track down a number of their backers through online searches and piecing together the wider network of related organisations. In total, we discovered that 60 US-based charities donated almost $41 million to … 14 organisations … promoting a right-wing anti-Islam agenda between 2009 and 2013. (Marusek, 2017: 195)

Furthermore, over 80 per cent of the funders support more than one organization, and Marusek (2017: 200) found a 'significant overlap between the funders of Islamophobia and Israel's occupation of Palestine'. Of the 60 charities or foundations that fund Islamophobia networks, '45 also finance organisations identified as supporting Israel's occupation and/or settlements, giving almost $169 million over five years (2009–2013)' (Marusek,

2017: 200). Zine (2022a: 24) refers to research by the Council for American Islamic Relations that found that 1,096 charitable groups provided funding for at least 39 groups involved in the Islamophobia industry between 2014 and 2016 of sums ranging from US$20 to US$32.4 million, granting them access to US$1.5 billion overall in that period.

The Islamophobia industry in the United States and Canada

Far from it being simply a bizarre group occupying the extreme margins, Lean (2017: 126) points out that there are two extremes to the Islamophobia industry, the first being 'a ferocious squad of propagandists who flood the internet with skewed information and outright falsehoods, and a more measured group of policy-oriented warriors who inject prejudiced views of Muslims and Islam into legislative and governmental arenas'. However, as Lean (2017) explains, although these groups appear somewhat distinct from each other, they mutually reinforce and benefit each other. The power and influence of the Islamophobia industry is such that it shaped the promotion of anti-Muslim narratives during the 2016 US presidential election. This industry 'had the ear of the most powerful leader of the so-called free world' (Lean, 2017: 124).

As a specific example of how the Islamophobia industry operates on the more explicitly Islamophobic propaganda end of the spectrum, Lean (2017) refers to the websites of Pamela Geller and Robert Spencer, which feature up to 400 Islamophobic blog posts each month about Islam and Muslims, all of which are shared on their social media accounts and re-posted on various other sites. Geller and Spencer's group significantly increased their funding between 2012 and 2013. Geller was being paid well over US$200,000 a year for ten hours' work per week, and Spencer received almost US$213,000 a year. Robert Spencer's *Jihad Watch* website is financially supported by the David Horowitz Freedom Center in California that routinely spreads messages of anti-Muslim hatred such as the Islamofacism Awareness Week on college campuses. Breivik's manifesto quotes Spencer 64 times (Iftikhar, 2016). As Lean (2017: 127) explains, such funding allows *Jihad Watch* to enjoy 'prime Internet real estate', which enables the mobilization of 'online foot soldiers into on-the-ground activists'. In this way, the influence and reach of the Islamophobia industry are such that its various components are very well financed, share human resources, and have a network of connections and highly influential online spaces in which to share their messages of hate. The proponents of these messages know no bounds, given their immediate access to online platforms and social media, enabling a fast and efficient method of sharing their propaganda. Iftikhar provides an example of Geller sharing conspiratorial pieces about the Norway terrorist attacks:

As you can probably imagine, Pamela Geller – America's favorite, camera-loving Islamophobe – also wasted no time in blaming Muslims for the Norway terrorist attacks. 'Jihad in Norway?' Geller wrote on her website soon after the news of the attacks started to break. Shortly after, she posted a second item, stating, 'You cannot avoid the consequences of ignoring jihad', while linking to a previous blog item she has bluntly headlined 'Norway: ALL Rapes in Past 5 Years Committed by Muslims'. (Iftikhar, 2016: 60)

At the other end of the spectrum – but mutually reinforcing the work of the likes of Geller and Spencer – Lean (2017) points to the work of Frank Gaffney in the world of anti-Muslim policy making (see also Uddin, 2024). Playing a very influential role in the 2016 presidential campaign, it was Gaffney's Center for Security Policy that produced a report from which Donald Trump quoted heavily when outlining his proposed 'Muslim ban' that was discussed in the last chapter. According to this report, 51 per cent of American Muslims want to be covered by Islamic law, and a quarter said that they felt it was justified to be violent against Americans. The poll used for this report was heavily critiqued, and Lean (2017) highlights the serious conflict of interest involved, given that the company that conducted the poll was led by Kellyanne Conway, who later became Trump's campaign manager. Interconnected with this too is Steve Bannon, Trump's senior advisor, whose platform *Breitbart* publishes pieces by the likes of Geller, Spencer, and Gaffney:

> Thus, Bannon and Conway, with their shared commitment to ramping up domestic surveillance of Muslim communities, curtailing immigration from Muslim-majority countries, and otherwise dismantling Islamic institutions within the US that they perceive as threatening, present extraordinary challenges for those who value civil rights and equality, and those who loathe prejudice. (Lean, 2017: 133)

Essentially then, Trump's approach was informed and supported by a group whose 'ideas about Muslims and Islam are not only conspiratorial, but dangerous' (Lean, 2017: 133).

Similarly, Kumar (2021: 178) has charted what she refers to as the 'right-wing Islamophobia network', but it is noteworthy that she also points to a set of 'liberal enablers'. What she refers to as the 'right-wing Islamophobic warriors' and the 'new McCarthyites' (Kumar, 2021: 179) are not marginalized and on the extremes of society but part of the political establishment, the security system, as well as from universities, think tanks and the media. Kumar (2021) is clear in her analysis that, although some of these groups are explicitly racist and others may appear to be less so, their work informs each other's, and they are webbed together in a complex network that supports and bolsters the interests of each other. Kumar (2021) points to four interconnected groups that have come together to promote Islamophobia. What she refers to as the 'new McCarthyites' include the neocons and Zionists, the Christian far right, and ex-Muslims. However, Kumar (2021) is clear that there is also a set of liberal racists that include human rights organizations, academics, and public figures whose approach and tenor is such that they support the work of the far-right Islamophobia network. Kumar (2021: 214) refers to this as the 'matrix of anti-Muslim racism', in which politicians and the security apparatus play a key role alongside think tanks and academia.

In reflecting upon the operation of the Islamophobia industry in Canada, Zine (2022b) refers to the media, politicians, the far right, white nationalists, Islamophobia influencers, and a range of other groups and organizations that work to exclude, marginalize, and stigmatize Muslims in Canada. Using a social network analysis, Zine (2022b: 236) examined the operation of the Islamophobia industry in Canada and included the groups outlined in Table 5.1 as part of this industry.

Zine (2022b: 237) also considers the strategies employed by these organizations and agencies in their attempts to promote Islamophobia, as their

Table 5.1: Key groups involved in the Islamophobia industry in Canada

Media outlets and Islamophobia influencers	Far-right media outlets such as *Rebel News* and those that contribute to such media and use social media to share their anti-Muslim rhetoric
Foot soldiers	Far-right, neo-Nazi, white nationalist and related groups that participate in demonstrations and spread Islamophobia online
Soft-power groups	A range of groups that are seeking to achieve specific religious or political goals and often do so using ideas associated with democracy. Such groups may advocate for free speech, human rights, or Judeo-Christian principles, but oppose Muslims and Islam in the process and clamp down quickly on any criticisms levied against their work
Native informers	Ex-Muslims and Muslim dissidents who can create and advance Islamophobic rhetoric while providing a form of 'cover' for the promotion of Islamophobia
Think tanks and designated security experts	Utilizing a discourse of expertise, these groups promote Islamophobia and support discourses that, for example, represent Muslims as security threats
Political figures and influencers	Politicians can contribute to this network through the sharing and endorsing of Islamophobia rhetoric

Source: Adapted from Zine (2022b)

connections are utilized to platform (or co-platform), to echo and amplify, legitimize, and validate, to enable and to act as a form of surveillance (see Table 5.2). While some of these tactics might not be surprising, Zine (2022b) points to two more unusual key developments that are further bolstering this network. Ex-Muslims or Muslim dissidents provide a level of support and validation for Islamophobic views and conspiracy theories and are often held in high esteem, given their presumed status as insiders. Moreover, concerns have been raised about the potential infiltration of Muslim organizations for the purposes of passing on information to the opposing side. In 2021, the Ohio chapter of the Council for American Islamic Relations sacked Romin Iqbal, its executive and legal director, claiming that he had been passing on confidential information to an organization heavily involved in the Islamophobia industry in the United States.

However, the key issue that I am exploring here is not the nature of the industry, the funding it receives, or who is and is not involved. It is the widespread and devastating impacts that the spreading of Islamophobia has on the everyday lives of Muslims and those mistaken for being Muslim. This industry is transnational in nature and impact; it is not only operational in the United States and Canada but has a global reach and impact. As Lean notes, 'the net impact of negative beliefs about Muslims was dangerous. The Islamophobia industry had whipped up a fear so toxic that it spilled out into its only logical conclusion: violence' (Lean, 2012: 12–13).

Table 5.2: Strategies used to promote Islamophobia

Platform and co-platform	Connections between different Islamophobic interest groups are employed to share Islamophobia across different platforms
Echo and amplify	Islamophobic ideas are circulated, shared, and promoted as different sectors of the Islamophobia industry reiterate and promote the messages of others
Legitimize and validate	Islamophobic ideas are given some legitimacy and validation through being shared by being 'leveraged simultaneously by different media outlets, influencers, organizations, think tanks and their designated security experts, and by Islamophobic special-interest groups' (Zine, 2022b: 237)
Enable	This involves a combination of actively engaging in events, demonstrations, rallies, and other activities alongside offering financial support for Islamophobia campaigns, speakers, or organizers. These enabling strategies are often financially supported by the organizations that fund the Islamophobia industry
Infiltrate and surveil	Muslim organizations or groups challenging Islamophobia are infiltrated by outsiders for the purposes of surveillance

Source: Adapted from Zine (2022b)

One example of this violence is the killing spree of Anders Breivik in Oslo, and there is no doubt that such events filter through to shape the ideologies of many groups and individuals.

Opposing the 'Ground Zero mosque'

A significant example of the Islamophobia industry in operation is the controversy associated with the so-called Ground Zero mosque (Selod, 2024). A local imam who has served the community for a long time proposed the development of a centre in Lower Manhattan that would promote understanding of Islam and of the Muslim community. Cordoba House was the suggested name for the centre, after Cordoba in Spain, which was an important centre for Muslims in the region because of its intellectual focus and peaceful interaction of the community with those of other faiths. The imam who proposed this – Feisal Abdul Rauf – regarded himself as a moderate Muslim and, as Kumar (2021) observes, the proposal was well received by many, including the New York Mayor. Its development was approved unanimously on 6 May 2010 by the city's Community Board.

Very quickly, the right-wing Islamophobia network kicked into action with the group Stop Islamization of America – led by Pamela Geller and Robert Spencer – launching a campaign to 'stop the 9/11 mosque', including a protest on 29 May to stop the '911 monster mosque' and Geller writing a blog about the proposals. Geller claimed that Muslims were trying to take over the United States. Kumar (2021) points out that Geller has connections with Geert Wilders in the Netherlands and holds the English Defence League in high regard. Geller's blog was picked up by the *New York Post*, which published an article that incorrectly stated the opening date of the mosque to be 11 September 2011 and, not surprisingly, this led to the story being very widely shared.

Kumar (2021) documents how the conservative blog, *Pajamas Media* (now *PJ Media*), received US$3.5 million from Aubrey Chernick to bring together a collection of voices in opposition to the centre. This enabled an explicit form of Islamophobia and racism to be platformed, with articles claiming that the centre embodied a form of Islamic triumphalism and promoting the idea that the mosque development was representative of the Muslim invasion of North America. Several other leading figures and organizations contributed to demonizing the Cordoba Centre, drawing upon racist stereotypes and assumptions in the process.

> The Islamophobia network's effort to brand the center as the 'Ground Zero mosque', even though it was several blocks from the site of the former World Trade Center, succeeded. Their construction of the victims of 9/11 erased the multiracial and multinational character of

the dead. The narrative was one of white victimhood at the hands of the racialized Muslim. (Kumar, 2021: 185)

The success was such that 54–68 per cent of Americans were opposed to the location of the centre. However, there were others who spoke out in support of it and of what the local community was seeking to achieve. Kumar (2021) argues that the right-wing Islamophobia network utilized a racist approach to advance its argument but that those of a more liberal persuasion – including politicians and academics – focused more on the location of the proposal and its possible offence to those who lost family or relatives during 9/11. What is interesting here is that 'what this controversy demonstrates is a dynamic in which Far Right-wing and liberal Islamophobia act as mutually reinforcing ideologies' (Kumar, 2021: 187). The debate around this proposal partly catalysed a growth in anti-Muslim groups in the United States, which tripled in 2011, and so the right-wing Islamophobia network was further bolstered and enabled.

Think tanks promoting Islamophobia

Playing a key role within the Islamophobia industrial complex are influential think tanks – many of which are positioned in deeply concerning close relationships with political leaders and governments – that act as a catalyst for the expression of Islamophobia while bolstering and supporting the work of the transnational Islamophobia industry. The Henry Jackson Society was founded in 2005 and named after the US senator of the same name. It was initially based in Cambridge, UK before relocating to London and has played a role in advancing a right-wing agenda, including promoting Islamophobia, especially from 2011 when it merged with the Centre for Social Cohesion. It has for a long time worked closely with the UK government and has included many leading UK politicians among its ranks. Its executive director stood for the Conservative Party in the Brent Central constituency in the 2015 election. Indeed, some of its founding signatories include conservative and labour MPs. Michael Gove, who was chair of another think tank, Policy Exchange, later joined the list of signatories (Mills et al, 2011; Griffin et al, 2015).

In 2009, members of the Henry Jackson Society participated in a conference in Washington about silencing criticism of radical Islam, for which one of the main sponsors was the Middle East Forum. A key agent in the global Islamophobia industry, its founder Daniel Pipes played a key role in spreading the myth that Obama was a Muslim and worked very closely with the US government. Frank Gaffney from the Center for Security Policy was a speaker at this conference and, as we learnt earlier, he produced a report that informed Trump's Muslim ban. As Manzoor-Khan (2022: 151) notes, the Henry Jackson Society 'provided much of the academic justification for Donald Trump's Muslim ban'. In 2011, the Centre for Social Cohesion merged with the Henry Jackson Society, and Douglas Murray became an associate director. This led to its budget increasing to £1.3 million in 2013 (Griffin et al, 2017). Murray was already known to have a somewhat ambiguous attitude towards the English Defence League and was a frequent critic of Muslims and Islam (Griffin et al, 2015), evidenced by his books about the death of Europe and the war on the West. He has been identified as an Islamophobic intellectual (Ekman, 2015) and critiqued for demonstrating Islamophobic views (Meer and Modood, 2019). Yet, even knowing this, supporters of the Henry Jackson Society include those from politics and academia, as well as defence and security figures (Griffin et al, 2017).

In an analysis of other right-wing think tanks – including the Policy Exchange, which was chaired for a period by Michael Gove – Griffin et al observe that they have

> used the fear of terrorism and of Islam to push an authoritarian political agenda. ... Funded by wealthy businessmen and financiers, and conservative and pro-Israel trusts and foundations. ... Their modern targets are politically engaged Muslims, liberals and leftists, as well as liberal institutions such as schools, universities and public libraries. (Griffin et al, 2015: 52)

Griffin et al (2015) note that several strong advocates for the approach used by these think tanks were powerfully located within British politics with portfolios that they could exploit to ensure that Islamophobia ideas help to share policy and practice.

> The Coalition Government's Prevent Strategy, published in June 2011, was clearly influenced by the kind of neoconservative ideas pushed by the Centre for Social Cohesion and Policy Exchange. It stated that: 'preventing terrorism will mean challenging extremist (and non-violent) ideas that are also part of a terrorist ideology', and later lamented that, 'work to date has not recognised clearly enough the way in which some terrorist ideologies draw on and make use of extremist ideas which are espoused by apparently non-violent organisations very often operating within the law'. (Griffin et al, 2015: 52)

We see here, then, that the work of right-wing think tanks not only promotes Islamophobia but also informs government policy through the close connections between these think tanks and experienced politicians. Moreover, these think tanks engage in a complex web of global relationships with other think tanks, organizations, and politicians, and benefit financially from these connections, as key agents in the Islamophobia industrial complex. Added to this is their intertwinement with wealthy funders who will support their work and with media platforms that enable them either to write Islamophobic pieces themselves or have quick and easy access to publications with a wide readership.

Manzoor-Khan (2022: 15) rightly questions the apparent independence of such groups: 'Although the HJS (Henry Jackson Society) and similar think tanks like Policy Exchange and the Centre for Social Cohesion (CSC) call themselves "independent" research bodies, it is unclear what exactly they are independent from.' So, what we see here are key participants in the transnational Islamophobia network or a 'well-greased and tightly woven cadre of people and groups that share funding and institutional structures … [with] the same cast of characters, and those characters have become more vocal, and more prominent, since the end of the twenty-first century's opening decade' (Lean, 2017: 123). The tricky issue with think tanks is that many do very good work but, within this, there are those that are espousing Islamophobia, often disguised by the careful use of terminology and shared by well-spoken, well-educated men in suits. These are often not easy to detect.

The role of the media

Working in liaison with many of the key actors in the Islamophobia industrial complex – and gaining both power and money in the process – is 'the media' and the engagements of large audiences with various forms of mass communication. The media are frequently pointed out as key generators of Islamophobia and this includes broadcast media – including films, radio, and television – and digital media, which includes diverse internet media such as social media networks and websites. There are also print media, such as newspapers, magazines, comics, and books, and forms of media promoted through advertising such as billboards, marketing on public transport or in shopping centres, or promotions on the walls of buildings. There are numerous – often very large – companies and organizations that run and control all these forms of media, many of which are responsible for multiple media sources.

Said (1997) observes that the media have played a very important role in making Islam 'known' to people. Yet, there is a large disjuncture between the Islam that is practised by millions of people in different parts of the world and the 'Islam' that is discussed in and projected by the media. The coverage of Islam in 'the news' is carried out in such a way that people are given a sense that they have engaged with it, learnt about it, and somehow have come to understand what it is and what it means. This has led to a situation in which 'there is an unquestioned assumption that Islam can be characterized limitlessly by a handful of recklessly general and repeatedly deployed cliches' (Said, 1997: ii). A lot of covering up has gone on. Said (1997) discusses the difference between 'covering' Islam and 'covering up' Islam in the media and how there has been a general tendency to oversimplify the complexity of social relations and to generalize in ways that are highly problematic. 'Of no other religion or cultural grouping can it be said so assertively as it is now said of Islam that it represents a threat to Western civilization' (Said, 1997: iii).

These diverse forms of media play a powerful role in shaping people's view of the world – including Muslims and Islam – by the ways in which they, the media, frame such issues. Thus the media set the agenda (Rane et al, 2014) and control what people see. In this context, the media perpetuate stereotypes about Muslims and Islam, including by mainstreaming far-right ideas and platforming conspiracy theories and mechanisms for circumventing, downplaying and avoiding Islamophobia. Given that the 'media is generally a visual medium' (Iftikhar, 2021: 95), it provides a powerful space in which not only to misrepresent Muslims and Islam using words and text but to do so through the employment of visual imagery (Gottschalk and Greenberg, 2019). Ali and Witham (2018) discuss how successive media scandals and policy initiatives in the UK have worked to create a 'Muslim problem'. They point to ideological fantasies constructed about Muslims in relation to child sexual exploitation, education, and halal meat. They argue that these imagined constructions of the 'conceptual Muslim' are due to the unbearable anxiety about factors and issues, structures, and practices underlying British society, which are not spoken about.

A crucial factor, besides the topics and issues covered, are the actors who are included in them and those who are not. Kassaye and van Heelsum (2020) note that the media are a competitive field and, even if Muslim groups have access, it may be restricted only to certain actors. They analysed national newspapers from six West European countries (Belgium, the UK, France, Germany, the Netherlands, and Switzerland) and selected five newspapers from each country. They found that most of the claims made in newspapers came from civil society actors rather than from politicians or state actors, the only exception being in Germany, where state actors made more claims. However, Muslims made less than one third of the claims being made about Muslims and so these are less visible than the claims made by other actors. There is some variation here: in Germany the figure is only 16 per cent, but in the UK it is 32 per cent. There are, in addition, powerful actors who can exploit their positions to gain key roles on television: 'Reverend Pat Robertson, the octogenarian evangelical polemicist who helped found the Christian Coalition ... spent many years spewing anti-Muslim rhetoric through his Christian Broadcasting Network (CBN) television channel and its flagship television show, The 700 Club' (Iftikhar, 2016: 14).

Print and broadcast media

Typical examples of print media include newspapers and magazines and of broadcast media television and radio, but there are other types of media in each of these categories. Both print and broadcast media have a lot to answer for in relation to Islamophobia. The controversy around *Charlie Hebdo* is possibly the best-known example here, when 'two Muslim extremists killed 12 people at the offices of *Charlie Hebdo*, a French satirical magazine with a history of ridiculing Islam' (Green, 2015: 3). In neighbouring Germany, Ehrkamp (2010) conducted an analysis of German newspapers between 1998 and 2008, focusing on articles that covered issues of forced marriages and honour killings. She found that there had been a significant increase in the number of articles since 2005, pointing to the compatibility of Islam with German citizenship and belonging becoming an increasingly significant issue. She observed that the media operate to locate issues associated with Islam as being outside of the German national space, so honour killings or forced marriage are badged as 'Turkish' or 'Kurdish'. Dress is also a powerful signifier in this analysis, and the veil is seen as a symbol of oppression (see Chapter 8), while the wearing of jeans or a miniskirt is symbolic of freedom from oppression. Poynting and Briskman (2017) relate that newspapers such as *The Australian* – which is regarded as having a more educated readership – produced a series of articles in 2015 that were directly hostile to Islam and about Muslims. Moreover, they observed that usage of terms such as 'asylum seeker' and 'Muslim' were often quickly interchangeable with 'terrorist' (Poynting and Briskman, 2017).

A key issue with print and broadcast media is the careless and sloppy usage of terminology, which can work to further stereotype Muslims and Islam in negative ways. For example, Bokhari (2023) discusses the use of the term '*jihad*', which is normally translated as 'struggle', 'determined effort', or 'exerted striving'. Yet the media overwhelmingly apply the term negatively and often in the context of terrorism or extremism. Similarly, Khan (2023) explores the use of 'Sharia', which translates as 'the correct path' or 'the correct way', yet the term is used in such a way as to provoke concern and anxiety among readers. In particular, he highlights two ways in which the usage of this word generates concerns about separateness: it provokes the idea of a separate legal framework to emerge from Muslim communities and this implies a sense of replacement. There are also of course the misunderstandings associated with '*Allahu Akbar*', which is typically associated with terrorism and violence rather than its usage in the call to prayer or in its meaning that 'God is greater' (Al-Azami, 2023b).

Beydoun (2018) notes specific issues about the coverage in the media of the Muslim ban in the United States discussed in Chapter 4:

Only seven of the ninety commentators (7.8%) CNN featured to discuss the ban during this five-day span were Muslim analysts. MSNBC, widely perceived to be the most progressive of the three major cable new networks, only featured two Muslim analysts out of twenty-eight (7.1%) invited to speak during that period. Fox News, on the other hand, has the highest proportion of Muslims on air, with five out of the fifty-eight contributors (8.6%) identifying as Muslims. The effective exclusion of Muslim analysts from a concern that directly impacts their communities and very lives demonstrates not only latent Islamophobia but also the corollary belief that others (overwhelmingly white men pegged as 'Muslim experts') are more qualified to speak on Islam and Muslims than Muslims themselves. (Beydoun, 2018: 32)

The risks of reinforcing negative stereotypes about Muslims and Islam or falling into the trap of drawing upon conspiracy theories or simplistic or reductionist framings also extends to other forms of media such as film production:

[M]any films depict Muslims negatively and play into harmful stereotypes, with some even claiming that the 'Muslim-as-terrorist' film has become a legitimate genre (or subgenre) in its own right. Despite an increasing number of positive depictions of Muslims in recent years, such depictions may justify discriminatory policies and Islamophobic sentiment by feeding a good versus bad Muslim binary. Various Western film and television producers also engage in the process of 'whitewashing' by depicting Muslim characters without having consulted with or cast any Muslims. (Shaheed, 2021: 5–6)

Versi (2023) – who is the founder of the Centre for Media Monitoring of the Muslim Council of Britain – refers to three recent examples of Islamophobic headlines in the mainstream press in the UK. The *Sun* front page blazoned '1 in 5 Brit Muslims' sympathy with Jihadis' and positioned a picture of a terrorist alongside it. The *Daily Mail* stated that 'more than 50 million Muslims are willing to support those who carry out terror attacks'. The *Daily Star* claimed, 'UK mosques give cash for terror'. Although it can be pointed out that these are tabloids, Versi (2023) is quick to challenge this: 'Some might claim that such hysterics and sensationalism [were] the purview of the tabloids alone. Even if this were true, these tabloids have the widest readership and a huge influence in public life' (Versi, 2023: 18). However, this Islamophobic reporting is not confined to the tabloid newspapers; the *Daily Telegraph* published a front-page story based on work by the Henry Jackson Society, claiming that a scout group based in Lewisham Islamic Centre had extremist links.

According to analysis conducted by the Muslim Council of Britain's Centre for Media Monitoring in its groundbreaking report, based on 'analysing over 48,000 online articles and 5,500 broadcast clips', … 'almost 60% of online media articles and 47% of television clips associate Muslims and/or Islam with negative aspects or behaviour'. The evidence shows that media reporting about Islam and Muslims is hugely problematic. (Versi, 2023: 19)

Some may suggest press regulation as the way forward. For example, there are numerous guidelines produced by organizations advising on different aspects of reporting about Muslims and Islam. Munnik (2023) reviewed the usage of the term 'Islamic State', noting the recommendations of the Centre for Media Monitoring style guide, which suggests 'Isil' or 'Isis', given that the group is neither Islamic nor a state. Al-Azami (2023a) discusses the usage of 'moderate' and 'radical Muslims' and the way that these terms are used to control and discipline Muslims. The style guide previously mentioned suggests that the term 'radical' is avoided. There are press regulators to which people can report if they deem that an article has breached the guidelines. However, Versi (2023) notes that the regulator saw no problem with Katie Hopkins referring to migrants as 'cockroaches', and of 800 complaints about discrimination made to the press regulator, the Independent Press Standards Organisation, one only was upheld as of 2018. This has meant that those seeking to challenge issues of media misrepresentation like Versi have had little option but to reach out to editors and others involved in the press to challenge directly any issues with the representation of Muslims.

Social media

Such is the extent of Islamophobia on social media and elsewhere on the internet that research routinely refers to online Islamophobia as a distinct form of anti-Muslim hatred. 'Online Islamophobia can be defined as Islamophobic prejudice that targets a victim in order to provoke, cause hostility and promote intolerance by means of harassment, stalking, abuse, incitement, threatening behaviour, bullying and intimidation of the person or persons, via all platforms of social media' (Zempi and Awan, 2016: 6).

The Center for Countering Digital Hate (2022) found 530 posts that broke platform standards of anti-Muslim hatred on Facebook, Instagram, TikTok, Twitter, and YouTube over the three-week period from 15 February 2022 until 9 March. In this period, these posts were viewed at least 25.5 million times. Their analysis concluded that these platforms failed to act on 89 per cent of Islamophobia reported to them. Only 11.3 per cent of posts that were reported were acted upon, resulting in fewer than 5 per cent of posts being removed and 6.4 per cent of the posting accounts being removed.

Among these, platforms failed to act on 85 per cent of posts, reported by the Center, that feature racist representations or caricatures about Muslims. Platforms failed to act on 90 per cent of these posts that claimed that Muslims are inherently violent and on 93 per cent of the posts that associated Islam with some sort of disease. Platforms failed to act on 89 per cent of the posts that associated Muslims with terrorism and on 94 per cent of the posts that associated Muslims with extreme or dangerous views. Platforms also failed to act on 89 per cent of these posts promoting the great replacement conspiracy theory. This includes Instagram not doing anything about a post that claimed that Muslims have outbred white Europeans, and Twitter failing to address a post that claimed that Muslim migration is part of a plan for demographic change. Moreover, researchers found 20 posts that celebrated the Christchurch terrorist, and only six of these were removed.

The research also explores the practice of sharing Islamophobia online using hashtags, especially on Instagram, TikTok, and Twitter. Instagram failed to act on a post using the hashtags #saveindia, #fuckislam, #stopislam, and #stopislamization and one that promoted the great replacement conspiracy theory and used hashtags #grandreplacement, #replacement, #islamisation, #stopislamisation, and #stopislam. Likewise, Twitter failed to address a tweet with the hashtags #RejectIslam and #IslamIsCancer.

This research further found that Facebook hosts pages and groups dedicated to Islamophobia that have a collective membership or following of 361,922, including several groups in the United States, the UK, and Australia, and at least one in Canada, South Africa, and India. Posts in these groups included false claims that Muslims are not telling the truth, that Islam is associated with disease, and that halal food is associated with terrorism. The serious issue here is that, even when complaints are raised about specific social media accounts or posts, little, if any, action is taken to address the Islamophobia, even when it is explicit. Khamis (2023) observes that there are cloaked Facebook pages on which Islamophobic ideas can be shared by a cloaked user profile who is taking on the identity of a political opponent to spread hate, and there are Twitter campaigns, such as #BanIslam, which promote anti-Muslim hatred and encourage the sharing of Islamophobia.

In another example, we can see that biased coverage of a specific issue can work to support the idea that Muslims and Islam are of less value or not as important as other groups. An analysis of Instagram posts of six Australian news outlets between 7 October and 7 November 2023 found a clear bias in favour of Israelis over Palestinians, the report claiming, 'The lives and deaths of Palestinians are of less relevance than those of Israelis, and this warrants less time and fewer – if any – new stories' (Carland, 2023b: 21). This research observed that 'anti-Palestinian racism is a specific form of Islamophobia, and there is a documented alignment of anti-Palestinian sentiment and Islamophobia both pre-dating the current war and during the current war, making anti-Palestinian racism a concern' (Carland, 2023b: 1). This example is what is referred to as a 'trigger event'.

Trigger events

The media play a key role in facilitating everyday Islamophobia by using particular incidents as specific trigger events to generate a focus on issues that will lead to the targeting of Muslims or others mistaken for being Muslim.

> The Special Rapporteur notes that surges in online hate speech are often sparked by offline 'trigger events'. Such events may include terrorist attacks (including attacks on Muslims), comments made by prominent public figures and political events such as elections or referendums. Following the attack in Christchurch, New Zealand, one civil society organization recorded an increase of 692 per cent in online attacks against Muslims, many using the same rhetoric as the attacker. Trigger events typically produce a strong response during the first 24–48 hours; these rapidly drop off but it can take months for online expressions of hatred to taper to the baseline. Notably, Muslims do not necessarily have to be perceived as 'at fault' in the context of the trigger-event to be targeted. (Shaheed, 2021: 7)

Indeed, it is often after trigger events that sharp increases in Islamophobia are experienced, as the engine of the Islamophobia industrial complex kicks into action and its many actors – especially the far right, politicians, and public figures – seek to utilize the avenues open to them on diverse media platforms, where they are freely able to share Islamophobic material and to have this easily promoted across the media.

One of the key issues about trigger events is that, following the sharp increase in Islamophobic incidents shortly after the specific event, the number of incidents rarely goes back to its previous level quickly and, indeed, can take some time to do so, resulting in reports of such incidents remaining at a higher level than normal for an extended period. TellMAMA (2023) charted the last ten years of their work to monitor anti-Muslim hatred in the UK and point to the ways in which trigger events lead to an increase in cases of Islamophobia. For example, following the murder of soldier, Lee Rigby, on the afternoon of 22 May 2013 by Michael Adebolajo and Michael Adebowale, TellMAMA (2023) recorded a 373 per cent increase in incidents reported to them, of many different types of anti-Muslim hatred, including abuse, anti-Muslim literature being distributed, assault, property damage, extreme violence, and threat. Likewise, Kundnani 'reported racist attacks on Muslims and those perceived to be Muslim increased sixfold in the weeks after 7/7' (Kundnani, 2007: 128), and in the week following Boris

Johnson's (2018) newspaper column about Muslim women looking like letter boxes (see Chapter 4), TellMAMA (2023) received a 375 per cent increase in reports. Following the Hamas-led attacks on Israel on 7 October 2023, there was a 1,300 per cent increase in Islamophobia in Australia (Carland, 2023b), mirrored in the UK, according to TellMAMA (2024: 4), which refers to 7 October 2023 as 'an earthquake that has shaken us all' (TellMAMA, 2024: 4) and relates that during the four months following the attacks, there were record numbers of anti-Muslim hate cases, involving Muslims being targeted on public transport, in their homes, when walking down the street, and at schools and universities in the UK.

Trigger events can include major incidents, such as those described, in which some would argue that Muslims or those perceived to be Muslims are involved or are to be held responsible. However, it is not only incidents of violence or aggression by Muslims or those committing acts in the name of Islam that lead to increasing levels of Islamophobia. For example, the terrorist attack in Christchurch, New Zealand, was carried out by a white man, yet in the week following this, TellMAMA (2023) reported a 692 per cent increase in incidents of anti-Muslim hatred. A similar pattern can be observed after the shootings in Oslo. The Islamophobic rioting in the UK in the summer of 2024 was catalysed by the actions of a young man of Rwandan heritage, who was born in the UK and whose family were committed to their local church. Moreover, there are still many accounts of increasing incidents of Islamophobia following October 2023, even given the violence towards Palestinians in Gaza. For example, Smits (2024) reports that several mosques in Brussels have been threatened following the start of this conflict.

What we see in all these examples is that the use of the media – and the ways in which key actors in the Islamophobia industrial network capitalize upon these events for financial gain and power – helps to facilitate and promote everyday Islamophobia.

Everyday Islamophobia and the Islamophobia industrial complex

And so, the transnational network of groups and individuals who accrue significant power and money in spreading everyday Islamophobia are all part of the global Islamophobia industry and key actors in the Islamophobia industrial complex. They work in close operation with the state and with politicians (see Chapter 4) and through think tanks and with diverse forms of media to capitalize on any opportunity or trigger event from which they can seek financial benefit and enhanced power. These all together form the powerful, well-resourced, highly organized, and well-networked Islamophobia industrial complex.

6

Communities, Public Spaces, and Mobility

Having considered the role that nation-states and politics, interconnected with and by networks of think tanks, the media, and other group and individual actors, play in global Islamophobia, a clearer picture of the Islamophobia industrial complex is now building, including insights into the key components of this complex. My reason for addressing these matters in the first half of this book is that the issues of everyday Islamophobia covered in the next three chapters are emboldened and empowered by their presence; indeed, without these components of the Islamophobia industrial complex, it is likely that many of the cases of everyday Islamophobia in people's communities, on their way to work, or when they are walking down the street would not happen; everyday Islamophobia might still be present, but its power, reach, and impact would be significantly curtailed.

The European Union Agency for Fundamental Rights (2024) report found that 55 per cent of incidents of racism against Muslims in Europe take place on the street, on a square, in the park, car park, or other public area. In this chapter, I focus on the domains of social life that are probably those that one would more likely expect to hear about in relation to everyday Islamophobia. However, it is crucial to remember that people's everyday lives – in their local neighbourhoods, on their journey to school or work, and on public transport and so on – are all shaped by the issues discussed in the previous two chapters. As Kundnani (2007) emphasizes about the Islamophobic culture in politics and the media, it has

> very little to do with the ways in which Muslims actually live their lives or practise their faith. The complexity of faith identity and the different levels from which it operates, comprising belief, practice and affiliation, tend to be erased. Nor is there recognition of the multi-faceted identity that a British Muslim citizen of Pakistani heritage,

for example, holds, in which faith, heritage and cultures are separable and potentially conflicting. Instead, to be 'Muslim' in the 'war on terror' is to belong to a group with common origins, a shared culture and a monolithic identity that can be held collectively responsible for terrorism, segregation and the failure of multicultural Britain. The 'Muslim community' becomes, effectively, an ethnicity rather than a group sharing a religion. (Kundnani, 2007: 126)

In this chapter, I consider how everyday Islamophobia presents in debates about communities and neighbourhoods, public spaces, and daily mobilities. These issues often arise through concerns about the apparent segregation of Muslims or their lack of willingness to integrate, or through anxieties about refugee resettlement and integration. I then consider issues relating to public space, where we find that Islamophobia presents through rioting in towns in cities, through Quran-burning protests, as well as the encounter with it in daily mobilities such as on public transport, on the journey to school, or when negotiating airport security.

Segregation and integration

As Ehrkamp (2010) noted – 15 years ago now – debates about the integration or assimilation of immigrants in Europe, alongside concerns about self-segregation and ghettoization, increasingly focus upon the presence of Islam and Muslims in the public sphere. I contend that this remains the case today and, if anything, these concerns have heightened further. This is a key mechanism for the expression of everyday Islamophobia, but it is disguised as a concern about community relations. When thinking about the complexities of spaces of multiculturalism (Nagel and Hopkins, 2010), it is often through local communities and neighbourhoods that the 'Muslim community' is imagined (Alexander, 1998), whether this be the 'Muslim area', or an area with a presence of migrants with a South Asian heritage, or an area where refugee communities have resettled (Ali, 2023). For example, the predominantly Muslim Molenbeek neighbourhood in Brussels is regarded as a 'hotbed of extremism' by the state and, following the terrorist bombings in Brussels in March 2016, far-right groups threatened to attack this area (Farmer and Majlesi, 2024: 176). As another example, Dobbernack (2022) refers to the Danish ghetto initiative to identify neighbourhoods for policy intervention, for which two criteria were ethnic background and the country of origins of the local community.

Indeed, Kundnani (2007) notes that following 9/11, issues of cultural diversity were increasing concerns, including for those on the left, and points to a change in messaging around this: 'What had before been interpreted as a problem of Asians living in separate *cultures*, has, since 9/11, been taken to be a problem of Muslims living by separate *values*' (Kundnani, 2007: 127). This generated a focus on concerns about integration, and

> in the cacophony of voices that make up this new media-driven 'integration debate', it is Muslims who are routinely singled out; it is their cultural difference that needs limits placed on it; it is they who must subsume their cultural heritage within 'Britishness'; it is they who must declare their alliance to (ill-defined) British values. (Kundnani, 2007: 123)

Increasingly, then, Muslims have been seen as having 'different' values, values that somehow do not accord with so-called 'British values', which are associated – ironically in the face of Islamophobia – with 'decency'.

> Since 9/11, however, it has become a regular refrain from high-profile 'muscular liberal' columnists such as Rod Liddle, Niall Ferguson, and Melanie Philips, who harangue Muslims for a supposed failure to share in the values around which Britishness is thought to coalesce: sexual equality, tolerance, freedom of speech and the rule of law. (Kundnani, 2007: 126)

Illogically, that vague premise can escalate to common assumptions that all Muslims are intolerant of these values and are, therefore, potentially working to destroy them, seeking to replace them with their own. There is a fear that 'Europe faced a gradual "Islamicisation" as increasing Muslim immigration creates Islamic ghettos across the continent' (Kundnani, 2007: 126).

A common stereotype associated with Muslim communities alongside other minority ethnic groups is that they have a preference to live separately in their own communities, promoting a form of ethnic residential segregation, or 'ghettos'. According to Mohammad (1999), the growth in interest in Muslim schools is partly where concerns about segregation arose. Sardar (2009) notes that Muslim segregation is seen as a serious problem. The standard argument here is that minority groups – including Muslims – self-segregate (Andrews, 2023). In the UK, following the riots in Burnley, Bradford, and Oldham in 2001, the focus of government policy was upon 'community cohesion', and claims were made that Asian and British communities were living 'parallel lives', and were sleep walking into segregation. Chan (2010: 34) clarifies that 'the suggestion was that different communities lived, worked, and socialised separately, thereby creating an uncivil atmosphere of mistrust, jealousy, and intolerance. The suggestion was that communities had slumbered into segregation and government policy had played a part in their sedation'.

As Phillips (1998) makes clear, patterns of segregation are complex and exist as they do for diverse reasons and vary from place to place. However, it is white communities that have most control to maintain divisions between communities. For example, Kundnani (2007: 123) notes that issues of segregation in the UK's northern mill towns were more to do with 'industrial decline, "white flight" and institutional racism'. In a sense, then, what we see here is a list of concerns associated with segregation, immigration, terrorism, community relationships, and other issues 'lumped together and misdiagnosed by the integrationists as resulting from an "excess" of cultural diversity. ... The fault-line of this new agenda is the perceived incompatibility between British society and Muslim communities in which supposedly alien values are embedded' (Kundnani, 2007: 125).

Phillips provides an excellent critique of the discourse of Muslim self-segregation, noting that both residential patterns and lived experience challenge this assumption:

> Although it emerged that many British Muslim families value residential clustering, for reasons of culture and tradition, familiarity, identity, and security, the desire for separation from others is not self-evident. Their spatial segregation in poorer neighbourhoods largely reflects bounded choices, constrained by structural disadvantage, inequalities in the housing market (past and present), worries about racism, and ... racist harassment. (Phillips, 2006: 34)

Brice (2009) supports this by suggesting that, although there may be residential segregation of Muslims in the UK, it can be regarded as 'good segregation', as people choose to live close to family, friends, and local services. Finney and Simpson (2009) challenge several myths about the discourse of self-segregation. For example, they found that those from minority groups have at least half of their friends from different ethnic groups (far more so than do white residents), and there are many shared aspirations across different ethnic groups in terms of a desire for better-quality housing, freedom from anti-social behaviour, and a preference to have family and friends close by. Considering a range of different indicators, they found that minority groups are eager to engage and integrate and it is, instead, sections of the white population that are far more intolerant, suspicious, and less likely to engage.

Furthermore, the issues discussed here are also shaped by those who work as estate agents or in property management. The European Union Agency for Fundamental Rights (2024) found that a third of Muslims encountered racism when trying to rent a property or buy a house, and this has increased sharply since 2016. In work about the housing preferences of South Asian Muslims in the UK, Phillips (2006) points to the important roles that those who work in and manage the housing market play in controlling who lives where.

She identifies issues of housing market manipulation as one factor among many, including questions about who mortgage lenders are willing to support:

> [I]t was evident that estate agents, in particular, still shape the structure of housing opportunities for people of South Asian origin and other (for example, white) purchasers. Although agents are aware of the law and are unlikely to express overtly discriminatory comments, interviews with key players in the private market uncovered a worryingly familiar use of racist stereotypes, an acknowledgement of vendor discrimination, and a distrust of 'Asian' clients. Many also held racialised views of the housing market, constructing certain areas as 'Asian' or 'white'. (Phillips, 2006: 34–35)

Evidence from interviews further suggests that racial steering is likely for both South Asians and white people and those wearing traditional dress, such as a hijab, are the most likely to be excluded from a full range of options. The message here is that estate agents contribute to the shape of the housing market in reinforcing Islamophobic stereotypes about the residential preferences of Muslim clients, thereby reinforcing narratives of segregation. Although I have so far focused on the UK in this discussion, concerns about segregation and integration in relation to Muslim communities can be found in many countries across Europe and in Australia and North America. What is often a problem of white communities living quite geographically bounded lives is turned on its head, and Muslims and other black and minority ethnic communities are scapegoated for their lack of 'integration' with something that is very rarely clearly defined or well articulated.

The survey work of Itaoui (2016) and the mental maps created by young Muslims in Sydney, Australia, provides another context in which we can see examples of how Islamophobia shapes public space usage. Participants expressed the opinion that Islamophobia is more likely in areas where there is a lower Muslim population. We find within all these debates, then, that concerns about specific urban communities, about issues of migration and resettlement, and about residential segregation are laced with an everyday Islamophobia. It can present itself explicitly but can also be disguised by these concerns.

Refugee dispersal, resettlement, and integration

Alongside – and often interconnected with – debates about segregation and integration, another way in which everyday Islamophobia presents is through concerns about the reception, dispersal, resettlement, and integration of refugees and asylum seekers (Ehrkamp, 2017; Fritzsche and Nelson, 2020). Much like the construction of Muslims as 'good Muslims' or 'bad Muslims', people seeking asylum can sometimes be constructed according to the extent of their deservingness of welfare or other forms of support. It can be here that Islamophobic sentiments come into play. For example, Kyriakidou (2021) conducted focus groups with members of the public in Greece, in 2018, on the topic of the 'refugee crisis' and found clear examples of Islamophobic sentiments being expressed about the arrival of Syrian refugees, which included stereotypical assumptions about Muslims being fanatical and not compatible with Greek society.

Focusing upon the United States, Nagel (2016) discusses changes in the narrative of 'southern hospitality', especially since 2015 when Barack Obama announced that 10,000 Syrian refugees would be resettled. There had already been growing concerns about the resettlement of Syrian refugees following the Paris terrorist attack and the shootings in San Bernardino, although Nagel is quick to point out that neither of these events involved Syrians. Anti-Muslim narratives had taken over concerns about refugee issues since 9/11, but a revised blend of anti-refugee, anti-Muslim, and anti-immigrant sentiment was growing. Especially among evangelical Christians, a narrative that the American way of life is under threat from various corners is a major concern, and Islam represents a key threat for these groups. Nagel (2016) refers to Senate hearings in South Carolina, in which anti-Muslim narratives have increasingly been aired alongside other concerns about crime, national decline, undocumented migrants, and so on. In the course of the speeches, refugees were represented as posing a threat to the wives and daughters of Americans and likened to criminal aliens. This is perhaps not surprising in a context where 74 per cent of the population agreed with Trump's Muslim ban. However, concerns about refugee resettlement issues are closely interwoven with and shaped by Islamophobia.

In the context of West Virginia, in the United States, Gorman and Culcasi (2021) explored the work of a national hate group in relation to its opposition to the proposed resettlement of Syrian refugees. They analysed the content of a public seminar run by the regional lead of the organization 'ACT! For America', called 'Invasion and colonization of West Virginia'. This organization is one of the most powerful anti-Muslim groups in the United States. Its leader is regarded as a key member of the Islamophobia industry and has close links with government. A key strategy of the organization is to work locally to promote anti-refugee and anti-Muslim sentiment, which then influences those in power. The authors detected four themes in their critical analysis of this seminar and the methods by which it promoted Islamophobia through resisting the resettlement of refugees:

> The first theme is 'smallness' ... [which] affixes a white and Christian identity to certain spaces and lays the foundation that these places are under threat. We find that the spatial metaphors of 'fresh territory' and 'sowing seeds' function as two related themes to stake a claim about

who is threatening to change America and its small spaces. Claims of invasion and colonization function powerfully through a fourth interrelated theme of the 'Other Islamic Bomb', which frames Muslim women's fertility as the vehicle of the invasion and colonization of West Virginia and the United States. (Gorman and Culcasi, 2021: 170)

Those seeking asylum in contexts that are unfamiliar to them often come up against everyday Islamophobia in their attempts to arrive and resettle in a new place. This can take many forms, from the local community and from border control or security staff or from people working in different areas of service provision. For example, Kirndörfer (2024) explored young refugees' negotiations of arrival and resettlement in the East German city of Leipzig, where she notes that reports of racism and Islamophobia have increased, especially since the founding of PEGIDA (Patriotic Europeans against the Islamization of the West) in 2015 and its sister organization Legida in Leipzig. Numbers of racist incidents in Leipzig were around 100 per year from 2012 until 2014, but increased to 260 in 2015, 500 in 2018, and 740 in 2021.

Public spaces, public transport, and daily mobilities

Another key context in which everyday Islamophobia happens are public spaces, on public transport – including train or bus stations or other transport hubs – and in negotiations of daily mobilities. In such encounters, Muslim women who display visible markers to their Muslim identity are more likely to be targeted: '[I]t is primarily visible Muslim women (wearing hijab) who are the main targets of Islamophobic violence across the West. And these crimes tend to mainly occur in "open spaces" such as on public transportation, in city streets, or at local markets and shopping centers' (Iftikhar, 2021: 95). Indeed, there is evidence across many studies of Muslims choosing to avoid using public spaces by staying at home in order to minimize the likelihood of experiencing Islamophobia (Zempi and Chakraborti, 2015).

There is a diversity of public spaces in which everyday Islamophobia takes place: in the street, in shopping malls, in the park, or outside of or close to religious buildings or venues. In her work in the San Francisco Bay area, Itaoui (2020) found that 33 per cent of participants mentioned public areas as the locations where they had experienced most Islamophobia, and just over 50 per cent mentioned shopping centres. When asked to note in what spaces they most anticipated Islamophobia to occur, the street was the most frequent response, followed by other public spaces such as shopping centres, and public parks, while public beaches, sports stadiums, and cinemas were also mentioned. In our research in the northeast of England, we found that 34 per cent of incidents occurred on the street and nearly 17 per cent on public transport (Hopkins et al, 2020).

Experiencing everyday Islamophobia can often lead to people feeling compelled to reconstruct their journey and social practices in the hope that they will not experience it again and will remain safe, as Iner et al (2022) observe from their work in Australia. Strategies include avoiding specific streets or shops, taking a different route to their destination, or dressing differently so they will be less noticeable and more likely to blend in with others.

Using public transport is a common experience for many people who commute to school, college, or work, or to visit the shops. This can be an everyday context in which people from a diverse range of backgrounds come into contact with each other, often occupying small, restricted, and crowded spaces, and spending time in very close proximity to others (Shaker, 2021). Everyday Islamophobia happens on public transport vehicles but also in transport hubs such as train and bus stations, where people are waiting for or changing between forms of transport. Drawing upon interviews and autoethnographic observations in Amsterdam, Shaker (2021: 2137) found that there was a wide variety of negative experiences encountered by Muslims using public transport: '[a]n assortment of feelings such as anxiety, fear, discomfort, and disgust; symbolic violence and harassment in the form of gestures, whispers, scrutiny, and "bitter" looks; avoidance including standing, sitting, or moving away from them; and poor or no service provision by public transport staff, verbal abuse, and physical aggression'. He suggests that these experiences are both performative and affective. In the performative category are those examples of explicit exclusion and avoidance, such as when people refuse to sit next to someone, or when there are verbal exchanges, and this was not only about relationships between passengers but also the ways in which the staff working on public transport or in stations treated Muslim passengers. The second category – the affective – includes more subtle experiences such as receiving awkward looks, suspicious glances, staring, or having a general sense of unease about the atmosphere.

Such is the extent of Islamophobia on public transport that several studies point to people preferring to commute by car instead of taking the bus or train. This is an issue not just for the person who feels obliged to change their behaviour: more people travelling by car has an impact on the environment. Itaoui et al (2021) refer to participants in their research who preferred to travel by car because of concerns that they would experience Islamophobia if they used public transport, as did Iner et al (2022). We also found this to be the case in our research with Muslims in northeast England, where many voiced a preference for driving rather than taking public transport in order to minimize the risk of experiencing Islamophobia. However, this led to them coming into conflict with other drivers (Hopkins et al, 2020).

Everyday Islamophobia is a serious issue, as people negotiate their daily travel and mobilities, such as when walking or taking the bus to school or college, on the commute to work, or while driving to meet friends or to go to the mosque. Nearly 20 years ago, Sheller and Urry observed:

> All the world seems to be on the move. Asylum seekers, international students, terrorists, members of diasporas, holidaymakers, business people, sports stars, refugees, backpackers, commuters, the early retired, young mobile professionals, prostitutes, armed forces – these and many others fill the world's airports, buses, ships, and trains. The scale of this travelling is immense. Internationally there are over 700 million legal passenger arrivals each year (compared with 25 million in 1950) with a predicted 1 billion by 2010; there are 4 million air passengers each day; 31 million refugees are displaced from their homes; and there is one car for every 8.6 people. ... Many different bodies are on the move and it is often through their movements and proximities that bodies are marked as 'different' in the first place (Ahmed, 2000) and this movement shows relatively little sign of substantially abating in the longer term. This is so even after September 11, severe acute respiratory syndrome (SARS), multiple suicide bombings of transport networks, and other global catastrophes, and the fact that many grand projects in transport do not at first generate the scale of anticipated traffic. (Sheller and Urry, 2006: 207)

In the context of these debates, Itaoui et al (2021) explored the mobility strategies employed by young Muslims in San Francisco in their attempts to minimize the likelihood of experiencing Islamophobia. Based on interviews with 28 young Muslims aged 19–35, in early 2017, they found a diverse set of strategies. Participants in this research talked about thinking carefully about their everyday behaviours such as making eye contact (or not), smiling at people, walking in a manner that would not appear to be aggressive, and some students involved in the research chose to organize public events that educated people about Islam and Muslims. There were also accounts of young people engaging in bystander action to prevent Islamophobia, such as taking turns to pray so that the person not praying could keep an eye out for anything untoward, and others would intervene in incidents to try to minimize the impact of the situation.

Itaoui et al (2021: 889) discuss what they refer to as 'Muslim mobility' as 'the range of movement controlling discourses and practices that structure the spatial lives of Muslims within the wider exercise of Islamophobia'. The practice and experiences of mobility – whether this be walking through a public square, commuting on a train or bus, or flying abroad for a holiday or for a business meeting – are racialized and used as a mechanism of control and surveillance. Itaoui et al (2021) report on three types of mobilities strategies that are used by racialized minorities to work through, resist, or counter the attempts made to constrain their spatial mobilities. First, there are strategies that employ technology to help facilitate movement across space, such as using social media or other forms of technology to minimize risk, avoid racism and Islamophobia, and enable safer movement through careful timing, planning of routes, and pacing of travel. Second, and related to what I will discuss in Chapter 8, there are embodied strategies that are 'the various performances, behaviours and choices of racialized individuals to negotiate and moderate the possible and actual experiences of racism while moving through different landscapes' (Itaoui et al, 2021: 891). Third, there are strategies that focus on the management of social relations to minimize the likelihood of stress or to employ a social network as a mechanism for avoiding police or surveillance.

'Proactively preventative ... socio-bodily anti-racism mobility practices' (Itaoui et al, 2021: 894) were employed by some participants. These involve careful use of eye contact. For some, this meant avoiding eye contact and getting on with their day by presenting as a happy person who is not scared. Others used eye contact with bystanders on public transport to defuse negative encounters that could turn violent, and others still were careful about how they approached people, so they did not come across as aggressive. 'When navigating everyday spaces, young Muslim Americans in the Bay Area employed a delicate balance in both being prepared for Islamophobic attacks, while also employing pro-social bodily anti-racist practices as a way of "softening" their encounters with others in public spaces and facilitating their mobility through public spaces' (Itaoui et al, 2021: 895).

There are direct experiences of everyday Islamophobia from others, such as fellow travellers. There is also the everyday Islamophobia that can be encountered through advertising on public transport or in transport hubs and stations:

> [I]n late 2012, Pamela Geller took her Islamophobia to new heights (or new lows) when she purchased prominent advertising space in several New York City subway stations to display her newest anti-Islam message. According to *The New York Observer*, Geller's belligerent ads feature a 'panorama of the sky the moment the World Trade Center burst into flames [on September 11], accompanied by a quote from the Quran that reads 'Sons shall cast terror into the hearts of Unbelievers'. (Iftikhar, 2016: 54)

Encountering airport security

Not surprisingly, the counterterrorism apparatus is such that negotiations of airport spaces can be very anxiety-provoking for Muslim travellers and those who may be mistaken for being Muslim (Blackwood, 2019).

'The encounters that take place when flying while Muslim are rooted in subjective determinations, Orientalist stereotypes, and racial fears and anxieties that require Muslims to be wary and at times hyper-conscious of how they are going to be perceived in these securitised contexts' (Zine, 2022a: 138). Travelling through airports has become particularly challenging since 9/11 and the launch of the global war on terror.

> Since 9/11, Muslim men and women, particularly those that visibly appear Muslim because of their religious attire, like the hijab, or men who don beards, have been removed from flights because of their religious identity. For example, Eaman Shebley, who wears the hijab, and her family were removed from a United Airlines flight in 2016 simply because she asked for a child harness for her toddler. (Selod et al, 2024: 15)

This form of policing is so common now that it is not only routinely conducted by security officials but also by lay members of the public. Blackwood et al (2013: 1097) note in their research with Muslims that 'all those who talked about airport [security] encounters were explicit that the basis of their treatment was that they were Muslims and that anyone who was Muslim (or fitted a Muslim stereotype) was open to similar treatment'. In his work in Ireland, Carr (2016: 84) found that apparently 'random checks' were a regular experience for his participants, and many said that they experienced checks frequently, compared to others. This was the case for Muslims from a diverse range of ethnic and cultural backgrounds, and such checks were happening in the airports of many different countries, including Ireland. He recalls one South Asian participant, whom he called Ehan, who was travelling to Turkey on holiday and was questioned by security while waiting in the lounge. He had his passport taken from him and was told to wait; his passport was returned to him ten minutes later, during which time he had to wait in full view of everyone else travelling on the same flight.

While the airport is a context in which national identities and citizenship are policed by border control staff, practices of 'racial and religious profiling occur where culture, bodies, and the state collide in a tension that renders Muslims as suspect citizens' (Zine, 2022a: 138). Blackwood et al (2015) interviewed 38 Muslims in three Scottish cities and found that some participants adopted a strategy of minimizing encounters while in the airport. 'Broadly speaking, these strategies took one of two forms: to withdraw and avoid all physical contact with others occupying that space (i.e. authorities, shopkeepers, and fellow travellers); and when that was not possible, to protect oneself through an inauthentic identity performance' (Blackwood et al, 2015: 155). Much of this points to the role of embodied Islamophobia (see Chapter 8), and operates to police, control, and stigmatize the mobility practices of those seen to be Muslim. In our own research, participants talked about avoiding specific airports, travelling less frequently, or considering in detail when and where to travel. Reflecting on an encounter in Edinburgh airport, Ananya, an Indian international student (aged 19–21) who was studying in Scotland, recalled:

> I flew into Edinburgh airport and, as we were coming out of the plane, we were walking down towards the immigration bit and this lady behind me, I think she was in a rush, or … I don't know. And, well, we were all walking in the same direction, but she wanted me to move, so instead of saying, 'Excuse me', she said, 'Hey Paki, can you get out of the way?' … which was really quite, it was really shocking because I hadn't really expected that. Never had that before. Really came out of the blue to be honest and, like, I was of course off an international flight and I was completely exhausted and so I turned around and I looked at her and I said that, I said, 'First of all, I'm Indian not Pakistani and, like, there's no need to be so rude,' and then I just moved out of the way. And she kind of, she was a bit taken aback that I didn't, I don't know, that I actually responded. (Hopkins et al, 2017: 941)

Islamophobic rioting in the UK, Australia, and India

In late July and early August 2024 – as I was writing this book – several days of rioting, violence, looting, and arson by the extreme far right took place in many towns and cities across the UK. The rioting appeared to be catalysed by an incident in Southport, north of Liverpool in the northwest of England, on 29 July, when children taking part in a Taylor Swift-inspired dance class were attacked by a young man armed with a knife. Three girls, aged six, seven, and nine, were killed in the incident and many other children and the young dance instructor were injured. As the offender was under 18 at the time, the police did not immediately name him while they undertook investigations. Very quickly, claims about the suspect being an immigrant who had arrived in a small boat and had a Muslim name appeared all over the media, especially social media. One of the first posts on social media was identified as belonging to Bernadette Spofforth (also known as Bonnie or Bernie), the owner of a clothing company, and described by the *Sun* newspaper as a 'millionaire fashion boss'. Her tweet read, 'Ali Al-Shakati was the suspect, he was an asylum seeker who came to the UK by boat last year and was on an MI6 watch list. If this is true, then all hell is about to break loose'. Although the tweet was deleted around one hour after it had been posted, it was mentioned in 2,632 posts across five platforms, and it is believed to have reached the attention of 1.7 billion people. It was also promoted to people through algorithms and features that recommend high-profile stories (Center for Countering Digital Hate, 2024). Some pointed the finger at a Muslim Pakistani journalist who released a story on *Channel3NowNews*, yet this news item appeared over an hour after the initial tweet from Spofforth. The Islamophobia industrial complex capitalized on this potentially profit-making opportunity by publishing pieces linked to this in the hope of making more money, and public figures such as Andrew Tate and Lawrence Fox shared posts about it too. Within a couple of days, the police named the suspect. Axel Rudakubana, who was about to turn 18, was born in Cardiff and now lived in Lancashire and was the son of a Christian family originally from Rwanda.

> In short, viral, unchecked falsehoods about the attack spread rapidly on social media, with the platforms seemingly unaware or incapable of moderating the spread. The impact of this violence has been profound. The targeting of mosques, hotels housing asylum seekers and public buildings has left communities across the UK deeply shaken. Members of these communities, and many law enforcement officers tasked with protecting them, have been verbally abused, physically attacked and otherwise targeted by rioters. Polling found that 92% of Muslim respondents felt less safe in the UK as a result of the riots. (Center for Countering Digital Hate, 2024: 7–8)

For a period of a week or so, towns and cities across the UK were targeted by far-right activists, leaving Muslims and other ethnic minority groups gripped with fear about possible violence. The mosque in Southport was attacked with bricks as the imam and another man were trapped inside. Hotels accommodating asylum seekers were targeted by the extreme far right, and some of these were set alight in explicit acts of racism, Islamophobia, and arson. Just an hour or so away from where I live, drivers in Middlesbrough were being stopped by the far right to assess whether they approved of them being allowed to proceed, much like border control officers at immigration services in the airport or police stop-and-search activities. An Asian man who worked as a carer returned to his car after leaving his job for the day to find it had been torched. A video was shared widely online of a group of white men physically attacking and beating up a black man in Manchester. Children walking down the street were heard shouting abuse like, 'Who the fuck is Allah?' TellMAMA reported that at least 14 mosques in the UK were targeted.

Of course, after any period of unrest like this, people are quick to point the finger. Some claimed that it was due to white working-class people having been 'left behind' in communities that had been under-invested in. The sense here, then, was that the rioters were simply voicing a set of grievances they had about being socially and economically marginalized and not listened to. Respected newspapers suggested that the riots were the result of 'populism', and others blamed the demise of the UK because of a Brexit vote based on lies about how much would be invested in the country if the UK were to leave the European Union. Many pointed the finger solely at Nigel Farage and were quick to label the 'Farage Riots'. Some said that the violence was down to genuine concerns about immigration, which is why hotels housing asylum seekers were a key target of many of those seeking to set buildings alight.

However, while it might seem logical to rely upon arguments about being 'left behind' or solely to blame Nigel Farage for these riots, the responsibility lies with key agents of the Islamophobia industrial complex, in enabling, facilitating, and promoting these opportunities. Farage was, indeed, part of the problem here, but there were also other politicians, such as Lee Anderson, former deputy chairman of the Conservative Party, prior to his defection to Reform UK, who tweeted that the problem was that a 'third-world culture' has been imported to Britain. Robert Jenrick, a Conservative politician, who served as the Minister of State for Immigration, as Secretary of State for Housing, Communities and Local Government from 2019 until 2021 and stood to be the leader of the Conservative Party, claimed in a television interview that Muslim men in the street who say '*Allahu Akbar*' should be arrested immediately. This phrase is used often by Muslims, including during prayer, and as an indication of appreciation, such as when enjoying a nice meal or on receipt of positive news about something.

> The Muslim culture of saying Allahu Akbar ... means glorifying the greatness of God. Allahu Akbar, which literally means 'God is Greater', is one of the most expressed terms in the life of a practising Muslim due to its repeated use in the rituals of everyday prayer. ... It is also uttered six times in the Adhan—the call to prayer chanted in every Mosque before each of the five daily congregational prayers. Besides its intrinsic links with the prayer rituals, this term is often used by Muslims as an exclamatory expression when receiving good news, viewing some beautiful scenery, or even for simply praising God. ... [W]hen a baby is born in a Muslim family, the culture of chanting the Adhan softly into the ears of the newborn baby is widely practised around the world. (Al-Azami, 2023b: 243)

In addition to these politicians, public figures such as Douglas Murray seized this opportunity to turn on immigrants and Muslims, saying that they had betrayed the country, and Lawrence Fox posted a video about the threat of Muslim extremists. All this was taking place while Tommy Robinson was on holiday in Cyprus with his family but regularly tweeting to over a million followers on X and generating what the Center for Countering Digital Hate estimate to be over 343 million views during the time of the rioting.

Three specific sets of issues here relate to the operation of the Islamophobia industrial complex. First, far from being the socially excluded voice of the working class, far-right political leaders and activists receive significant financial benefit from doing what they do. An investigation by the *Guardian* in 2018 found that Tommy Robinson is essentially funded by some of the key players in the Islamophobia industrial complex. For example, the Middle East Forum confirmed that it spent £47,000 on his legal fees and to support a far-right rally in London in December 2018 (Halliday et al, 2018). The Australian Liberty Alliance – that has hosted Geert Wilders – has helped to raise funds for Tommy Robinson, but did not admit how much. Robert Shillman, a US tech billionaire, funded a position with the right-wing media website, *The Rebel Media*, so that Robinson could be paid a monthly salary of approximately US$5,000. The David Horowitz Freedom Center – that supports a lot of the work of Robert Spencer and Pamela Geller mentioned in Chapter 4 – has published several articles defending him, as has the Gatestone Institute, a New York City-based think tank (Halliday et al, 2018). Essentially, characters like Tommy Robinson are receiving significant sums of money to promote Islamophobia and to catalyse racist violence.

Second, working in close partnership with the likes of Tommy Robinson are various branches of the media. Many shared images of a series of *Daily Mail* front pages with headlines such as 'UK Muslims helping jihadis', 'Migrant numbers hit new records', 'True toll of mass migration on UK life', '100,000 illegals stopped at the UK border', '1m more migrants are on their way', 'The "swarm" on our streets', 'Britain's broken borders', 'Migrants spark housing crisis', and 'Foreign workers get 3 in 4 jobs'. I recall the editor of the *Daily Mail* being interviewed and looking rather pleased with himself. X actively supported the promotion of tweets about the situation, and Elon Musk aimed a provocative tweet at Keir Starmer, the UK prime minister. In both cases, these media platforms will have financially benefited from sharing such division and hate-filled narratives. Furthermore, reporters on the apparently balanced and well-considered BBC referred to those participating in the rioting as 'pro-British protesters'. While all this was happening, there was almost no mention in the media of the rioting being Islamophobic, even though mosques were being targeted, and Muslim communities were under fire. All these examples confirm the key role that the media plays – in many ways – in platforming ideas that promote Islamophobia. Brown and Mondon (2024) point to specific approaches in the press that either helped to enable these riots to happen or restricted a proper analysis of them (see Table 6.1).

Third – and increasingly supporting the mainstreaming of far-right narratives and the media – is the role played by mainstream politicians from across the political spectrum. The Conservative Party routinely shares

Table 6.1: Media strategies to help mainstream and platform the extreme far right

Exceptionalization	Depicting the far right as outside the norms of society
Amplification	Giving the far right an exaggerated platform
Deflection	Distracting from the wider power dynamics by focusing on narrow understandings of the processes at play
Euphemization	Using passive, less accurate, and less objectionable language in reporting that distorts accurate understandings

Source: Adapted from Brown and Mondon (2024: 83)

far-right discourses such as David Cameron's 2011 speech about the failure of multiculturalism, Boris Johnson's (2018) *Daily Telegraph* piece mentioned in Chapter 4, Michael Gove's connections to the Islamophobic Henry Jackson Society, Priti Patel's obsession with deporting asylum seekers despite legal advice, and Suella Braverman's association of asylum seekers with drug-dealing, exploitation, and prostitution, to name only a few examples (Community Policy Forum, 2024). Moreover, Rishi Sunak made several speeches as prime minister in his failed campaign to be re-elected, standing at a lectern adorned with the motto 'Stop the Boats'. What is notable here is that these are all senior figures in the party being in or having held key leadership roles and thereby having significant influence. However, this is not only about the Conservative Party. Labour has focused a lot on immigration and concerns about asylum. Notably, the MP Sarah Edwards claimed that 'we want our hotels back' only a couple of days before hotels in her constituency were targeted by the far right. All of this encourages the mainstreaming of far-right narratives and gives a platform to racist and Islamophobic ideas.

Playing into the hands of these issues is the slow response of the state. Miller-Idriss (2021) observes that states are set up to deal with so-called Islamic terrorism, but the system is not fit for purpose in dealing with the type of rioting discussed here. The Islamophobia industrial complex is such that the well-resourced counterterrorism strategies of the global war on terror can quickly kick into action at any talk of Islamic extremism; however, they remain dormant when other issues arise. When thousands of people from diverse ethnic and religious groups marched in solidarity with the people of Gaza, Suella Braverman, then Home Secretary, referred to them as 'hate marches', yet she said very little – if anything – about those who were burning down shops, community centres, and hotels or those engaging in aggression and violence towards ethnic minority groups. This is a key example of how silencing and absence are a form of Islamophobia.

The UN Committee on the Elimination of Racial Discrimination (2024) launched a report on 23 August 2024 that focused on several countries, including the UK. In its press release, it noted:

> The Committee expressed its concern about the persistence of hate crimes, hate speech and xenophobic incidents on various platforms and by politicians and public figures. It was particularly concerned about recurring racist acts and violence against ethnic and ethno-religious minorities, migrants, refugees and asylum-seekers by extremist far right and white supremacist individuals and groups, including the violent acts committed in late July and early August 2024. In calling for action, the Committee urged the United Kingdom to implement comprehensive measures to curb racist hate speech and xenophobic rhetoric, including from political and public figures. The Committee emphasized the need for thorough investigations and strict penalties for racist hate crimes, and effective remedies for the victims and their families.

On 7 July 2024, thousands of anti-racists demonstrated in towns and cities across the UK to voice their opposition to what had been happening. While there was a sense of relief that the rioting appeared to have subsided, the Muslim Council of Britain reported that 75 per cent of Muslims in the UK were very concerned about their safety after the rioting, compared with 16 per cent during the month before. This is a key issue. While the rioting stopped being in the news headlines and other issues dominated the press, for Muslims – and other ethnic and religious minority groups – there remained a sense that they should remain in lockdown, confined to their homes, as the fear, concern, and anxiety about possible violence looms large and continues to do so.

It is not only in the UK that there are cases of rioting or civil unrest connected with Islamophobia. In Australia, in December 2005, around 500 young men – most of whom were white – rioted at Sydney's Cronulla beach, targeting anyone of Middle Eastern appearance. Apparently, an incident the previous weekend was the catalyst for this: some off-duty lifeguards had had a disagreement with a group of Lebanese men. Noble (2009) points to two key events that had important influence here. The first was the role of the media in maximizing the sense of panic by bringing in politicians and other public figures to debate the issues, turning what was a largely local issue into a debate about Australian culture and society. The second factor was the use of text messaging, partly by right-wing groups, to activate the interests of others to engage in 'Leb and wog bashing day' (Noble, 2009: 2). Itaoui and Dunn (2017: 316) are clear that the 'Cronulla riot was a blatant manifestation of Islamophobia. ... The rioters and their sponsors racialised the Muslim Other on the grounds of both religion and culture'.

Although the riot was directed at the Lebanese community and at 'Arabs', Itaoui and Dunn (2017) describe how this quickly turned into anti-Muslim sentiment, conveyed through racist chants being used and some young people painting offensive slogans about Islam on themselves and attacking people whom they perceived to have a Middle Eastern heritage.

Islamophobic rioting is also an issue in India. Bonnett (2024) notes that what he refers to as 'racism' is often called 'communalism' and 'casteism', and that there is a messy overlap between these. Bonnett (2024) points out that India's National Crime Records Bureau found that there are, on average, 161 riots every day, with 247 people killed or injured. In 2017, 713 riots were recorded as being 'communal', meaning that they were religious clashes between Muslims and Hindus. There are around 200 million Muslims in India yet

> this violence has, at times, appeared to be officially endorsed, particularly under the national and regional government of the Hindu nationalist Bharatiya Janata Party (BJP). Thus, for example, in February 2020 Delhi's police refused to intervene for several days in an ongoing communal riot that took place in a once mixed neighbourhood and that left fifty-three people dead, mostly Muslims. (Bonnett, 2024: 99)

Oza (2007) notes that the ideological project of Hindutva promotes the idea that Hindus are the original residents of India, and other groups such as Christians and Muslims are unwelcome newcomers. The intention of the Hindu right has been to make public spaces into Hindu spaces, and they have utilized organized forms of sectarian violence to do this. Their focus is on using a Hindu claim to the nation as a mechanism for justifying their actions. Oza focuses on specific cases in which the Hindu right sought to override Muslim claims to specific public places and, in doing so, worked to transform such spaces into Hindu spaces. Yet, such claims never fully succeed, and this results in further violence.

Islamophobic public protests in Scandinavia

Bangstad and Linge (2024) explore the increasing tendency since the late 2010s for far-right and Islamophobic activists to engage in public burnings of the Quran in the Scandinavian countries of Denmark, Sweden, and Norway. Since 2019, the Stop Islamization of Norway (SIAN) group has been visiting Norwegian cities to engage in such activities and to provoke Muslims, mobilize the protection of the police, and garner attention from the media (Døving, 2024). They also deliberately employ anti-Muslim discourses, such as there being a war between the West and Islam, and they wear military outfits. Different strategies of Quran desecration are engaged with, including spitting on the Quran, wrapping it in bacon, and burning it; these emerged as tactics particularly after 9/11 and the global war on terror. Bangstad and Linge (2024) focus on SIAN's first public Quran burning, which took place in Kristiansand in southern Norway on 16 November 2019. It is believed that the chair of this organization has burned the Quran 50 times since 2019. The activities of SIAN have been informed by a set of international, European, and Scandinavian networks, including organizations such as Forum Against Islamisation, Stop Islamisation of Denmark, and Stop Islamisation of Europe. As its name suggests, SIAN is a single-issue group that focuses on the alleged threat that Islam and Muslims pose to Norwegian society. Yet, the organization claims to be non-violent and non-racist. It was suggested that it had 1,000 members in 2020, with most members being male, white, over the age of 50, more likely than the population as a whole to be employed, earning a higher annual income, and more highly educated than the population. So it is by no means a marginalized group but an organization with broader appeal.

> Some of the claims of the group are that Muslims are 'sexual predators' and 'murderous zombies', that Islam is a 'machine for genocide' and 'at war' with Norway, and that raping and murdering children are acts 'sanctioned by the Qur'an'. ... Their new messaging also includes regular calls for the ethnic cleansing of Muslims from Norway by means of forced deportations. (Bangstad and Linge, 2024: 949)

A key inspiration for the activities of this organization come from Rasmus Paludan, a far-right politician who sought to ban Islam from Denmark and rid the country of all Muslims. Paludan's strategies were to engage in hate-filled speeches targeted at Muslims, to set alight copies of the Quran that were covered in bacon or pig's blood, and to draw pictures of the Prophet Muhammed in front of those demonstrating against him. His fellow campaigners would film events and upload them immediately to social media. Although the videos were eventually removed from YouTube for violating hate-speech policy, they had been watched over 20 million times, demonstrating the powerful role of social media contexts in catalysing everyday Islamophobia. He also started to target Swedish neighbourhoods, and, in 2023, he burned the Quran outside the Turkish embassy in Stockholm (Bangstad and Linge, 2024).

Such Islamophobic tactics and strategies are not new, and there are many other examples such as the evangelical pastor in Florida, Terry Jones, who announced plans to commemorate 9/11 by organizing the burning of over 200 Qurans on a 'Burn the Quran Day', or the desecration of the Quran at Guantanamo Bay in 2005, when it is alleged that it was urinated on and flushed down a toilet (Bangstad and Linge, 2024).

Everyday Islamophobia and the Islamophobia industrial complex

The power of the key actors in the Islamophobia industrial complex is such that they impact the ways in which Muslims engage with and experience communities, public spaces, and how they negotiate their daily mobilities. Through binaries such as segregation versus integration and concerns about refugee dispersal, resettlement, and integration, expressions of everyday Islamophobia seep into neighbourhoods and communities, facilitate Islamophobic encounters and hostile experiences in public spaces and on public transport, generating heightened security at airports. More than this, these concerns can result in Islamophobic rioting and public protests, which further generate explicit forms of everyday Islamophobia in towns and cities.

7

Mosques and Institutions of Education and Employment

In this chapter, I discuss some of the many ways that Islamophobia is expressed through and within institutional contexts, and I focus on those associated with mosques and other religious buildings, educational institutions, and the workplace. These are diverse institutions but are interconnected by the references to such contexts as being the most obvious domains of institutional Islamophobia and institutional racism. The UN Special Rapporteur on Freedom of Religion and Belief pointed to the specific targeting of such institutions in his report about Islamophobia:

> The Special Rapporteur received numerous reports documenting attacks on Muslim properties, including mosques, community centres, family homes and businesses, that have been desecrated with offensive graffiti or animal carcasses, as in the case of a pig's head being nailed to the door of a school in Georgia. Such attacks have been reported widely, including in Bosnia and Herzegovina, France, Greece, India, Latvia, North Macedonia, Norway, Sri Lanka, Switzerland and the United States. According to OSCE, attacks on property, mainly on Fridays and religious holidays, are the most common manifestation of Islamophobic violence. (Shaheed, 2021: 14)

As Clayton et al (2022) point out, buildings such as mosques demonstrate the physical presence of Muslims and offer a material target for those wanting to enact everyday Islamophobia. Perhaps it is not surprising, then, that resistance to mosque development and a suspicion about the presence of religious buildings or symbols are key mechanisms for the expression of Islamophobia. We have already explored the controversy generated by the Park 51 proposal in New York (Ruez, 2012) and how this was used by key members of the Islamophobia industry to promote Islamophobia.

I also consider places of education, focusing on universities. It is important to note here the relationship between these contexts and other state institutions alongside the requirement for most to comply with national legislation, including in relation to issues such as counterterrorism. Although educational institutions may be seen to be locally embedded and providing a service to local communities, their connection with the apparatus of the state positions them as key players in the Islamophobia industrial complex. In the final section of this chapter, I turn to Islamophobia in the workplace and discuss issues of recruitment, promotion, and progression.

Approvals for mosque development

The issues that arise around proposals for the development of new religious buildings involve several different groups. Local Muslims are involved in proposing the development, in raising the funds for the work and finding sites where the building could be located. As well as involving their own communities, this is likely to include conversations with architects, designers, builders, and others needed in the construction of the building should permission be forthcoming. In the UK, the system of being granted permissions for such developments relies on local authority planning approval (for example, Gale and Naylor, 2002; Gale, 2004, 2005) and so will involve planners and consultants employed by local councils who inform elected local authority officers to decide whether the proposal should proceed. The process of applying for permission can generate attention in the local community, and planning processes include neighbourhood notification followed by a period of time in which anyone may submit formal objections to proposals. One of the most explicit forms of Islamophobia can be found in the resistance and opposition demonstrated against proposals for the development of a mosque or other religious building or centre. Such objections demonstrate assumptions that Muslims are a homogeneous group, have a desire to self-segregate, and are a threat to the local community.

In Sydney, Australia, Dunn (2001, 2005) found that debates associated with the development of mosques were some of the most politically significant in terms of considerations of cultural diversity and the changing landscape of the city. He notes that nearly all the 30 or so mosques and Islamic centres that had been proposed in Sydney since the 1980s were met by some sort of resistance from the city authorities and from the local community. Dunn (2001, 2005) explores the role of stereotypes of Islam and Muslims in the decision-making process and the interplay of these with debates about multiculturalism and national identity. One of the stereotypes he found in his analysis was that of the fanatical Muslim, leading to claims that Muslims would want to worship at times that would be disruptive to the local community. This was an issue both of timing and frequency, which presented as concerns and objections on the grounds of traffic congestion, parking, and noise disturbance. Indeed, the fanatical discourse was used to differentiate mosque proposals from those for a church that was supposedly not used as fanatically as a mosque.

An additional concern raised by opponents was that Muslims would want to congregate around mosques and live close by, leading to residential concentration, which would in turn change the landscape of the city. This was often expressed by a narrative of intolerance, which included assumptions that non-Muslims would be forced to move elsewhere or even to convert to Islam. Some objectors used militaristic language, such as the area being 'occupied', 'intruded upon', or 'taken over'. Dunn (2001) also found that those opposing some mosques drew upon the stereotype that Islam is sexist and exclusionary and oppressive towards women. In a sense, then, Dunn's findings show a combination of stereotypes of Islam and ideas about what makes for strong local citizenship. He also considers how a mosque proposal invokes constructions of nationhood and discussions about who can and cannot be allowed to belong within the Australian nation, and these often arise through troubling and repetitive processes (Dunn, 2005). It was not all about opposition, however. Those in support of new mosques, especially Muslims in Sydney, and others who voiced their support, often engaged in a process of countering misrepresentations of Muslims and their faith. This included confirmation that Muslims are indeed moderate, respectable, tolerant, law-abiding, and family-oriented people.

In Copenhagen, the first large purpose-built mosque was opened on 19 June 2014 and was called the Khayr El-Bareya Mosque and Hamad Bin Khalifa Civilisation Centre. It is located just north of the city centre in the neighbourhood of Norrebro, where approximately 35 per cent of the population have family heritages in countries such as Turkey, Somalia, Iran, Iraq, Pakistan, Lebanon, and Syria (Simonsen et al, 2019). As Simonsen et al (2019: 650) note, the opening of the mosque was 'moving Islam from the private to the public sphere and rendering it visible in urban space', and so 'is a contested issue'. They note that there had been several previous attempts to gain permission to build a new mosque, but many of these had failed. They identify this as characteristic of the strength of Islamophobia in Denmark and bolstered by welfare nationalism and a focus on cultural homogeneity (see also Koefoed and Simonsen, 2011).

Similarly, in the Netherlands, Verkaaik and Tamini Arab (2016) have explored the ways in which proposals for mosques are managed by local government, and they note that there is a controversial and heated debate whenever permission for a mosque or religious centre is applied for. However, although right-wing political leaders often generate hype around such proposals, the authors note that many new mosques have been built and so those working on the approval processes for such developments must be taking a different perspective.

Lundsteen (2020) considers the challenges to the construction of a purpose-built mosque in Catalonia. He notes that there were conflicts about mosques in 1981 in Granada and three more recent cases in Catalonia in 1990, 1995, and 1996, but it was not until a conflict in 1997 in Barcelona that this became regarded as a social problem. In contrast to much of the literature, Lundsteen (2020) argues that socio-economic and spatial matters need to be given more consideration rather than only focusing on the different reasons for rejection and opposition. The case of the Premia de Mar in Barcelona is one of which Lundsteen (2020) considers the different factors leading to opposition. The main conflict centred around housing and issues of space and noise, so essentially this was a neighbourhood-level dispute. When the proposed location was adjusted, based on a suggestion by the local council, the focus was more on equality of access between groups and about having a place to worship. Following media attention, the discussion moved to a regional or state level and focused more on possible tensions between migrants and locals. Concerns were expressed by less socio-economically privileged residents that this was adding an additional burden to their local area and was symbolic of its historical exclusion and marginalization, while those living in a nearby middle-class area expressed concerns about the maintenance of the quality of their area and whether property prices would rise, remain stable or fall. Lundsteen (2020: 57) concludes by referring to such conflicts as being 'Islamophobia located' and points to the diversity of issues that should be considered when studying mosque conflicts, including socio-economic factors and institutional racism.

Many of the issues highlighted arise in research in other contexts and, although it is not always about opposition, the contestation over these issues is often laced with Islamophobia. For example, Gale (2004, 2005) considers the racist and exclusionary sentiments that can be expressed through the planning system in resistance to mosque development in the UK, although Gale and Naylor (2002) found that some proposals for new religious buildings were positively received and actively incorporated into the local multicultural landscape of cities.

Such expressions of Islamophobia are not limited to mosques but operate towards other religious buildings or aspects of religious architecture. For example, Cheng (2015) explored the minaret ban in Switzerland, noting that the 2013 census found that 5.1 per cent of the population aged over 15 identified with the Islamic faith. Despite being a small group, Muslims in Switzerland are often associated with suspicion and regarded as the least likeable population and the most culturally remote. She observes that the Swiss government is harsher than both those of Germany and Austria when addressing the claims of Muslim residents. This has been heightened further since 9/11, and many political groups in the country have a strong stance against Muslim immigration. Muslims are more likely to receive rejections when applying for naturalization than Christian migrants. The Swiss People's Party strongly encouraged voters to say 'no' to a vote to naturalize second- and third-generation migrants in 2004 and issued posters with Osama Bin Laden pictured on a Swiss identity card to provoke voters.

The history of the minaret ban can be traced to 2007, when there was a campaign to prevent the building of any further minarets in Switzerland, following the erection of one by the Turkish Cultural Association in Wangen bei Olten in 2006. This proposal was initially rejected but subsequently overturned and, when completed, this was the fourth minaret to be built in Switzerland.

> The malignment of Muslims in Switzerland came to the fore on 29 November 2009 when 57.5% of Swiss voters in the Swiss Constitution in a national referendum voted in favour of prohibiting the building of minarets. As the required double majority was reached, both in the percentage of voters and number of cantons, the Swiss Constitution now reads under Article 72, Section 3 'The building of minarets is prohibited'. (Cheng, 2015: 571)

Cheng (2015) argues that this ban was not so much about buildings *per se* but about fears about Islam and Sharia law, and concerns about democracy (see also Lean, 2012). She analysed parliamentary debates and documents about campaigns against minarets to explore how Islamophobia and racism presented. Although there were some points raised about worries about loudspeakers being mounted on minarets, most politicians who promoted the ban did so on the grounds that successful applications lead to more applications, rather than on the specific impacts of those minarets already in place. Indeed, most issues raised in the analysis were not necessarily linked to the built environment at all. Concerns were expressed about Sharia law, halal food, forced marriages, honour killings, misogyny, homophobia and so on. Essentially, there was a mixture of anti-Islamic and anti-Muslim discourse found in this analysis.

I turn to Paris, as Hancock (2020) explores the provision of places for Muslims to pray, rather than on mosques or other official religious buildings. Despite the explicitly Islamophobic discourses of politicians in France, local communities are often more accommodating. Hancock (2020) cites one case study on the Goutte d'Or, which has a long-standing reputation as a rough area located in the 18th arrondissement, has a high proportion of first-generation migrants, and is the kind of area that receives a lot of media attention. The area has attracted many Muslims wanting to pray, especially on Fridays. They would pray in the street as there was no space left in the mosques or other buildings that had been adapted for their use. Concerns were expressed about men taking over the streets to pray, feeding into moral panics about Arab men in public spaces, heightened by the fact that most new arrivals were to be found in that location. The authorities offered them the opportunity to rent a disused barracks, while the longer-term solution was that a second venue would be built – the Institut des Cultures d'Islam (ICI). 'While the most extreme mobilizations against the street prayers display straight-forward Islamophobia, the complex negotiations surrounding the ICI show the pervasiveness of subtler forms of Islamophobia among the left-wing majority running the municipality of Paris' (Hancock, 2020: 536).

The focus here was on Islam as a culture rather than a religion. Moreover, there was a backlash against the ICI initiative following the January 2015 terrorist attacks, and plans for a new building, library, and auditorium were scrapped by the mayor of Paris. It is important to consider how Islamophobia operates at different scales, be these at the micro neighbourhood level, at the local community level, or at a more administrative urban level. Some might demonstrate more openness than one would expect, but others less so.

There is evidence that it has been made very difficult to secure permission for mosques or religious buildings in some places. Sakellarious (2019) observes how Muslims in Athens must meet and pray in warehouses or basements of buildings, as the proposal for a Mosque of Athens has had a long and challenging history, meeting resistance from specific political parties and from the Orthodox Church. Furthermore, Shaheed reports that:

> Slovakia has reportedly increased the number of signatures required to register a mosque or religious community from 20,000 to 50,000, effectively barring Muslims from registration due to their low population. It was also reported to the Special Rapporteur that law enforcement and intelligence officers in some Western countries surveil mosques and their attendees in the name of counter-terrorism. (Shaheed, 2021: 9)

Attacks on mosques and religious venues

Even when mosques are the subject of permission to be built and start to provide services to the local community, Islamophobia does not stop, as mosques and religious centres are often the target of violent, aggressive, and offensive attacks. For example, 'the Council on American-Islamic Relations (CAIR) reported seventy-eight attacks on U.S. mosques in 2015, the highest number since the immediate aftermath of the 9/11 terror attacks. Many of these attacks took place in heavily concentrated Muslim neighborhoods and enclaves' (Beydoun, 2018: 33), and several mosques were targeted in the UK in the rioting of summer 2024.

In Sweden, Gardell (2015) notes that nearly 60 per cent of mosques have been subject to some form of vandalism or threat. He recalls:

> On New Year's Eve 2014 /2015, a masked man dressed in black tried to burn down the grand mosque in the university city of Uppsala, north of Stockholm, Sweden. Witnesses saw him throw a brick through a window followed by a Molotov cocktail. When the flames took off, the masked assailant quickly disappeared from the scene. Five years earlier, during New Year's Eve 2009 /2010, lone wolf race warrior, Peter Mangs, sneaked through the bushes outside the Islamic Centre's grand mosque in Malmö, Sweden. When he saw Imam Edmir Smajlaj sitting at the computer by the mosque's office window, he raised his gun. The sound of his Glock 19 was drowned out by the rattle of New Year fire crackers. Smajlaj escaped death by a whisker, as the 9 mm bullet touched a flowerpot, changed direction and only grazed his neck. (Gardell, 2015: 92)

Younis (2024) refers to the Quebec City Mosque massacre in 2017, when Alexandre Bisonnette entered the building with an assault rifle and fired towards the backs of the 53 people who were praying, killing six in the process (see also Perry, 2019). And Iftikhar (2016: 36) recalls that in November 2015, a mosque in Irving, Dallas, United States, became the target of a demonstration: '[I]n a brazen display of intimidation, some of the protesters carried guns, including at least one assault rifle and shotgun. The group further invited violence by also posting on Facebook the names and addresses of local Muslims and what they term "Muslim sympathizers".'

Karcic (2024) recounts that on 14 January 2023, a man was recorded urinating on the wall of a mosque in Bijeljina, Bosnia and Herzegovina. During Ramadan in March 2023, there was an attack in the Great Mosque of Échirolles in France. A man was punched by the attacker, who was armed with a knife and ran off after being overpowered by those worshipping (Najib, 2024). Hafez (2024b) reports that, in September 2023, pigs' heads were placed at the entrance to a mosque in Graz, Austria, noting that three men were found guilty of doing something similar in 2020, including smearing pigs' blood in the area surrounding the building. Goldmann (2024) notes that a masked gang vandalized the Selimiye Mosque in Siegburg, Germany, in early October 2023, and around three weeks later a different mosque received a threatening letter in a package that included burnt pages of the Quran as well as pork and faeces. Similar incidents have taken place at mosques in several other German cities, including Bochum, Dortmund, Berlin, and Hamburg.

As a result of these issues, matters of security and surveillance are often given a high priority at mosques and other religious centres. For example, in some contexts the police are asked to protect mosques because of concerns about safety (Iftikhar, 2016), and there are also examples of mosques paying for security personnel, developing local volunteer security rotas, and having detailed and well-understood processes for evacuation and lockdown (Itaoui et al, 2021).

Islamophobia in spaces of education

Conflict, tension, and disagreement about the provision of religious facilities, buildings, and spaces not only happens in community settings but is increasingly a feature of spaces of education. Everyday Islamophobia is, sadly, endemic in the culture of many schools across the world in interactions between teachers, parents, and pupils, as well as in the format and content of the curriculum. In the UK context, Gilliat-Ray (2010: 150) argues that 'for example, a Euro-centric curriculum, poor home-school communications, racist/Islamophobic bullying of pupils, and stereotypical views held by some non-Muslim teachers (especially in relation to girls) now provide evidence for low self-expectations on the part of some Muslim pupils'. Teachers and other educators have powerful roles in reinforcing everyday Islamophobia through the use of simplistic and reductionist stereotypes, or indeed, in challenging the culture and providing an empowering space for anti-racism.

However, I intend to focus on universities and other higher education institutions that recruit students from across the globe, including many Muslim students (Allen, 2023). Jones (2014) studied the issues relating to proposals for a mosque at a UK university and consulted archives of university meetings and media sources to explore this issue. The initial campaign to establish a mosque took place in the early 1980s when the UK higher education sector was allowed to recruit international students. At this time, there were no local facilities on campus or in the town for Muslims to pray so a common room at the university had to be used, and the furniture re-arranged. The university appeared to have no issue with a mosque being present on campus but was unable to fund the cost of it. 'The university's approach indicates a tolerant position towards religious difference ... but of a "blind-eye" variety that allows provision at arm's-length and originating from students. This approach facilitates religious provision from a passive position, placing the responsibility with service users' (Jones, 2014: 1989). A new registrar was appointed in 1984 and objected to a building that would segregate students by gender and would mostly be used by men, so plans to develop a mosque were put on hold and Muslim students continued to use 'makeshift sacred spaces in a commonroom' (Jones, 2014: 1989). The registrar did try to help Muslim students by suggesting that they used a vacated sports hall as a short-term solution. This was in the suburbs of the town and it had to have a supply of water to enable ablutions.

The second attempt to open a mosque arose in the early to mid 1990s as Muslim students were finding the sports hall solution impractical, given its location and limited parking. A 'Mosque project steering group' was established in February 1993, set out the key requirements for the community and shortlisted an architect to lead on its design, which included a blend of Islamic features and construction of local stone and slate. Attempts to raise funds for the project throughout 1993 and 1994 did not succeed, the group failing to achieve its target of £500,000. Furthermore, changes in international recruitment meant that there were likely to be fewer Muslim students studying at the university. Tensions increased between the university and Muslim students, who were frustrated by the lack of progress and pointed to issues they had with the process. In 1995, the mosque project was abandoned, and Muslim students were left to continue using the old sports hall as a space for prayer (Jones, 2014).

Far from being liberal and open spaces of learning, it is important to note that university campuses do not necessarily shield Muslim students from Islamophobia (Possamai et al, 2016; Akel, 2021). Zine (2022a: 100) observes that 'organised campaigns of Islamophobia promoted by groups such as US-based Campus Watch are some of the most egregious examples of campus-based Islamophobia', pointing to the Islamophobia industrial complex and those actors intent on spreading Islamophobia often seeing university campuses and students as prime targets. Some groups employ the narrative of free speech to justify spreading Islamophobia: 'Universities are grappling with the rise of the alt-right, White supremacist, and neo-fascist groups on campus that use free speech as a rhetorical prop for their ideological campaigns of hate' (Zine, 2022a: 101).

However, everyday Islamophobia on university and colleges campuses comes not only from external sources, as many members of the educational community promote everyday Islamophobia themselves and on their own terms. Saeed (2016) points to the complex ways in which Muslim women students are securitized on campuses in the UK. Kara (2012) observed how Muslim students and Islamic societies on university campuses in the UK increasingly had to respond to being positioned as potential terrorists. Suggestions for addressing this include new legislation (especially legislation that includes Muslims, given their current omission), campaigns to raise awareness about Islam and Muslims on campus, better responses to the dietary needs of Muslim students, and greater flexibility about timetabling in order to accommodate Muslim prayer times and other religious commitments. Chaudry (2021) refers to two types of microaggressions experienced by Muslim students studying in the UK. One is 'microinsults', such as other students not sitting near to you and being stared at when wearing Islamic dress. The second type is more explicit and involves the use of jokes in which there is a racist element.

Scott-Baumann et al (2020) conducted an impressive study about Islam on UK university campuses, generating a sample of over 250 interviews and over 2,000 survey responses. The research team found that there were cultures of anxiety and suspicion across the six different university campuses they studied and that discourses of radicalization resulted in Muslim students being stigmatized on campus. There was, however, a general hostility towards counterterror initiatives: 'Such resistance is also triggered by a sense that universities are being appropriated by the state for surveillance purposes, a pattern also reflected in monitoring international students, which universities are required to carry out as a means of checking compliance with UK immigration regulations' (Scott-Baumann et al, 2020: 167). Indeed, such initiatives often evoke strong responses from academics employed at universities and broader opposition among students, including Muslim students.

Thus, we see how everyday Islamophobia can be perpetuated by the ways in which specific services are – or are not – provided on university campuses. Based on interviews with Muslim students studying at a university in northern England, we found that students struggled to find halal food on campus and were frustrated that the campus mosque is located on an isolated part of the campus, separated from other student facilities, and by the dominance of a student drinking culture on campus. Students were also concerned that a senior university staff member had added themselves to the email list of the Islamic Society, resulting in students expressing concerns about being under surveillance (Hopkins, 2011).

Employment and workplace cultures

Experiences of everyday Islamophobia extend into the domain of employment and workplace culture. Issues explored here include approaches to recruitment, such as interviewing practice, opportunities for promotion, and progression once employed, as well as the broader culture and environment of specific workplaces. It is important to note that such issues are not limited to sectors in which there are more Muslim employees. Hamid and Jones (2023), for example, found evidence of Islamophobia for those working in the arts, culture, and heritage sectors in the UK.

Lloyd Evans and Bowlby (2000) explored the labour market experiences of Pakistani Muslim women in Reading in the UK. Some women they interviewed had moved from Pakistan and, despite being well qualified, it had often taken them several years – up to ten years in some cases – to achieve a role with a similar level of responsibility and status to that which they had previously held. Some mentioned issues of racism from white colleagues as being a barrier to promotion. Most women positioned themselves as Asian when discussing issues of racism, and they referred to Islam when talking about issues of dress choice and related matters.

In Lewis's (2015) influential work about Muslim women and cultures of fashion and dress, participants noted that not wearing Muslim dress made them more likely to be identified as glamorous in the workplace but, if they wore a headscarf or other item of Islamic dress, they were seen to be militant. There was also a sense among some that Muslim women were seen to be lacking intelligence, and some suggested that employers were surprised when Muslim women had a voice, were articulate, or made recommendations for change. This was similarly a challenge for those who had achieved some success in the workplace and were earning reasonably good salaries yet were still stigmatized because they wore a hijab. 'As the numbers of young Muslim women wearing hijab have increased, so too has the sense that a widely perceived "Muslim penalty" turns wearing the hijab into an obstacle for employment success' (Lewis, 2015: 207).

The context of the job interview is one in which these issues appear to be particularly heightened, as the stereotypes associated with hijab-wearing Muslim women come to the fore.

> [W]omen are paying the penalty more than their male peers and face worse job discrimination than other minority ethnic women. Muslims account for half of the cases brought to employment tribunals on the grounds of religion or belief, a jurisdiction that overall shows 88 percent of cases with a secondary jurisdiction, of which 66 percent were about racial discrimination. (Lewis, 2015: 207)

As an example in the United States, Iftikhar (2021) recounts the experiences of Samantha Elaud, who was refused a job at Abercrombie and Fitch in Tulsa, Oklahoma, because she did not comply with their 'look policy' as she wore a hijab and this was considered to be 'headgear', which was forbidden. She filed a claim based on employment discrimination through the US Employment Opportunity Commission stating that she was refused employment based on her religious affiliation. Nearly seven years later, the Supreme Court ruled in favour, and she was awarded US$44,653 to include damages and court costs.

Similar challenges can be experienced by Muslim men in relation to finding work and negotiating stereotypes around dress. Zine (2022a: 81) discusses the challenges of securing employment, based on her extensive research with young Muslims in Canada, and she talks about 'challenges for Muslim men who choose to wear religious attire such as a topi (hat)' or political symbols like a kaffiyeh (Palestinian scarf) while on the job hunt: 'There's guys who'll be wearing the traditional outfit and say, "'We're gonna go out and get jobs." In the workforce you have the right to wear what you feel comfortable with religiously, but in the time we live in it's like, "Buddy, good luck getting a job!"'

Everyday Islamophobia and the Islamophobia industrial complex

In this chapter, we see how the reach of the Islamophobia industrial complex extends into the domains of resistance over mosque development and the promotion of attacks on religious buildings and community centres. The key apparatus in place to endorse state-sponsored Islamophobia through counterterrorism measures permeates institutions of education, and the stereotypes promoted through all this impacts on workplace cultures and experiences of employment, thereby facilitating the spread of everyday Islamophobia into the crucial and central domains of education, work, and religious observance.

8

Home, Family, and the Body

The home has been, for some Muslims, one of the few contexts in which they can feel shielded from the everyday Islamophobia they experience on the street, when shopping, on the way to school or work, or while out walking with family or friends. Kwan (2008) worked with a sample of 37 Muslim women in Columbus, Ohio, and used oral histories to explore how their lives had changed after the events of 9/11. Through an in-depth exploration of the lived experience of these Muslim women, Kwan (2008) charted what had changed after 9/11, and she used 3D Geographic Information System mapping and coded participants' sense of fear and anxiety. She focused in depth on the experiences of Nada, an Egyptian-born Muslim woman who had lived in the United States for 16 years, and mapped how fear played a key role in shaping her use of public spaces and increasing the likelihood that she would stay at home, given the sense that this was the safest place to be. Yet, some women overcame this and, as Kwan (2008) notes, some contacted local non-Muslims to offer to educate them about Islam.

However, increasingly, it is becoming apparent that even home is not a sanctuary for some. A context in which everyday Islamophobia takes place is when neighbours come into conflict. In the UK, TellMAMA found that anti-Muslim incidents targeting the home or property of a victim are a common form of Islamophobia:

> Many of these cases involve conflict with neighbours and often include ongoing 'low-level' harassment such as abusive comments, social exclusion, or repeated inconveniences such as parking in front of driveways, emptying bins in front of the victim's house, or playing loud music at night. These instances regularly escalate to more serious incidents of vandalism, threats, or physical violence. Experiencing abuse in and around their home can have serious physical and psychological implications for victims as they are often unable to avoid their perpetrators. (TellMAMA, 2019: 24–25)

Focusing on the home, the family, and the body, in this chapter, I consider how everyday Islamophobia can literally come home; it invades the intimate and personal spaces of home and is not something that happens only in the public sphere. I then discuss embodied Islamophobia (Mansson McGinty, 2020) and explore everyday Islamophobia as a deeply personal experience that is felt on and in the body, lived out through an individual sense of personhood, and experienced deeply both on and under the skin. This is about the ways in which specific bodies and types of bodies become stigmatized, marginalized, and associated with suspicion and negative stereotypes.

> Members of oppressed groups frequently experience … avoidance, aversion, expressions of nervousness, condescension, and stereotyping. For them, such behavior, indeed the whole encounter, often painfully fills their discursive consciousness. Such behavior throws them back onto their group identity, making them feel noticed, marked, or conversely invisible, not taken seriously, or worse, demeaned. (Young, 1990: 133–134)

I then consider the important subject of dress and the excessive focus that is so often placed upon specific items of clothing associated with the Muslim faith. Finally, I look at experiences of misrecognition, as bodies that are read as Muslim experience everyday Islamophobia even though the person may be Sikh, Hindu, Christian, or of no faith.

Islamophobia comes home

Although often regarded as a public issue and something that happens on public transport, or in encounters with institutions, everyday Islamophobia has important consequences for those more personal and intimate spaces of belonging and connection, such as the home, the family, and the body. Such is the power and influence of the Islamophobia industrial complex and its many actors that everyday Islamophobia can literally come home. Manzoor-Khan tells this story:

> Adam was eight years old when counterterrorism police interrogated him. He wasn't being held at a police station or stopped at the border. Adam was interrogated at primary school. His teacher took him to a classroom just after lunch, where three adults he has never met were waiting for him: two counter-terrorism officers and a social worker. [His teacher] left him alone with them. They asked whether he liked school, and what games he played at home. Did he play them with his father? Which relatives did they visit? Did he pray? Go to

mosque? What did he read at mosque? The officers asked Adam if he could recite some of the Quran in Arabic and then asked if he knew the meaning of the words. Apparently, they were looking to have a theological discussion with an eight-year-old. (Manzoor-Khan, 2022: 62)

When Adam's mother arrived at the school to collect him, the teacher informed her that he was being spoken to by the police. Adam's mother was surprised that she had not been informed. 'The officers did not greet or give their names to Adam's mum. Instead, they asked why she thought the London Bridge attack and 7/7 had happened. She suggested, maybe it has something to do with the Middle East? "No, it's all happening because of the Quran", they told her' (Manzoor-Khan, 2022: 62–63). The officers then followed Adam and his mother home and started asking Adam's father whether he thought the UK should become an Islamic country. 'After they left, Adam did not tell his parents the details of his interrogation for a week. What thoughts were going through his eight-year-old mind? Did he think he was in trouble? That he had done something wrong at school? That his teacher didn't like him?' (Manzoor-Khan, 2022: 62–63). Manzoor-Khan further notes that many questions like this are left unanswered by those who are referred to Prevent by teachers, doctors, or other public servants. 'In fact, people under 20 made up 54% of Prevent referrals between 2019–20, and between 2015–2018, 532 children under the age of six were referred' (Manzoor-Khan, 2022: 63).

There are many similar accounts such as the incident at a school in Texas, when Ahmed Mohamed's teacher assumed that the clock he had made was a bomb, which I explored in Chapter 1, and the experiences of Rizwan Sabir and Farid Hafez in relation to counterterrorism initiatives in the UK and Austria. Far from being a public issue and something that the home and family can shield Muslims from, everyday Islamophobia can easily – and sometimes aggressively – enter those spaces that are the most personal and intimate. As we have seen, while many people understandably chose to stay home when the Islamophobic riots were happening in the UK, sometimes the safety and security of the home can be directly threatened. A concerning example of this was reports of Muslim households and businesses in UK receiving letters through their postboxes. This letter was announcing 'Punish a Muslim Day', to be held on 3 April 2018.

> They have hurt you, they have made your loved ones suffer. They have caused you pain and heartache. What are you going to do about it? Are you a 'sheep' like the vast majority of the population? Sheep follow orders and are easily led, they are allowing the white majority nations of Europe and North America to become overrun by those who would

like nothing more than to do us harm and turn our democracies into Sharia law police states. Only you can help turn this thing around, only you have the power. Do not be a sheep!

The letter then outlined a system of 'rewards': points to be scored for specific actions undertaken against Muslims:

- 10 points: Verbally abuse a Muslim
- 25 points: Pull the head-scarf off a Muslim 'woman'
- 50 points: Throw acid in the face of a Muslim
- 100 points: Beat up a Muslim
- 250 points: Torture a Muslim using electrocution, skinning, use of a rack
- 500 points: Butcher a Muslim using gun, knife, vehicle or otherwise
- 1,000 points: Burn or bomb a mosque
- 2,500 points: Nuke Mecca

The date of 3 April was chosen, as it is the birthdate of Dylann Roof, the white supremacist who murdered nine black African Americans at a church in Charleston, South Carolina, in June 2015. A second set of letters was issued in May for 'Punish a Muslim Day 2'. TellMAMA (2019) reported an increase in Islamophobic incidents targeting households and personal property in 2018, which may have been the result of these letters.

Embodied Islamophobia

Mansson McGinty (2020) advances the idea of embodied Islamophobia and differentiates this from systematic Islamophobia, which she sees as being more about geopolitical concerns. She focuses on embodied Islamophobia as being about 'how Islamophobia – anti-Muslim ideas and actions – is ultimately lived, experienced and embodied in the context of the everyday in particular spaces and within particular interpersonal relationships, but without losing sight of the parallel construction of belonging' (Mansson McGinty, 2020: 405).

Embodied Islamophobia focuses then on aspects of everyday Islamophobia that target the body, including forms of Islamophobia connected to the way someone looks, how they dress, and how they are racialized as belonging to specific ethnic or racial groups. Work about embodied Islamophobia is informed by feminist research and pays attention to the most intimate, emotional, and personal aspects of everyday Islamophobia (Schenk et al, 2022). We have already discussed some examples of embodied Islamophobia in this book because, ultimately, a lot of everyday Islamophobia is embodied, the greatest impact of it often being felt on or in the body, regardless of whether the issue is about national Islamophobic policies, negotiations of airport security, or challenging discourses of self-segregation. Indeed, one way in which the Islamophobia industrial complex causes most damage is by intervening into the personal, psychological, and interpersonal aspects of people's everyday lives (Schenk et al, 2022; Mansson McGinty, 2023).

In research in Milwaukee, Mansson McGinty (2020) focuses on the experiences of siblings, Mona and Kareem, who were in their early 20s when she interviewed them. They were both born in Milwaukee, and their father had come to the United States from the Middle East to study, and he met their mother – a white American who converted to Islam. Both siblings felt at home in Milwaukee; it is the city they were born in, grew up in, studied in, and have their friends in. However, Mona experienced anti-Muslim sentiment from her grandmother, who was white and not a Muslim. Mona had started to wear a hijab in the last year or so and recalls:

> Until this day, there was an incident that happened when I was twelve with my grandmother. She had taken my older sister and I and one of my cousins down to Florida for vacation. My grandpa was there too. And we were going to go to Disney World and you're a kid and so excited. But the minute when we got out of Wisconsin, she had packed my sister and I an entirely different wardrobe, and none of it was stuff that we could wear. It was shorts and short sleeves. And again, we were both covering. And she basically forced us to not wear our scarves. That is when this whole issue started. If I know that my grandma is capable of doing such a thing, I don't trust her. ... You should love your family, but I always question that. For me, it is a very thin line between love and respect. Obviously, I can't change who I'm related to and I still love them. But if I don't necessarily trust them, there is always that conflict. (Mansson McGinty, 2020: 412)

Here we see a specific example of embodied Islamophobia, but the source of this is from a family member rather than from someone on the street, on public transport, or encountered while shopping. Not surprisingly, embodied Islamophobia is often highly gendered (Carland, 2011, 2023a; Listerborn, 2015; Iner et al, 2022; Thorpe et al, 2022; Beydoun, 2023; Easat-Daas and Zempi, 2024; Khandoker et al, 2024); indeed, much research refers to Islamophobia as *intersectional* – as simultaneously racialized and gendered and shaped by other markers of social and cultural difference (Ansari and Patel, 2024) – and when the focus of the work is also on the body and about embodiment, it can also be classified as *embodied* Islamophobia. For example, Shaker et al (2023) recall the accounts of 34 young Muslims' experiences of embodied marginalization in Amsterdam. The young people involved in this study pointed out that they were not only marginalized and excluded because of their Muslim faith but also because of the complex ways that this intersects with other aspects of themselves, such as their socio-economic status, or style of dress, as well as the stereotypical assumptions made about them, thus providing examples of everyday Islamophobia as being both intersectional and embodied.

Gendered stereotypes and tropes interplay with everyday Islamophobia in complex ways, often changing the operation of Islamophobia in the process. For example, 'the figure of the Muslim woman is constructed as oppressed, voiceless, and submissive … whilst the figure of the Muslim man is constructed as threatening, violent, and barbaric' (Easat-Daas and Zempi, 2024: 1), and so gendered Islamophobia may operate differently depending on the gendered assumptions of those involved. This often helps to explain why specific segments of the Muslim community may be targets for Islamophobic abuse.

> Muslim women are disproportionately targeted in Islamophobic hate crimes, experiencing 90 per cent of such incidents in the Netherlands and 81 per cent in France. Similarly, in Australia and the United Kingdom, the victims of Islamophobic attacks are mostly women, and perpetrators are predominantly men. Muslim women and girls are subjected to verbal abuse, profanities, physical intimidation, and death threats in public spaces, with 96 per cent of female Muslims in one Australian survey reporting having been targeted while wearing a headscarf. Perpetrators are often not deterred by the public visibility of their attacks (60 per cent of reported incidents occurred in places with security officers and surveillance) or the vulnerability of their targets (57 per cent of women victims were unaccompanied). In Slovakia, a male passer-by in the street reportedly tried to strangle a Muslim woman with her hijab while she held her baby in her arms. (Shaheed, 2021: 14)

Muslim women continue to be key targets of everyday Islamophobia, and many reports record many more incidents against women than men. In the Netherlands, over 90 per cent of the victims of Islamophobic hate crime incidents in 2015 were Muslim women. In France, 82 per cent of Islamophobic violence in 2014 were against Muslim women. In Germany, 59 per cent of Muslim women responding to a survey said they had been victims of verbal abuse or physical assault. In Belgium, 64 per cent of Islamophobic hate crimes in the three-year period between January 2012 and September 2015 targeted Muslim women (Iftikhar, 2021). Soltani et al (2022: 413) demonstrate that even countries like New Zealand are not immune from the spread of Islamophobia, as Muslim women in Hamilton, New Zealand, prioritized addressing the stereotype that they were 'oppressed, unfashionable and out of date beings'.

However, sometimes gendered Islamophobia is written about as if it is only women who are gendered. It is important to remember that men are gendered too, and stereotypes about Muslim men and masculinities intersect with Islamophobia in complex ways (for example, Dwyer et al, 2008; Allen, 2024). Much research about Muslim masculinities 'reveals how a Muslim identity marks men and young boys as potential terrorists and threats to security' (Selod et al, 2024: 24), which is identified in their bodies as having the potential to engage in violence, aggression, and, if needed, terrorism.

Many Muslims are highly sensitized to the ways in which embodied Islamophobia works. For example, from our work in Scotland, Botterill et al (2019) refer to young people from diverse ethnic backgrounds – including Muslims – using pre-emptive security strategies of self-surveillance and self-protection that they had developed, in response to their previous experiences, or expectations of experiencing, racism and Islamophobia. They employed a range of strategies, such as staying alert, checking things out carefully, deciding whether to cover their head. A second set of security strategies was more proactive and focused on more direct attempts to resist dominant discourses or challenge exclusions. This included behaviours such as smiling, looking people in the eye, or outperforming what might be expected of them. For example, they talked about standing aside to let everyone get onto the bus before them or tidying up after people in the weights room at the gym. A Muslim asylum seeker living in Glasgow said:

> I think if you take the first step and smile and say, 'hi how are you' or 'how's the weather' and stuff and you know just be normal, be who you are even if I'm wearing scarf or even if I'm a Muslim, it doesn't change me, I'm still a human being. So, I have felt then I find it easier that they find, well people find it easier to talk with me if I'm open and smiling rather than the person who is closed or you know doesn't talk to them regularly. (Botterill et al, 2019: 478)

Dress choice

Probably the most overdetermined marker of Muslim identity (Dwyer, 1999) – and therefore a key focus for those wanting to enact everyday Islamophobia – is the dress choice of Muslims, and particularly the dress choice of Muslim women (Hussein et al, 2019). The obsession, preoccupation, and paranoia associated with this can be bolstered by the conspiracy theories, mechanisms for circumventing Islamophobia, and stereotypes about Muslims: 'Hijabs, niqabs, female-genital-mutilation, forced marriages, honour killings, strict dads and overbearing brothers are the tropes used to refer to an apparently culturally-specific, barbaric misogyny that comes with Muslim presence in the West. These issues are raised in everyday conversations as fact' (Manzoor-Khan, 2022: 136). While dress is an important marker of Muslim identity and a key mechanism for ensuring that women's sexual purity is protected and any unwanted attention from men is minimized (Mohammad, 1999), the obsession with dress – and especially with the veil or headscarf (Chakraborti and Zempi, 2012) – is such that specific forms of Muslim attire are banned in several European countries, including Austria, Belgium, Denmark, France, the Netherlands, and Switzerland (Najib and Hopkins, 2019). Norway announced formal legislative plans in June 2017,

> to ban all face-covering Muslim veils in universities, schools, and kindergartens across the country … in the Norway ban, any female Muslim employees who insisted on wearing hijab could risk losing their jobs. Furthermore, many female Muslim students could face expulsion from their colleges and universities if they were found in violation of this ridiculous law. (Iftikhar, 2021: 81)

There are other national and localized bans in several other countries across the globe. In France, a law was introduced in 2004 banning the wearing of religious symbols in schools, and Najib (2024) reports that this was extended in September 2023 to include the abaya and qamis (thobe). As Iftikhar observes, what is supposed to be an important symbol of Muslim femininity has been politicized:

> The Islamic headscarf has always been a powerful symbol of Muslim women's defiance against the male gaze, against colonialism, and against Islamophobia as we know it today. Now in the West, it has become a racially politicized garment; there is every reason to think it will sadly remain at the center of a socio-political tug-of-war for the foreseeable future. (Iftikhar, 2021: 106)

A challenge with this issue is that Muslim dress choice is very diverse and influenced by a range of factors, including links to specific regional traditions and local customs, many of which have little, if anything, to do with religious identity.

> Saris, for example are popular amongst Muslims in Bangladesh, but they are also worn by Hindus and Christians in India, Similarly, the shalwar kamiz (tunic and trouser) is a form of regional dress, sometimes considered to have Muslim connotations in North India and Pakistan, but also worn by Hindus and Sikhs. (Tarlo, 2010: 5)

There are serious contradictions at the heart of the debate about the veil. For example, concerns are often raised about Muslim women's dress practices in relation to the perception that these make them invisible, hidden, and concealed, which is frequently overloaded with assumptions about docility, oppression, and women being limited to the home. Yet, as Tarlo (2010) argues, the veil brings with it a strong visibility, rather than concealment, and Soltani et al (2022) likewise argue, from their work in Hamilton, New Zealand, that it can lead to hypervisibility, especially in contexts where there is a very small Muslim population. After 9/11, many Muslim women chose to wear a headscarf as a political statement to confirm their identity and to challenge the negativity associated with their religious faith (Lewis and Almila, 2020), which is quite the opposite of what the stereotypes about veiled Muslim women would have us believe. The Dutch marathon gold medallist who wore her hijab while receiving her medal at the Paris Olympics is an excellent example of the veil being worn politically and as a strategy of resistance.

The veil then is a 'contested signifier' (Meer et al, 2010: 84) for Muslim women and 'a powerful and overdetermined marker of difference' (Dwyer, 1999: 5). As Dwyer (1999) explains, the headscarf is something that young Muslim women wear at certain times and not at others. In a sense, then, they do so strategically.

> Thus, despite the power of the rhetoric of the veil, individuals argued it could mean nothing about the sexual and moral propriety of the wearer. Participants recounted the ways in which headscarves could be worn strategically to negotiate different spaces—for example, being worn by pupils to and from school but then removed in the classroom. Individuals also questioned the commitment of those who chose to wear a headscarf by insisting that wearing it could not be done casually and required an all-encompassing commitment to Islam. Those who did not wear a headscarf therefore argued that they were not yet ready for such a commitment, and to pretend otherwise would be hypocritical and, thus implicitly, even more irreligious. (Dwyer, 1999: 18)

Focusing on the Swedish context, and the city of Malmo in particular, Listerborn (2015) notes that Swedish authorities only collect data on 'foreign background' and not on ethnicity, religion, or race. She explains that estimates suggest around 20 per cent of Muslim women wear a veil, but that covering the face is very rare. Listerborn interviewed 19 women who covered their hair and shoulders. Participants shared accounts of violent encounters in the form of hostile expressions and bodily gestures, nasty examples of verbal abuse including swearing, often when Muslim women are with their children, with most incidents taking place in central parts of the city, in shopping centres, on public transport or in parks. They were so accustomed to it that they were prepared for encounters like this.

Based on in-depth life narratives with five Palestinian Muslim women who live in Milwaukee, United States, Mansson McGinty (2014) explores the emotional dimensions of veiling practices. While wearing the hijab points to the embodiment of a visibility and activism among Muslim women, it also presents emotional challenges. She approaches the hijab as a symbol that has personal, psychological, and social/political meanings. She interviewed the women for a long time, often carrying out follow-up interviews to understand the depth of their everyday lived experiences. Most of the women viewed wearing the hijab as a religious obligation, in contrast to the dominant narrative that it is something they are forced to do. Wearing the hijab is, then, an important way for these women to embody openly their religious faith and to demonstrate what a Muslim woman should be like to wider society. The women did not wear the hijab lightly and saw it as a sign of their commitment to their faith and as something that requires strong personal conviction.

One woman talked about choosing to wear the veil because she felt excluded from mainstream society and many other identities were not available to her. Following the events of 9/11 and then starting college, another of Mansson McGinty's (2014) participants discussed her strong feelings about needing to present her religious identity visibly, and starting college gave her the ideal chance to start wearing the veil: 'After September 11, she felt a need to defend who she was and her political affiliation. The group she was identifying with, "Muslims" in a broader sense, was being attacked, and as a result, she felt an urgency to show her stance' (Mansson McGinty, 2014: 693). This is about political connection and solidarity and takes a stance against Islamophobia. It is also about imagining community, embodying the existence of your religious faith, and demonstrating your right to belong in your city. In this context, some women saw this as a form of activism and wanted to engage in cross-cultural, inter-faith dialogue, to educate others to address social injustices.

Some of the most fraught dress choices present themselves in contexts where the veil is banned or where there are localized restrictions on it. For example, 'several laws were passed in France, in 2004 and 2010, prohibiting "ostentatious" religious signs in public schools and full-face veils in public space, as part of a tendency to question the compatibility of the practice with French citizenship' (Hancock and Mobillion, 2019: 2). Hancock and Mobillion (2019: 1) consider what they refer to as the 'geopolitics of veil-wearing' in the Paris context, as Muslim women's bodies have become a key site through which debates about French citizenship are played out. They use the idea of 'femonationalism' – by which feminist principles are utilized for nationalistic ends – to consider the social mobility of women who wear the veil in Paris and the ways this restricts their access to education. Although there are policies targeted at helping women, many of these exclude Muslim women, and key gatekeepers and communities police access. They consider 'ways in which issues of security and territorial defence come to focus on the bodies of women – with forms of dress determining whether they are identified and treated as enemies or friends, whether they are entitled to protection or designated as scapegoats' (Hancock and Mobillion, 2019: 1). This work was based on lengthy interviews with Muslim women in Paris, as well as with city officials.

Paris itself was identified as the context in which Muslim women reported feeling most uncomfortable and more likely to experience harassment. The women reported Islamophobic aggression in the affluent areas of central Paris, and most were more comfortable in working-class areas, where they reported being more likely to feel protected and supported by the local community.

> A typical statement is that of Fatia, one of our interviewees who is 41 years old and an unemployed separated mother of one: 'Before I started wearing a veil, people didn't know whether I was a Muslim or not, whether I practiced my religion or not. When I started I encountered difficulties, stares, even insults.' (Hancock and Mobillion, 2019: 5)

Many women pointed to the media as being responsible, and several felt more confined and enclosed in the city when they started to veil yet were eager to emphasize that it was their decision to wear a veil and that it was not imposed upon them. Some even sought to find employment in other countries that have less restrictive policies on dress.

Among the women who face discriminations on a regular basis, the degree of violence of the Islamophobic acts seems to vary according to the size of the veil. Wearing a hijab exposes them to stares and taunts. Those who wear a jilbeb (or a niqab in one case) are assaulted more violently, sometimes physically, for example having water thrown on them, being spat on, having their veil torn off, being hit and pushed to the ground. 'These frequent occurrences point to the way in which ordinary citizens take on a role in "policing the borders" through aggression and violence, as though national discourse and local public policies enabled and sanctioned their harassment of women wearing veils as "enemies" or threats to public safety' (Hancock and Mobillion, 2019: 6). Two women were rejected for university places – one for business and one for journalism – because they wore a veil. No participants veiled when working in private companies, even though restrictions do not directly apply in such contexts. Ironically, Hancock (2015) explains that, in French discourse, short skirts are regarded as something symbolizing the opposite of the veil, held up as a signifier of French femininity and a form of dress to be promoted and encouraged.

Although most research focuses on Muslim women's dress choice, as we saw in the previous section of this chapter, there is also evidence of Muslim men's embodied presentation shaping the likelihood of them experiencing everyday Islamophobia. In some of my earlier work, I make the point that men wearing what were often referred to as 'Asian clothes', as well as having a beard and being of South Asian ethnicity, made them more likely to be targets of Islamophobic abuse (Hopkins, 2004). This has been compounded since 9/11, given that the 'construct of the terrorist is one of the ways we see Muslim men racialized as dangerous and violent' (Selod et al, 2024: 23).

Misrecognition: being mistaken for being Muslim

One way in which we see everyday Islamophobia play out in relation to readings of the racialized body is through a process of misrecognition, whereby people who have skin colour and other embodied features that are not read as white are regarded as Muslims and, consequently, seen as a possible threat. This includes those who follow other faiths, such as Sikhs, Hindus, Christians, and Jews (Iftikhar, 2016, 2021). Sian (2010) notes 'Don't freak, I'm Sikh', Beydoun (2018: 35) describes how 'Sikh men continue to be routinely perceived as Muslims', and Kwan (2008: 655) refers to 'Muslim-looking individuals'. It would be easy to dismiss such experiences of being mistaken for being Muslim as simple mistakes. However, experiences of misrecognition can be very damaging to those who encounter them, especially if they happen frequently. Fraser (2000: 113) explains that misrecognition 'is not simply to be thought ill of, looked down upon or devalued by others' attitudes, beliefs or representations'. Instead, it is to be 'denied the status of a full partner in social interactions', and places the target in a position of being 'unworthy of respect or esteem' (Fraser 2000, 113–114). Likewise, Taylor (1994: 26) believes that 'misrecognition shows not just a lack of respect. It can inflict a grievous wound, saddling its victims with a crippling self-hatred' and that '[n]onrecognition or misrecognition can inflict harm, can be a form of oppression, imprisoning someone in a false, distorted, and reduced mode of being' (Taylor, 1994: 26).

Beydoun (2018) recounts the experiences of Balbir, an Indian Sikh who was persuaded by his brother to leave India and move to California in 1988, to live closer to his brother. He worked in several jobs in California, including in a 7-Eleven convenience store and as a cab driver, devoting long hours to provide for his family. He bought his own home in Arizona in 2000 and a gas station that helped him to provide for his two daughters, while also sending money to his family in India. He was living the American dream as a citizen of the United States: he had his own home and was able to provide for his family. He watched the events of 9/11 in shock and his patriotism for his country led him to flying an American flag from his home to show support for those who had lost their lives. He even sold American flags from his gas station.

> While gardening and arranging the flags in front of his station, a Chevrolet S-10 pickup pulled up to one of the pumps. The man driving the truck looked at Balbir's direction, sizing up the brown man wearing a turban, black beard, and friendly smile. He remained inside his truck, staring squarely at Balbir. The Sikh American assumed the man was just another customer. However, this was the furthest thing from the truth, and Balbir realized this when he heard the first shot ring out from the truck. He would not hear the next four. (Beydoun, 2018: 94)

As Beydoun (2018) notes, Balbir was not a follower of the Islamic faith, but he looked 'Muslim' according to many, as he had a beard, dark skin, and a turban similar to those worn by the terrorists shown on television. 'In America, the trouble with wearing turbans, a spiritual mandate for Sikh men, is their nexus to the ingrained stereotype of the Muslim terrorist and the hatred that stereotype activates' (Beydoun, 2018: 35; see also Iftikhar, 2016).

We have found diverse experiences of misrecognition in my collaborative work about the lived experiences of ethnic and religious minority young people growing up in urban, suburban, and rural Scotland. We worked with 382 young people aged 12–25, who participated in 45 focus groups and 223 interviews. They were from six different groups: Muslims, South Asian non-Muslims (such as Sikhs, Hindus, or other South Asian heritage), asylum seekers and refugees, international students, Central and Eastern European migrants, and white Scottish young people. We recognized that these categories often overlapped, as some young people fell into two or more, such as Muslim refugees from the African continent. Our analysis of this data found that young people from diverse backgrounds recalled experiences of being mistaken for being Muslim, and, although these experiences varied, all relied upon 'a racist reading of the phenotypical features of our participants – such as skin colour, facial features, hair texture, and style – that problematically (and often incorrectly) associated them with specific countries of origin and with the Islamic faith' (Hopkins et al, 2017: 939). Nearly all the Sikhs we interviewed referred to being misrecognized as Muslims. In a focus group in suburban Glasgow, a participant said, 'Even if you are Sikh, they call you a Muslim.' These are the words of another participant:

> I remember when I first made, like, one of my friends, like, someone, like, two years ago and she was, like, 'What are you?' And I was like,

'Well, Sikh.' She was like, 'What like a Muslim?' And I was like, 'No like Sikh.' And she was like, 'Is that not the same as Muslim?' And I was just like, 'Oh god, no!' And she was like, 'I don't get it, so you are Muslim.' 'No.' People actually just think that if you are brown you are Muslim, and [I] was in school, and I was just like, and this was only like two years ago. She was like fifteen. And she didn't even know what a Sikh was. I was just like, oh god! Ha ha. But I think that it is everywhere in Scotland.

Hindu young people also talked about people assuming they were Muslims. Moreover, a young Indian boy – to whom we gave the pseudonym Donald – attended a Catholic school but was assumed to be Muslim. He recalled being questioned regularly about his faith and about the faith of his parents. Donald was a practising Catholic, as were both of his parents.

Young people with African and Caribbean heritage also shared accounts of people assuming they were Muslims and being asked why they were not off school for Eid, even though many of them were Christians. Misrecognition also extended to some of the young Central and Eastern European migrants. In a focus group with young men from Slovenia, Romania, and the Czech Republic, participants agreed that some people assume they are Muslim and say that this is because they look Pakistani. Across the interviews, there were commonalities in where the incidents of misrecognition took place. Four everyday contexts were the most common: at school, in taxis, at the airport and in other public spaces.

Young Muslims – and other young people who 'look Muslim' – often responded to incidents of misrecognition in creative ways, such as using humour or clarifying what they see as the true meaning of their religious faith or ethnic heritage. Others chose to ignore the situation, and some socially withdrew. Young people had sophisticated explanations for what was going on. They were sensitive to geopolitical events, such as the aftermath of 9/11 and the Woolwich incident, that took place on 22 May 2013, when soldier, Lee Rigby, was killed by two black men, Michael Adebolajo and Michael Adebowale, who claimed they did this in response to the killing of Muslims by British forces. Moreover, these young people were also aware that multiple and diverse Asian identities are often homogenized – the assumption being that all Asians are the same, practise the same religion, and hold similar views.

Everyday Islamophobia and the Islamophobia industrial complex

We have seen how everyday Islamophobia – powered by the actors who make up the Islamophobia industrial complex – is felt on and in the body, lived through the bodily movements of individuals, and can seep into experiences of the most intimate, personal, and private spaces of everyday life, such as those associated with home and the family. Accessing the private spaces of the home through the mailbox or through social media, everyday Islamophobia is also promoted through the obsession placed on Muslim clothing cultures and dress choice.

9

Impacts and Solutions

In this chapter, I discuss the major impacts that everyday Islamophobia has on those who experience it, including the processes of weathering, the role of stigma, the impact of fear, and issues of recognition, coupled with the damage that comes from the regularity of incidents. I then address a question that I am asked often when speaking, writing, and talking about everyday Islamophobia: what can be done about this? This is a challenging question to address, and I by no means have all the answers, but I try to consider some of the key issues in this concluding chapter. I consider the role of the Islamophobia industrial complex and what can be done to demolish this, so that it can be abolished and destroyed. I emphasize the need to stop the global war on terror and the initiatives supporting it. I discuss the need for states to fund proper reporting processes, to collect reliable data about Islamophobia, and to recognize it as a fully fledged form of prejudice and discrimination, rather than deny its existence. Finally, I put forward some of the engaging and innovative strategies that Muslims and non-Muslims take against Islamophobia.

Impacts of everyday Islamophobia

Given the complex operation of the Islamophobia industrial complex and its transnational reach, it is not surprising that the everyday Islamophobias that it is responsible for generating can have deeply concerning impacts on those who experience them (Vakil and Sayyid, 2023). These issues are sometimes referred to as 'racial battle fatigue' or as 'minority stress', and are, in many ways, an extreme form of structural violence negotiated in the everyday.

> Structural violence is the manifestation of systemic racism or classism through the complex web of overlapping and repeated harms faced by members of marginalized groups. It takes many forms, but, in the context of weathering, structural violence refers to the chronic physical, environmental, material, and biopsychosocial stressors that members

of a socially stigmatized and discriminated-against group face in their daily round. (Geronimus, 2023: 48)

Some of the most significant impacts of everyday Islamophobia are the ones that damage the health and wellbeing of those who encounter it. As Essed explains, although everyday racism has 'such an informal ring that it may sound as if it concerns relatively unharmful and unproblematic events, it has been shown that the psychological distress due to racism on a day-to-day basis can have chronic adverse effects on mental and physical health' (Essed, 2002: 204). In constantly having to negotiate everyday Islamophobia, those who experience it encounter weathering, which is

> a process that encompasses the physiological effects of living in marginalized communities that bear the brunt of racial, ethnic, religious and class discrimination, [and] is critical to understanding and eliminating population health inequity. Weathering afflicts human bodies – all the way down to the cellular level – as they grow, develop, and age in a systematically and historically racist, classist society. (Geronimus, 2023: 3)

Essed (2002: 204) further discusses the toll of stress on the body, resulting in people dying younger than they should, and notes that stress can lead to high blood pressure as a result of the 'continuous disrespect and hostilities' that are experienced from 'alienation from society' (Essed, 2002: 204). We know from the influential work of van der Kolk (2014) that 'the body keeps the score' in how we respond to trauma. For those who must constantly fight against Islamophobia, and

> who must struggle for validation or success against strong headwinds, a set of physiological pathways are chronically activated that can lead to cardiovascular disease, cancer, accelerated ageing, weakened immune systems, and other life-threatening vulnerabilities. The triggers of these physiological processes are social and dynamic, even while they occur in individual bodies. (Geronimus, 2023: 12)

The serious consequences of Islamophobia on the health and wellbeing of individuals are beyond the damage already caused by issues of educational inequalities, socio-economic exclusions, and injustices based on residential location and lack of government investment in specific neighbourhoods (Geronimus, 2023). Exclusions, discrimination, and marginalization extend to issues of accessing housing, healthcare, education, employment, and other local services – contexts that should provide opportunity and enhance quality of life. The experience of everyday Islamophobia, then, adds more layers of exclusion to Muslims who already face racism. One in ten Muslims in Europe has to face this (European Union Agency for Fundamental Rights, 2024). Remember too, that the effects of these restrictions and discriminations are cumulative.

The role of *stigma* is important here: 'it is society's racialization of certain groups as being essentially "irresponsible," "inferior," "deficient," "naturally suited to harmful occupations," "insensitive to physical pain," and "threatening" – a classification in which both dominant and marginal are fluent – that damages their health' (Geronimus, 2023: 4–5). It is not only active and explicit everyday Islamophobia that leads to these negative outcomes. It can be societal processes of stigmatization. However, understanding stigma can also be a force for generating networks of support: 'While stigma is a disabling force, a form of power that is inscribed on bodies, places and communities in ways that often leave profound and permanent scars, understanding the wounds of stigma as social and political injuries can assist in the forging of networks of care and solidarity' (Tyler, 2020: 29).

The role of *fear* is also central. The issues discussed in this book can generate significant fear, anxiety, and worry for Muslims and those mistaken for being Muslim, whether this be the fear of being caught up in Islamophobic rioting, worries about travelling by any form of public transport, concerns about far-right activism, or anxieties about negotiating specific neighbourhoods or public spaces. Chaudry (2021) explores the fears of university students, aware that they are marginalized on university campuses. Pain (2001) talks about fear of crime, and the exclusion from society that can result from being constructed as a threat, through policing strategies, through precautionary behaviours, as well as the experiences of crime or sub-criminal acts. We have seen how concerns about experiencing everyday Islamophobia can lead to people limiting their everyday movements, avoiding specific places or contexts where they perceive the risk to be heightened.

Research points to the burden, which is often carried by the individual of responding to and managing these issues. People have to work at managing encounters with others, thinking through how to respond to any tension and minimize conflict, or how to appear cooperative, well-meaning, and friendly. In work with British Bangladeshi Muslims in London, Luton, and Birmingham in the UK, Redclift et al (2022) found that there are further specific burdens associated with ensuring that other people are at ease in everyday encounters, including that of educating and explaining, of understanding racism, and simply of blending in and appearing unremarkable.

We know that *recognition* is important and, indeed, without it, Muslims and other ethnic minority groups can 'feel noticed, marked, or conversely invisible, not taken seriously, or worse, demeaned' (Young, 1990: 133–134). Yet, everyday Islamophobia leads to people working to conceal aspects of their Muslim identity and thereby to reduce the positive recognition they should receive for who they are. Based on a survey that 1,123 Muslims responded to, Elsheikh and Sisemore (2021) found that nearly a third of Muslims in the United States have tried to conceal their religious identities at some point in their lives in response to Islamophobia. Nearly 90 per cent have censored their speech or what they were doing because of fear about how people might respond, and women are more likely to be careful here than men. Significantly, 93 per cent feel that Islamophobia affects their emotional and mental wellbeing, and 79 per cent feel that it prevents them from building social relationships with non-Muslims. This is not surprising, given that concealing aspects of who you are means that you are not bringing your full self into relationships and encounters with others.

The frequency and repetition of experiences of Islamophobia add further damage to what is already a very troubling dynamic. Much research points to the regularity of Islamophobia rather than it being a one-off or rarely occurring experience. It is this regular 'activation of the physiological stress response over years and eventually decades' (Geronimus, 2023: 18) that has such significant impacts. While certain more affluent groups might be able to mitigate these impacts, to some extent, with better healthcare, counselling, and psychotherapy, more privileged education, healthier diets, and other interventions, it is not possible to eliminate the effects completely.

Given the global and transnational nature of Islamophobia, there are increasing examples of cases of Muslim lives being deemed to be less significant, less important, and of lower value than the lives of others. Butler (2016) suggests that there are frames through which we capture – or fail to capture – the lives of those who are lost or injured, and these framings are forms of political power. The lives of Muslims are, more often than not, framed as being less important than the lives of others. While problematic in itself, this lack of recognition can lead to experiences of disenfranchised grief, as Muslim communities are left to grieve alone over relationships, connections, and ties that are not regarded as important or significant.

Manzoor-Khan (2022) provides an insightful account of the direct consequences of Islamophobia on her everyday wellbeing. While drafting her book, she was contacted by Fiona Hamilton from *The Times* newspaper, inviting her to comment on a piece Hamilton wanted to write about the Henry Jackson Society, which had queried the suitability of Manzoor-Khan to present a BBC Radio 4 documentary. Apparently, the Henry Jackson Society's query mostly concerned the supposed links that Manzoor-Khan had with the group, CAGE. As she notes:

> CAGE are a Muslim-led grass-roots human rights organisation working against the injustices of the War on Terror and therefore often face

charges such as Hamilton's description of them as 'an organisation accused in the past of being apologists for terrorists'. I can only presume that made me terrorist-apologist-aligned and therefore a danger to Radio 4 listeners. (Manzoor-Khan, 2022: 149)

Although she never replied to this query and an article was never published, Manzoor-Khan said that it 'left me hypervigilant. My body went into fight-or-flight mode when I received the email and adrenaline surged into my bloodstream. With my arms physically shaking, I spent hours typing a draft response to an article that never appeared and spent weeks or more in anticipation of it being published' (Manzoor-Khan, 2022: 150). As the target of an attempted Islamophobic smear-campaign, she was aware of how global capital and profit-making groups 'played out in my nervous system and my heartbeat' (Manzoor-Khan, 2022: 150).

We know that 'members of populations subject to weathering are rarely – if ever – responding to a single acute stressor. Their bodies are in constant biopsychosocial motion fulfilling their many and compelling responsibilities, which also steal their chances of having "me time"' (Geronimus, 2023: 43). We have seen how everyday Islamophobia has serious impacts on physical, mental, and emotional health and wellbeing, and the psychological effects include fear, embarrassment, humiliation, and a damaged sense of self and of self-esteem. As Manzoor-Khan (2022: 7) explains, 'Islamophobia lives under the skin of those of us who it marks. Islamophobia alters our physiologies through trauma, lives in our nervous systems, makes us hypervigilant and afraid'.

I cannot emphasize enough that a key factor in all of this is *repetition*, the constant reappearance, recurrence, and re-emergence, again and again, powered by the Islamophobia industrial complex.

Possible solutions: tackling everyday Islamophobia

As this book has highlighted, everyday Islamophobia presents in so many ways and has many different forms. Bonnett (2024) reminds us that there are multiple forms of *racisms* (rather than a singular racism), and that there is a spatial diversity to this. This diversity presents substantial challenges to thinking about solutions to racisms and Islamophobias; if everyday Islamophobia were only to present itself in one form all the time, then it would be much easier to address. Unfortunately, this is not the case, and so a diversity of tactics to tackle Islamophobia is needed, including a whole-of-society approach. There is no shortage of guidance about how to tackle Islamophobia, and many people, groups, and organizations have been working for a long time to challenge, counter, and overcome it. For example, Law et al (2019) have brought together a range of contributors to their book about how to counter Islamophobia in Europe, and there are chapters focusing on different national contexts, including Greece, Hungary, Czech Republic, Portugal, France, Belgium, Germany, and the UK. The European Coalitian of Cities against Racism (Hyokki and Cubelic, 2023) has produced a useful guidebook about local actions against anti-Muslim racism aimed at city administrators and those who work with them. Other examples include a focus on how Islamophobia can be countered in North America (el-Aswad, 2021), and there are a whole range of guidance leaflets, factsheets, booklets, and other resources provided by community organizations, civil society groups, and agencies seeking to counter Islamophobia and to support those who experience it.

To tackle everyday Islamophobia seriously, however, the Islamophobia industrial complex has to be abolished and destroyed. As this is a multifaceted and complicated system that is well funded and resourced, this will not be an easy task. Some components of the Islamophobia industrial complex would be easier to abolish than others, while some are so multifaceted, complex, and multidimensional that it will be very challenging to remove them completely and so the tactic, in these areas, might be to constrain, contain, or confine the extent to which Islamophobia can be promoted. Furthermore, these components are not fixed and static; they can be agile and adaptable, making them more elusive, more difficult to challenge and overcome. Moreover, the nature of everyday Islamophobia is such that, while there may be general trends or patterns in what drives it, it is often shaped by specific local issues, regional challenges, or national policies, and so a blanket solution, untailored to specific contexts, is unlikely to succeed.

I now explore some of the key steps that might be useful in considering how to tackle and counter everyday Islamophobia. Most crucially, the global war on terror must come to an end, and all governments must disinvest from, and work quickly to abolish, counterterrorism measures that unfairly target Muslim communities (Selod et al, 2024). More than this, there must be an end to the type of thinking and supposed logic behind such initiatives (Manzoor-Khan, 2022); simply abolishing them will only leave those who have spent decades generating and enabling these systems and processes to exist to continue as they are. Many alternatives to such problematic approaches have been proposed (Blakeley et al, 2019). O'Toole et al (2016) point to the different ways in which counterterrorism strategies, like Prevent in the UK, are practised and note that different levels of government are likely to implement them in different ways. So, such initiatives, then, are not only employed differentially, but even if they were to be removed, people would continue to use what they have learnt from these systems in their work. As such, there needs to be a concerted effort to abolish both the system, the thought processes behind it, and the apparent logic and presumed rationality of such an approach.

The wider role of the state in promoting Islamophobia, therefore, needs to be addressed. This includes abolishing the global war on terror, and it involves the state taking a more active role in ensuring that Islamophobia is regarded as a real issue and not rejected as a problematic concept. There are too many contexts in which the very idea of Islamophobia is not accepted, as we see in France, discussed in Chapter 4, or where it is not incorporated meaningfully into national or legislative frameworks and comes to be regarded with less significance than it should be; so, effectively, it is sidelined or de-prioritized as it is in the UK. Or it is simply ignored. How can this be addressed? Alongside giving it the legitimacy it deserves as a serious form of discrimination and prejudice, clear processes must be in place for the recording of incidents and for reporting. First, robust data needs to be collected about Islamophobia. Based on work in Ireland, Carr (2011) advocates for a national approach to the collection of data about Islamophobia – data that disaggregates it from racism – as this would help to assess levels of Islamophobia and enable Irish state policy to be more effective. Under-reporting of Islamophobia is often a serious issue. For example, equalities bodies in many European countries report no cases, despite it being known that Islamophobic incidents are taking place. Of course, collecting robust data alongside having well-resourced and clearly available reporting services all costs money. However, the savings made from abolishing the very expensive global war on terror and its associated counterterrorism apparatus will leave significantly more than enough funding to cover the costs of this.

Next, the mainstreaming of traditionally right-wing issues needs to be addressed, as clearly demonstrated in the important work of Mondon and Winter (2020, 2024). '"Discursive elites" (such as the media, politicians, and academics)' (Mondon and Winter, 2020: 199) must stop legitimizing the issues raised by the far right. Tackling the problems generated by this normalization of right-wing ideas would also greatly restrict the opportunities to spread Islamophobic sentiment that are available to Islamophobic think tanks, public intellectuals, and other public figures. While this restriction might not change their views, they would have very limited platforms from which to share their anti-Muslim narratives and, consequently, their impact and reach would be minimized.

A further crucial issue that needs to be tackled is the negative media coverage, stereotyping, and imagery about Muslims and Islam. Addressing the problems generated by mainstreaming of far-right ideas would, likely, filter through here, so that these components of the Islamophobia industrial complex would feature less often in some forms of media, such as television news programmes and mainstream newspapers. However, this is not enough. A suggestion that is frequently put forward is that journalists and other people who work in media are trained to avoid reinforcing problematic stereotypes about Islam and Muslims, and about migrant communities that are often racialized in similar ways to Muslims. In Scotland, we produced a set of media guidelines – and there are lots of other examples available too – for those working in print, broadcast, and digital media. We were clear that the guidance was for a broad group that included broadcasters, reporters, picture editors, columnists, writers, commentators, bloggers, as well as editors, correspondents, and news presenters. We produced a full report and a shorter version for people to have at their desk, which were organized around the acronym PART – portrayal, accuracy, representation, and terminology (Mir and Hopkins, 2019). The inquiry into Islamophobia in Scotland recommended that all journalists use this guidance, that it is incorporated into all journalism training, and that journalists receive regular training on such issues. While such training would by no means solve all the issues relating to the media, it would help to ensure that journalists are well informed and that what they produce is less likely to contain Islamophobic sentiment.

An even greater challenge than that presented by television and print media is social media, and related platforms, and the speed at which Islamophobia can be shared and then spread very quickly across multiple platforms. As Brown and Mondon (2024) note, some coverage of far and extreme right-wing politics and groups in the media is important, but uncritical coverage that has become increasingly normalized is very unhelpful and counterproductive and, indeed, can promote and platform far-right actors. The Center for Countering Digital Hate (2024: 23) suggests that the 'big tech' companies need to be 'proactive in addressing the online harm and misinformation before it becomes viral and communities are exposed to it', and that they must be 'responsive to reports from users who have been exposed to harmful content and misinformation, and are raising the alarm'. The Center makes a range of other useful recommendations. It proposes that legal frameworks need to be transparent and responsible and that behaviour that is illegal offline should be in online contexts too. It suggests that there need to be stronger controls on harmful content and clear complaints systems, which allow action to be taken quickly. Indeed, as a key agent in the Islamophobia industrial complex, the media financially benefit from the sharing of hate. The Center therefore recommends that, instead, financial penalties be introduced when harmful content is not removed quickly. It also recommends that platforms should hire and train moderators to remove hateful content and that anti-Muslim groups should be removed, as should hashtags that are Islamophobic, and the accounts of those who publish Islamophobic content should be closed. Empowering and enabling those who monitor the quality and standards of the media could be useful here, and this relies on Islamophobia being given proper recognition in national policy making. Some of these suggestions in relation to social media could usefully be applied to other media, although some might only be appropriate in dealing with the most explicit forms of Islamophobia.

Interconnected with the issues around media is the importance of offering strong counter-narratives to overturn the problematic stereotypes and mechanisms for circumventing Islamophobia discussed in Chapter 3. Law et al (2019: 323) conducted important work on the use of counter-narratives, which have a strong tradition in anti-racist work as they 'can be used to expose, critically analyse and reject dominant narratives, and they can be used to give voice to marginalised and silenced groups'. Working with data from 278 respondents, including politicians, policy makers, non-governmental organizations, activists, professionals working in the media and arts, and a range of people in other relevant organizations across Europe, they considered the role of counter-narratives employed by these people, to assess their effectiveness (Law et al, 2019). In doing so, they identified ten dominant counter-narratives to Islamophobia (see Table 9.1).

Alongside strong counter-narratives, it might be useful to work to enhance community resilience, to ensure that people are better informed and less likely to see the appeal of the extreme right, or to engage with problematic conspiracy theories (Miller-Idriss, 2021) or mechanisms of circumvention, and indeed to challenge the acceptance of these ideologies and ways of thinking head on, rather than allowing them to fester in the background. This can be done in various ways, and many Muslims and the organizations they work with are alert to these opportunities.

Table 9.1: Ten dominant counter-narratives to Islamophobia

1	Challenging and contextualizing constructions of Muslim 'threat'
2	Building inclusive nations: challenging exclusive and discriminatory national projects
3	Cultural compatibility and conviviality: challenging the narrative separation of cultural and ethnic groups
4	Elaborating plurality: challenging narratives of Muslim singularity
5	Challenging narratives of sexism
6	Building inclusive futures
7	Deracializing the state: challenging institutional narratives
8	Emphasizing humanity and Muslim normalization: challenging narratives of division
9	Creating Muslim space(s)
10	Challenging distorted representation: verity and voice

Source: Law et al (2018: 14)

Collaboration, partnership, and collective working

In this final section, I focus on the importance of working collaboratively, collectively, and, where appropriate, in partnership, to tackle Islamophobia. It is important to note here that many of the suggestions in this section come from research in which Muslims led on taking solutions forward. Collaborations between academics and civil society groups or organizations working to challenge anti-Muslim hatred can play an important role here, and the Muslim Milwaukee Project is an excellent example (for example, Mansson McGinty, 2012; Mansson McGinty et al, 2013; Sziarto et al, 2014). 'The Muslim community and its allies must work to engender social movements, enact dedicated advocacy and powerful lobbies to combat the formidable and lucrative business of Islamophobia, its industry, and purveyors, as well as the underlying conditions that allow its ecosystem to thrive before more tragedies occur' (Zine, 2022b: 246).

These collaborations and partnerships might be different nations working together multilaterally as well as diverse sectors that include academia, the voluntary and community sector, local authorities or city governments, non-governmental organizations, organizations working to tackle Islamophobia, alongside Muslim organizations or groups focused on addressing racism in all its forms. Kundnani (2007) suggests that it makes sense to organize as 'Muslims', given the way that anti-Muslim racism has been institutionalized in the war on terror. While this is useful, it is inappropriate to leave Muslims to address Islamophobia on their own, hence the focus here on partnership, collaboration, and a whole-of-society approach. There are many issues on which these partnerships and collaborations could work collectively, to tackle Islamophobia. I explore some of the possibilities here.

Promoting and advancing anti-racism

A central focus on tackling Islamophobia should be on the promotion and advancement of approaches that centre anti-racism and anti-Islamophobia (Joseph-Salisbury and Connelly, 2021). It is important to adopt a fully inclusive approach to the issues faced by Muslims and other ethnic minority communities and not to reinforce problematic stereotypes of Muslims or of Islam: 'Anti-racism that shows solidarity with Muslims as racialised subjects, but still sees Islam itself as embarrassingly unmodern, remains counter-intuitively invested in racial logics that construct Islam as backwards, barbaric and unenlightened' (Manzoor-Khan, 2022: 106–107). Committing to anti-racism involves describing and understanding racism and Islamophobia and to call this out and to do this on every occasion it arises. This is about being vigilant to Islamophobia and speaking out against it, to dismantle it in all cases, and to be an ally to those experiencing it.

Educational initiatives

One of the most powerful approaches to tackling Islamophobia is to engage in education and advocacy work. This includes educating people about Islamophobia, how it operates, and how to challenge it. There are already many organizations and initiatives working on educating people about and against Islamophobia. Akhtar and Robert (2021) have written an excellent book, specifically targeted at children, focusing on what Islamophobia is and how it works. Itaoui and Elsheikh (2018) produced a very useful reading resource pack about Islamophobia in the United States, including themes of theorizing the field, foreign policy, legal issues, media, discrimination, gender, health, public space, strategies for countering Islamophobia, and work with Muslim youth. Crucially, it was not only targeted at academics/universities but a wide range of stakeholders who might find it useful.

Of course, although the internet is a key site through which Islamophobia is spread, it can also be a useful location through which to take a stand against Islamophobia and for the Muslim community and others to stand in solidarity against racism and Islamophobia (Khamis, 2023). Moreover, it can be a potential space from which to educate people about Islamophobia. Part of the challenge here is about empowering organizations and agencies to call out Islamophobia, including in online contexts, and it is important, too, to challenge stereotypes such as those about the veil and Muslim women's bodies (Soltani et al, 2022). Education initiatives that target specific areas can be useful, such as those that focus on reporting processes in the workplace, recruitment practices, or promotion and progression, in which workplace cultures of Islamophobia may arise.

Developing strategies of resistance

Much research points to the ways in which Muslims – and those who are assumed to be Muslim – have developed sophisticated strategies of resistance to stand up against and challenge Islamophobia. There are examples of this provided throughout this book, such as the mobility strategies outlined by Itaoui et al (2021) or the examples of engaging in politics and activism (Finlay and Hopkins, 2019, 2020). Al-Sabawi et al (2024) refer to grief activism as one of the responses of Muslim youth to the tragic killing in London, Ontario. Khamis (2023) advocates the use of humour for challenging Islamophobia in online contexts, given that it can be a useful mechanism for discussing difficult topics or sensitive issues: 'By appropriating the meme #MuslimRage in the funniest, wittiest, and most sarcastic ways, they were able to successfully ridicule Islamophobia, while telling their own stories and narratives in their own voice. There is no better way to counter anti-Muslim rhetoric' (Khamis, 2023: 29).

In the face of the challenge of the scale and speed of Islamophobia being shared online, forms of online activism can have potentially powerful impacts. Saeed (2017) talks about young Muslims using the internet as a platform through which to challenge Islamophobia and racism. He observes that much research about Muslims and online contexts focuses on counter-radicalization, and there is less on the ways such spaces might be used to resist and challenge racism. Using the example of Amir Khan, a highly successful and popular British Pakistani Muslim boxing champion, Saeed (2017) explores the racist and Islamophobic attention received by Khan online and the ways in which the racist comments made online were responded to and reacted against by young Muslims in humorous and creative ways. In a different example, Jiwani (2022) has considered how online contexts can be used to resist and challenge Islamophobia through the use of hashtags such as #RememberJan29 and #QuebecMosqueShooting, where people shared images, photographs, artwork, and other symbols to express solidarity and shared political values with their followers. Following the killing of four members of the Afzaal family in London, Ontario in 2021, that I refer to in Chapter 1, the hashtag #OurLondonFamily generated waves of support and solidarity for Muslims and others close to the family. Jiwani (2022: 266) recounts the attention generating 'enough traction to harness the grief, anger, and feelings of exclusion into a movement for social justice', leading to imagery and artwork being taken up by wider national initiatives to challenge Islamophobia and promote equality.

Engaging with the community

Another strategy that can promote a positive image of a marginalized community is what Khamis (2023: 31) refers to as 'doing good and telling people about it'. The American Muslim community engaged in a range of meaningful and helpful activities during the COVID-19 pandemic, including acting as first responders, providing medical support, helping the whole community, and not only other Muslims.

> Therefore, the impressive acts of charity and philanthropy which Muslims from different countries, backgrounds, races, genders, and ethnicities initiated and contributed to worldwide during the pandemic could be considered the best and most effective weapons to fight Islamophobia through enhancing the image of Muslims globally and boosting their positive representation, both online and offline. (Khamis, 2023: 32)

This was even more poignant, given the circulation of negative stereotypes about Muslims being more likely to spread the virus through their apparent lack of engagement in adequate hygiene.

Political and community activism

Interconnected with initiatives that engage with the community, there is much research evidence pointing to the use of political and community activism in tackling Islamophobia. Examples mentioned by Khamis (2023) include the viral #CanYouHearUsNow campaign, when Trump suggested that Ghazala Khan's religion might have been the reason she remained silent during a Democratic National Convention. In fact she stood silently next to her husband as she had just witnessed a display that included an image of her son who was a fallen American soldier. Shortly after this, she wrote a piece in *The Washington Post*, entitled 'Donald Trump said I have nothing to say. I do'. This led to a widespread Twitter campaign, as Muslim women came together on social media to challenge the stereotype that they are silenced, oppressed, marginalized, and controlled by their husbands. In a different example, Al-Sabawi et al (2024) refer to the creation of the Youth Coalition Combatting Islamophobia that was formed after the attack directed at the Afzaal family in London, Ontario. On the first anniversary of the attack, this group arranged a vigil, a march to the local mosque, and a mural at the site of the attack. There is a power in bringing people together to remember and memorialize events like this and to show solidarity, grieve, and stand against all forms of hatred and division. Indeed, the group continues to organize events such as education activities and outreach. The authors refer to this as a form of grief activism.

Cultural production and fashion

There are excellent examples of everyday Islamophobia being challenged through cultural production and fashion cultures. Warren (2022: 235) refers to 'Muslim creative activism' to explore ways in which Muslim women employed in the creative and cultural industries engage with activism to resist racism and Islamophobia (Warren, 2019), and Zine notes that 'Canadian Muslim youth are engaged as storytellers, spoken word artists, political cartoonists, hip hop artists, filmmakers, actors, visual artists, musicians, digital media producers, as well as participating in other forms of literary and cultural production' (Zine, 2022a: 189), much of this targeted at challenging and overcoming Islamophobia. Tarlo (2017) discusses how stereotyping of Muslims and the issue of Islamophobia can be challenged through clothing and fashion. She refers to the clothes marketed by Anas Sillwood of SHUKR, which blend some components traditionally associated with garments worn by Muslims in North Africa, Asia, and the Middle East with some of the major trends in Western fashion.

Conclusion

The different sources of Islamophobia explored in this book and the complex ways that it can arise in different contexts mean that there is not a simple answer about how to address it. Carr (2019) suggests awareness raising, work with the media and education, and the introduction of hate crime legislation as some of the approaches to combine in tackling Islamophobia. Just as there are many racisms (Bonnett, 2024), there are also many Islamophobias, and this complexity requires a sophisticated set of strategies, or attempts at addressing everyday Islamophobia are unlikely to be successful. Moreover, it is often best to be targeted in seeking to address specific forms of Islamophobia, as this is more likely to enable change.

An example of this, and in bringing this book to a conclusion, I am reminded of the powerful work undertaken in my home city of Newcastle upon Tyne. Members of Tyne and Wear Citizens were reporting sharp increases in Islamophobia following the Brexit vote in 2016 (for example, Burrell et al, 2019). This included verbal and physical abuse, which was typically happening in public places, on public transport, in medical centres, and in supermarkets. Despite Muslim women raising concerns about such incidents, these were largely being ignored or downplayed. Members of Tyne and Wear Citizens formed an action group focused on creating safer cities. Members of this group included representatives from local universities, religious groups, and civil society organizations, including several Muslim women. Over time, this action group listened to the powerful testimonies of Muslim women, and their greatest concern was that they were not going out or were using private vehicles when they did, instead of public transport. A collective decision was made by the action group to focus on public transport issues.

This was the time when the Punish a Muslim Day letters (see Chapter 8) were being sent out. A human chain around the mosque was organized by the action group, and those of all faiths and none enjoyed tea and cake in the mosque following this action. This was a very powerful demonstration of solidarity with the Muslim community, and it took place in the context of the police advising people to stay at home.

In seeking to address the issue of Islamophobia on public transport, the action group pressed transport providers to adopt a hate crime charter so that drivers and passengers would know what to do and what to expect should an incident arise. The charter remained unpublished for over a year. However, the action group planned to 'Reclaim the Metro' (the light-rail transit system that serves Tyne and Wear), and on 13 October 2018, along with over 200 people from diverse backgrounds, I attended the speeches at Grey's Monument in the city centre. Afterwards, we travelled together to Whitley Bay at the coast and shared fish and chips. T-shirts and hoodies, with the letters HIJAB spelling out 'Hi I'm Just Another Being', were worn. The threat of this day had forced the hands of the transport providers, and they published the hate crime charter just days before. The day was therefore one of celebration, as those involved in organizing it could witness what they had achieved, while also raising awareness and challenging stereotypes.

The positive outcomes here included the publication of the hate crime charter by local transport providers and the commitment to educate drivers on how to manage reporting of incidents. In addition, those attending the mosque had been trained on how to report incidents of Islamophobia. Crucially, the Muslim women involved in organizing the group were empowered by their actions leading to change and by the widespread support they received on social media. New relationships were developed across diverse communities as people learnt more about Islam and about the experiences of Muslim women.

More recently, on Wednesday 7 August 2024, more than 3,000 people gathered in the West End of Newcastle to stand in unity against the Islamophobic riots that had been happening across the country (see Chapter 6). Although many were very concerned about the prospect of further violence, the large turnout and demonstration of solidarity by many communities was considered by many to have minimized the likelihood of further outbreaks of violence in the city in the days that followed.

I do not share these two examples to show that Islamophobia has been addressed here. Far from it. The ongoing presence of diverse forms of everyday Islamophobia remains a deeply concerning factor in the lives of many people in Newcastle upon Tyne, UK, as it does in so many places across the globe. However, our hope for the future must be that, although we know that Islamophobia 'had a beginning, and it has beneficiaries', through collaboration, partnership, and collective working, the Islamophobia industrial complex, which – through the research explored and the many examples in this book – we have come to understand as the foundation on which everyday Islamophobia is built, can be 'ended, uprooted, and upturned' (Manzoor-Khan, 2022: 169).

References

Abbas, Tahir (2021) 'Reflection: the "war on terror", Islamophobia and radicalisation twenty years on', *Critical Studies on Terrorism*, 14(4): 402–404.

Afshar, Haleh (2013) 'The politics of fear: what does it mean to those who are otherized and feared?', *Ethnic and Racial Studies*, 36(1): 9–27.

Ahmed, Sara (2010) 'Foreword: secrets and silences in feminist research', in Roisin Ryan-Flood and Rosalind Gill (eds) *Secrecy and Silence in the Research Process: Feminist Reflections*, London: Routledge, pp xvi–xxi.

Akel, Sofia (2021) *Institutionalised: The Rise of Islamophobia in Higher Education*, London: London Metropolitan University, Centre for Equity and Inclusion.

Akhtar, Sabeena and Robert, Naima B. (2021) *Talking about Islamophobia: What is It and How Do We Challenge It? A Beginners' Guide for Children*, London: Wayland Books.

Al-Azami, Salman (2023a) 'Reclaiming the spiritual meaning of "Allahu Akbar" from media misrepresentation', in Salman Al-Azami (ed) *Media Language on Islam and Muslims: Terminologies and their Effects*, Cham: Palgrave Macmillan, pp 243–268.

Al-Azami, Usaama (2023b) 'The embedding of an Islamophobic trope in the media: radical versus moderate Muslims', in Salman Al-Azami (ed) *Media Language on Islam and Muslims: Terminologies and their Effects*, Cham: Palgrave Macmillan, pp 149–172.

Alexander, Claire (1998) 'Re-imagining the Muslim community', *Innovation*, 11(4): 439–450.

Alexander, Claire (2000) *The Asian Gang: Ethnicity, Identity, Masculinity*, Oxford: Berg.

Ali, Nadya (2023) *The Violence of Britishness: Racism, Borders and the Conditions of Citizenship*, London: Pluto.

Ali, Nadya and Witham, Ben (2018) 'The unbearable anxiety of being: ideological fantasies of British Muslims beyond the politics of security', *Security Dialogue*, 49(5): 400–417.

All Party Parliamentary Group on British Muslims (2018) *Islamophobia Defined*, London: Westminster.

Allen, Chris (2005) 'From race to religion: the new face of discrimination', in Tahir Abbas (ed) *Muslim Britain: Communities under Pressure*, Oxford: Zed Books, pp 49–65.

Allen, Chris (2010) *Islamophobia*, Aldershot: Ashgate.

Allen, Chris (2015) '"People hate you because of the way you dress": understanding the invisible experiences of veiled British Muslim women victims of Islamophobia', *International Review of Victimology*, 21(5): 287–301.

Allen, Chris (2020) *Reconfiguring Islamophobia: A Radical Rethinking of a Contested Concept*, Cham: Palgrave.

Allen, Chris (2024) 'From terrorist to paedophiles: investigating the experience and encounter of Islamophobia on Muslim men in contemporary Britain', in Amina Easat-Daas and Irene Zempi (eds) *The Palgrave Handbook of Gendered Islamophobia*, Cham: Palgrave Macmillan, pp 147–161.

Allen, Chris (2025) 'Everyday experiences of Islamophobia in university spaces: a qualitative study of the United Kingdom', *Education, Citizenship and Social Justice*, 20(1): 168–180. https://doi.org/10.1177/17461979231210996

Al-Sabawi, Maryam, Ilsam, Ayesha, Khorshed, Jenna, McLean, Lisa and Jisrawi, Athir (2024) '"It's how we are leaving a mark": youth coalition combatting Islamophobia and grief activism', in Carrie Traher, and Lauren J. Breen (eds) *The Routledge International Handbook of Child and Adolescent Grief in Contemporary Context*, London: Routledge, pp 309–320.

Andrews, Kehinde (2023) *The Psychosis of Whiteness: Surviving the Insanity of a Racist World*, London Allen Lane.

Ansari, Saima N. and Patel, Tina G. (2024) 'Islamophobia as intersectional phenomenon', in Amina Easat-Daas and Irene Zempi (eds) *The Palgrave Handbook of Gendered Islamophobia*, Cham: Palgrave Macmillan, pp 11–27.

Archer, Louise (2001) '"Muslim brothers, black lads, traditional Asians": British Muslim young men's constructions of race, religion and masculinity', *Feminism and Psychology*, 11(1): 79–105.

Awan, Imran (2014) 'Islamophobia and Twitter: a typology of online hate against Muslims on social media', *Policy and Internet*, 6(2): 133–150.

Awan, Imran and Zempi, Irene (2020a) *Islamophobic Hate Crime*, London: Routledge.

Awan, Imran and Zempi, Irene (2020b) '"You all look the same": non-Muslim men who suffer Islamophobic hate crime in the post-Brexit era', *European Journal of Criminology*, 17(5): 585–602.

Aziz, Sahar F. and Esposito, John L. (2024) 'Introduction', in Sahar F. Aziz and John L. Esposito (eds) *Global Islamophobia and the Rise of Populism*, New York: Oxford University Press, pp 1–20.

Bagguley, Paul and Hussain, Yasmin (2005) 'Flying the flag for England? Citizenship, religion and cultural identity among British Pakistani Muslims', in Tahir Abbas (ed) *Muslim Britain: Communities under Pressure*, Oxford: Zed Books, pp 208–221.

Bakali, Naved and Hafez, Farid (2022) 'Introduction: understanding Islamophobia across the global North and South in the context of the war on terror', in Naved Bakali and Farid Hafez (eds) *The Rise of Global Islamophobia in the War on Terror: Coloniality, Race, and Islam*, Manchester: Manchester University Press, pp 1–16.

Bangstad, Sindre (2013) 'Eurabia comes to Norway', *Islam and Christian-Muslim Relations*, 24(3): 369–391.

Bangstad, Sindre (2014) *Anders Breivik and the Rise of Islamophobia*, London: Zed Books.

Bangstad, Sindre and Linge, Marius (2024) 'Qur'an burning in Norway: stop the Islamisation of Norway (SIAN) and far-right capture of free speech in a Scandinavian context', *Ethnic and Racial Studies*, 47(5): 941–962.

Bayrakli, Enes and Hafez, Farid (eds) (2023) *European Islamophobia Report 2022*, Austria: Leopold Weiss Institute.

Bayrakli, Enes and Hafez, Farid (eds) (2024) *European Islamophobia Report 2023*, Austria: Leopold Weiss Institute.

Bazian, Hatem (2018) 'Islamophobia, "clash of civilizations", and forging a post-Cold War order!', *Religions*, 9(9): Article 282. Available from: https://doi.org/10.3390/rel9090282

Bechrouri, Ibrahim (2023) '"L'espirit n de defense"': separatism, counterinsurgency and the dissolution of the Collective Against Islamophobia in France', *Modern and Contemporary France*, 31(2): 199–218.

Benwell, Matthew C., Hopkins, Peter and Finlay, Robin (2023) 'The slow violence of austerity politics and the UK's "hostile environment": examining the responses of third sector organisations supporting people seeking asylum', *Geoforum*, 145: Article 103845.

Beydoun, Khaled (2017) 'On Islamophobia, immigration, and the "Muslims bans"', *Ohio Northern University Law Review*, 43: 443–458.

Beydoun, Khaled A. (2018) *American Islamophobia: Understanding the Roots and Rise of Fear*, Oakland: University of California Press.

Beydoun, Khaled A. (2023) *The New Crusades: Islamophobia and the Global War on Muslims*, Oakland: University of California Press.

Birt, Jonathan (2009) 'Islamophobia in the construction of British Muslim identity politics', in Peter Hopkins and Richard Gale (eds) *Muslims in Britain: Race, Place and Identities*, Edinburgh: Edinburgh University Press, pp 210–227.

Blackwood, Leda (2019) 'Flying while Muslim: should we be concerned about Islamophobia at the airport?', in Irene Zempi and Imran Awan (eds) *The Routledge Handbook of Islamophobia*, London: Routledge, pp 340–351.

Blackwood, Leda, Hopkins, Nick and Reicher, Stephen (2013) 'I know who I am, but who do they think I am? Muslim perspectives on encounters with airport authorities', *Ethnic and Racial Studies*, 36(6): 1090–1108.

Blackwood, Leda, Hopkins, Nick and Reicher, Stephen D. (2015) '"Flying while Muslim": citizenship and misrecognition in the airport', *Journal of Social and Political Psychology*, 3(2): 148–170.

Blakeley, Ruth, Hayes, Ben, Kapoor, Nisha, Kundnani, Arun, Massoumi, Narzanin, Miller, David, et al (2019) *Leaving the War on Terror: A Progressive Alternative to Counter-Terrorism Policy*, Amsterdam: Transnational Institute.

Bokhari, Saarah (2023) '"The myth of Jihad": examining the multivalent nature of the term', in Sakman Al-Azami (ed) *Media Language on Islam and Muslims: Terminologies and their Effects*, Cham: Palgrave Macmillan, pp 195–224.

Bonnett, Alastair (2024) *Multiracism: Rethinking Racism in Global Context*, Cambridge: Polity Press.

Botterill, Katherine, Hopkins, Peter and Sanghera, Gurchathen (2019) 'Young people's everyday securities: pre-emptive and pro-active strategies towards ontological security in Scotland', *Social and Cultural Geography*, 20(4): 465–484.

Bowlby, Sophie, and Lloyd Evans, Sally (2009) 'You seem very Westernised to me': place, identity and the othering Muslim workers in the UK labour market', in Peter Hopkins and Richard Gale (eds) *Muslims in Britain: Race, Place and Identities*, Edinburgh: Edinburgh University Press, pp 37–54.

Bowlby, Sophie, Lloyd Evans, Sally and Mohammed, Robina (1998) 'Becoming a paid worker: images and identity', in Tracey Skelton and Gill Valentine (eds) *Cool Places: Geographies of Youth Culture*, London: Routledge, pp 229–248.

Bowler, Rick and Razak, Amina (2022) 'Speaking back and seeing beyond the landscapes of hate', in Edward Hall, John Clayton and Catherine Donovan (eds) *Landscapes of Hate: Tracing Spaces, Relations, and Responses*, Bristol: Bristol University Press, pp 196–216.

Brice, Kevin M.A. (2009) 'Residential integration: evidence from the UK census', in Richard Phillips (ed) *Muslim Spaces of Hope: Geographies of Possibility in Britain and the West*, Oxford: Zed Books, pp 222–235.

Bridge Initiative (2024) *Factsheet: Operation Luxor*. Available from: https://bridge.georgetown.edu/research/factsheet-operation-luxor/

Brown, Katy and Mondon, Aurelien (2024) 'The role of media in the mainstreaming of far- and extreme-right politics', in Community Policy Forum (ed) *From Hate Speech to Politically Motivated Violence: Far-Right Islamophobia in the UK*, London: Community Policy Forum, pp 83–98.

Burrell, Kathy, Hopkins, Peter, Isakjee, Arshad, Lorne, Colin, Nagel, Caroline, Finlay, Robin, et al (2019) 'Brexit, race and migration', *Environment and Planning C: Politics and Space*, 37(1): 3–40.

Butler, Judith (2016) *Frames of War: Where is Life Grievable?* London: Verso.

Cada, Karel and Frantova, Veronika (2019) 'Countering Islamophobia in the Czech Republic', in Ian Law, Amina Easat-Daas, Arzu Merali and Salman Sayyid (eds) *Countering Islamophobia in Europe*, Cham: Palgrave Macmillan, pp 153–181.

Caksu, Ali (2020) 'Islamophobia, Chinese style: total internment of Uyghur Muslims by the People's Republic of China', *Islamophobia Studies Journal*, 5(2): 175–198.

Campbell, Elaine (2013) Transgression, affect and performance: choreographing a politics of urban space', *British Journal of Criminology*, 53: 18–40.

Carland, Susan (2011) 'Islamophobia, fear of loss of freedom, and the Muslim women', *Islam and Christian-Muslim Relations*, 22(4): 469–473.

Carland, Susan (2023a) '"We're Islam in their eyes": using an interpellation framework to understand why being a woman matters when countering Islamophobia', *Religions*, 14(5): Article 654.

Carland, Susan (2023b) *A War of Words: Preliminary Media Analysis of the 2023 Israel-Gaza War*, Melbourne: Islamophobia Register.

Carr, James (2011) 'Regulating Islamophobia: the need for collecting disaggregated data on racism in Ireland', *Journal of Muslim Minority Affairs*, 31(3): 574–593.

Carr, James (2016) *Experiences of Islamophobia: Living with Racism in the Neoliberal Era*, London: Routledge.

Carr, James (2019) 'Islamophobia in Ireland: challenges from below?', in Irene Zempi and Imran Awan (eds) *The Routledge Handbook of Islamophobia*, London: Routledge, pp 135–146.

Carr, James and Haynes, Amanda (2015) 'A clash of racializations: the policing of "race" and of anti-Muslim racism in Ireland', *Critical Sociology*, 41(1): 21–40.

Center for Countering Digital Hate (2022) *Failure to Protect: Social Media Platforms are Failing to Act on Anti-Muslim Hate*, Washington, DC: CCDH.

Center for Countering Digital Hate (2024) *Social Media's Role in the UK Riots: Policy Responses and Solutions*, Washington, DC: CCDH.

Center for Uyghur Studies (2023) *Islamophobia in China and Attitudes of Muslim Countries*, Washington, DC: Center for Uyghur Studies.

Center for Uyghur Studies (2024) *The Plight of the Uyghurs 2014–2024*, Washington, DC: Center for Uyghur Studies.

Cesari, Jocelyn (2019) 'Civilization as disciplinization and the consequences for religion and world politics', *The Review of Faith and International Affairs*, 17(1): 24–33.

Chakraborti, Neil and Zempi, Irene (2012) 'The veil under attack: gendered dimensions of Islamophobic victimization', *International Review of Victimology*, 18(3): 269–284.

Chan, Wun Fang (2010) 'A shared or multicultural future? Community cohesion and the (im)possibilities of hospitable social capital', *Space and Polity*, 14(1): 33–46.

Chaudry, Izram (2021) '"I felt like I was being watched": the hypervisibility of Muslim students in higher education', *Educational Philosophy and Theory*, 53(3): 257–269.

Cheng, Jennifer (2015) 'Islamophobia, Muslimophobia or racism? Parliamentary discourses on Islam and Muslims in debates on the minaret ban in Switzerland', *Discourse and Society*, 26(5): 562–586.

Cho, Sumi, Crenshaw, Kimberle and McCall, Leslie (2013) 'Toward a field of intersectionality studies: theory, applications, and praxis', *Signs: Journal of Women in Culture and Society*, 38(4): 785–810.

Clayton, John, Donovan, Catherine and Macdonald, Stephen J. (2022) 'Becoming visible, becoming vulnerable? Bodies, material spaces and affective economies of hate', in Edward Hall, John Clayton and Catherine Donovan (eds) *Landscapes of Hate: Tracing Spaces, Relations, and Responses*, Bristol: Bristol University Press, pp 98–117.

Cohen, Stanley (1972) *Folk Devils and Moral Panics: The Creation of the Mods and Rockers*, London: Granada.

Collins, Patricia Hill (2000) *Black Feminist Thought*, London: Routledge.

Collins, Patricia Hill and Bilge, Sirma (2016) *Intersectionality*, Cambridge: Polity Press.

Combahee River Collective (1983) 'The Combahee River Collective statement', in B. Smith (ed) *Home Girls: A Black Feminist Anthology*, New York: Kitchen Table Press, pp 272–282.

Community Policy Forum (2024) *From Hate Speech to Political Motivated Violence: Far-Right Islamophobia in the UK*, London: Community Policy Forum.

Considine, Craig (2017) 'The racialization of Islam in the United States: Islamophobia, hate crimes, and "flying whilst brown"', *Religions*, 8(9): 1–19.

Crenshaw, Kimberle (1989) 'Demarginalizing the intersection of race and sex: a black feminist critique of antidiscrimination doctrine, feminist theory and antiracist politics', *University of Chicago Legal Forum*, 140: 139–167.

Crenshaw, Kimberle (1991) 'Mapping the margins: intersectionality, identity politics, and violence against women of color', *Stanford Law Review*, 43: 1241–1299.

Davis, Angela and Shaylor, Cassandra (2001) 'Race, gender, and the prison industrial complex: California and beyond', *Meridians*, 2(1): 1–25.

Davis, Mark (2024) 'Violence as method: the "white replacement", "white genocide", and "Eurabia" conspiracy theories and the biopolitics of networked violence', *Ethnic and Racial Studies*, 48(3): 426–446. https://doi.org/10.1080/01419870.2024.2304640

De Koning, Martijn (2016) '"You need to present a counter-message": the racialisation of Dutch Muslims and anti-Islamophobia initiatives', *Journal of Muslims in Europe*, 5: 170–189.

Dobbernack, Jan (2022) 'Civic inclusion for permanent minorities: thinking through the politics of "ghetto" and "separatism" laws', *Ethnic and Racial Studies*, 45(16): 568–590.

Døving, Cora Alexa (2024) 'Islamophobia in Norway: national report 2023', in Enes Bayrakli and Farid Hafez (eds), *European Islamophobia Report 2023*, Vienna: Leopold Weiss Institute, pp 485–497.

Dunn, Kevin (2001) 'Representations of Islam in the politics of mosque development in Sydney', *Tijdschrift Voor Economische en Sociale Geografe*, 92(3): 291–308.

Dunn, Kevin (2005) 'Repetitive and troubling discourses of nationalism in the local politics of mosque development in Sydney, Australia', *Environment and Planning D: Society and Space*, 23(1): 29–50.

Dunn, Kevin and Kamp, Alanna (2009) 'The hopeful and exclusionary politics of Islam in Australia: looking for alternative geographies of "Western Islam"', in Richard Phillips (ed) *Muslim Spaces of Hope: Geographies of Possibility in Britain and the West*, Oxford: Zed Books, pp 41–66.

Dunn, Kevin and Hopkins, Peter (2016) 'The geographies of everyday Muslim life in the West', *Australian Geographer*, 47(3): 255–260.

Dunn, Kevin, Klocker, Natasha and Salabay, Tanya (2007) 'Contemporary racism and Islamaphobia in Australia: racializing religion', *Ethnicities*, 7(4): 564–589.

Dwyer, Claire (1998) 'Challenging dominant representations of Muslim women', in Tracey Skelton and Gill Valentine (eds) *Cool Places: Geographies of Youth Culture*, London: Routledge, pp 50–65.

Dwyer, Claire (1999) 'Veiled meanings: young British Muslim women and the negotiation of differences', *Gender, Place and Culture*, 6(1): 5–26.

Dwyer, Claire, Shah, Bindi and Sanghera, Gurchathen (2008) '"From cricket lover to terror suspect": challenging representations of young British Muslim men', *Gender, Place and Culture*, 15(2): 117–136.

Easat-Daas, Amina (2019) 'The gendered dimension of Islamophobia in Belgium', in Irene Zempi and Imran Awan (eds) *The Routledge Handbook of Islamophobia*, London: Routledge, pp 123–134.

Easat-Daas, Amina (2021) 'Misogyny, hate crimes and gendered Islamophobia: Muslim women's experiences and responses', in Irene Zempi and Jo Smith (eds) *Misogyny as Hate Crime*, London: Routledge, pp 140–154.

Easat-Daas, Amina and Zempi, Irene (2024) 'Introduction', in Amina Easat-Daas and Irene Zempi (eds) *The Palgrave Handbook of Gendered Islamophobia*, Cham: Palgrave Macmillan, pp 1–10.

Ehrkamp, Patricia (2007) 'Beyond the mosque: Turkish immigrants and the practice and politics of Islam in Duisburg-Marxloh, Germany', in Cara Aitchison, Peter Hopkins and Mei-Po Kwan (eds) *Geographies of Muslim Identities: Diaspora, Gender and Belonging*, Aldershot: Ashgate, pp 11–28.

Ehrkamp, Patricia (2010) 'The limits of multicultural tolerance? Liberal democracy and media portrayals of Muslim migrant women in Germany', *Space and Polity*, 14(1): 13–32.

Ehrkamp, Patricia (2017) 'Geographies of migration II: the racial-spatial politics of immigration', *Progress in Human Geography*, 43(2): 363–375.

Ekman, Mattias (2015) 'Online Islamophobia and the politics of fear: manufacturing the green scare', *Ethnic and Racial Studies*, 38(11): 1986–2002.

Elahi, Farah and Khan, Omar (2017) (eds) *Islamophobia: Still a Challenge for Us All*, London: Runnymede Trust.

el-Aswad, al-Sayed (2021) *Countering Islamophobia in North America: A Quality-of-Life Approach*, Cham: Springer.

Elfenbein, Caleb Iyer (2021) *Fear in our Hearts: What Islamophobia Tells us about America*, New York: New York University Press.

El Sayed, Fatima (2023) 'Confronting anti-Muslim racism and Islamism: an intersectional perspective on Muslim women's activism in Germany', *Journal of Women, Politics & Policy*, 44(4): 486–507.

Elsheikh, Elsadig and Sisemore, Basima (2021) *Islamophobia through the Eyes of Muslims: Assessing Perceptions, Experiences, and Impacts*, Report, Berkeley: Othering and Belonging Institute.

Esposito, John L. and Kalin, Ibrahim (eds) (2011) *Islamophobia: The Challenge of Pluralism in the 21st Century*, Oxford: Oxford University Press.

Essed, Philomena (2002) 'Everyday racism', in David Theo Goldberg and John Solomos (eds) *A Companion to Racial and Ethnic Studies*, Oxford: Blackwell, pp 202–216.

European Commission against Racism and Intolerance (2022) *ECRI General Policy Recommendation No. 5 (revised) on Preventing and Combatting Anti-Muslim Racism and Discrimination*, Strasbourg: Council of Europe.

European Union Agency for Fundamental Rights (2024) *Being Muslim in the UK: Experiences of Muslims*, Luxembourg: Publications Office of the European Union.

Farmer, John and Majlesi, Ava (2024) 'Muslim life in Belgium: in search of a *vivre ensemble*', in Sahar F. Aziz and John L. Esposito (eds) *Global Islamophobia and the Rise of Populism*, New York: Oxford University Press, pp 169–180.

Finlay, Robin and Hopkins, Peter (2019) 'Young Muslim women's political participation in Scotland: exploring the intersections of gender, religion, class and place', *Political Geography*, 74: Article 102046.

Finlay, Robin and Hopkins, Peter (2020) 'Resistance and marginalisation: Islamophobia and the political participation of young Muslims in Scotland', *Social and Cultural Geography*, 21(4): 546–568.

Finlay, Robin and Hopkins, Peter (2024) 'Spatialising Islamophobia: responding to and resisting anti-Muslim racism in Scotland', in Amina Easat-Daas and Irene Zempi (eds) *The Palgrave Handbook of Gendered Islamophobia*, Cham: Palgrave Macmillan, pp 239–254.

Finney, Nissa and Simpson, Ludi (2009) *'Sleepwalking to Segregation'? Challenging Myths about Race and Migration*, Bristol: Policy Press.

Fraser, Nancy (2000) 'Rethinking recognition', *New Left Review*, 3 (May–June): 107–120.

Fritzsche, Lauren and Nelson, Lise (2020) 'Refugee resettlement, place, and the politics of Islamophobia', *Social and Cultural Geography*, 21(4): 508–526.

Gale, Richard (2004) 'The multicultural city and the politics of religious architecture: urban planning, mosques and meaning-making in Birmingham, UK', *Built Environment*, 30(1): 30–44.

Gale, Richard (2005) 'Representing the city: mosques and the planning process in Birmingham', *Journal of Ethnic and Migration Studies*, 31(6): 1161–1179.

Gale, Richard and Naylor, Simon (2002) 'Religion, planning and the city: the spatial politics of ethnic minority expression in British cities and towns', *Ethnicities*, 2(3): 387–409.

Ganesh, Bharath, Frydenlund, Iselin and Brekke, Torkel (2024) 'Flows and modalities of global Islamophobia', *Ethnic and Racial Studies*, 47(5): 895–906.

Gardell, Mattias (2015) 'What's love got to do with it? Ultranationalism, Islamophobia, and hate crime in Sweden', *Journal of Religion and Violence*, 3(1): 91–116.

Geronimus, Arline T. (2023) *Weathering: The Extraordinary Stress of Ordinary Life on the Body in an Unjust Society*, London: Virago Press.

Gilliat-Ray, Sophie (2010) *Muslims in Britain: An Introduction*, Cambridge: Cambridge University Press.

Gilmore, Ruth Wilson (2022) *Abolition Geography: Essays towards Liberation*, London: Verso.

Gökariksel, Banu (2017) 'The body politics and Trump's "Muslim ban"', *Journal of Middle East Women's Studies*, 13(3): 469–471.

Gökariksel, Banu and Smith, Sara (2017) 'Intersectional feminism beyond US flag hijab and pussy hats in Trump's America', *Gender, Place and Culture*, 24(5): 628–644.

Goldmann, Fabian (2024) 'Islamophobia in Germany: national report 2023', in Enes Bayrakli and Farid Hafez (eds) *European Islamophobia Report 2023*, Vienna: Leopold Weiss Institute, pp 317–351.

Gorman, Cynthia S. and Culcasi, Karen (2021) 'Invasion and colonization: Islamophobia and anti-refugee sentiment in West Virginia', *Environment and Planning C: Politics and Space*, 39(1): 168–183.

Gottschalk, Peter with Greenberg, Gabriel (2019) *Islamophobia and Anti-Muslim Sentiment: Picturing the Enemy*, London: Rowman & Littlefield.

Green, Todd H. (2015) *The Fear of Islam: An Introduction to Islamophobia in the West*, Minneapolis: Fortress Press.

Griffin, Tom, Miller, David and Mills, Tom (2017) 'The neoconservative movement: think tanks as elite elements of social movements from above', in Narzanin Massoumi, Tom Mills and David Miller (eds) *What is Islamophobia? Racism, Social Movements and the State*, London: Pluto Press, pp 215–233.

Griffin, Tom, Aked, Hilary, Miller, David and Marusek, Sarah (2015) *The Henry Jackson Society and the Degeneration of British Neoconservatism: Liberal Interventionism, Islamophobia and the 'War on Terror'*, London: Spinwatch Public Interest Investigations.

Hafez, Farid (2020) 'Unwanted identities: the "religion" line and global Islamophobia', *Development*, 63: 9–19.

Hafez, Farid (2023a) 'Criminalizing Muslim agency in Europe: the case of "political Islam" in Austria, Germany, and France', *French Cultural Studies*, 34(3): 313–328.

Hafez, Farid (2023b) 'Criminalising critical scholarship: Austria's intelligence service and Islamophobia studies', in Simone Pfeifer, Christoph Gunther and Robert Dorre (eds) *Disentangling Jihad, Political Violence and Media*, Edinburgh: Edinburgh University Press, pp 99–118.

Hafez, Farid (2024a) 'Postcolonialism, post-national socialism, German reunification, and the rise of the far right: making sense of Islamophobia in Germany', in Sahar F. Aziz and John L. Esposito (eds) *Global Islamophobia and the Rise of Populism*, New York: Oxford University Press, pp 75–93.

Hafez, Farid (2024b) 'Islamophobia in Austria: national report 2023', in Enes Bayrakli and Farid Hafez (eds) *European Islamophobia Report 2023*, Vienna: Leopold Weiss Institute, pp 89–122.

Hajjat, Abdellali (2021) 'Islamophobia and French academia', *Current Sociology*, 69(5): 621–640.

Hajjat, Abdellali and Mohammed, Marwan (2023) *Islamophobia in France: The Construction of the 'Muslim Problem'*, Athens, GA: University of Georgia Press.

Halliday, Josh, Beckett, Lois, Barr, Caelainn and Garcia, Carmen Aguilar (2018) 'Revealed: the hidden global network behind Tommy Robinson', *The Guardian*, [online] 7 December. Available from: https://www.theguardian.com/uk-news/2018/dec/07/tommy-robinson-global-support-brexit-march

Hamid, Sadek and Jones, Stephen (2023) 'Introduction', in Sadek Hamid and Stephen Jones (eds) *Contemporary British Muslim Arts and Cultural Production: Identity, Belonging and Social Change*, London: Routledge, pp 1–20.

Hancock, Claire (2015) '"The Republic is lived with an uncovered face" (and a skirt): (un)dressing French citizens', *Gender, Place and Culture*, 22(7): 1023–1040.

Hancock, Claire (2020) 'Accommodating Islamophobia: how municipalities make place for Muslims in Paris', *Social and Cultural Geography*, 21(4): 527–545.

Hancock, Claire and Mobillion, Virginie (2019) '"I want to tell them, I'm just wearing a veil, not carrying a gun!" Muslim women negotiating borders in femonationalist Paris', *Political Geography*, 69: 1–9.

Hassan, Oz (2017) 'Trump, Islamophobia and US-Middle East relations', *Critical Studies on Security*, 5(2): 187–191.

Hilal, Mahu (2021) *Innocent until Proven Muslim: Islamophobia, the War on Terror, and the Muslim Experience since 9/11*, Minneapolis: Broadleaf Books.

Hopkins, Peter (2004) 'Young Muslim men in Scotland: inclusions and exclusions', *Children's Geographies*, 2(2): 257–272.

Hopkins, Peter (2007) 'Young Muslim men's experiences of local landscapes after September 11 2001', in Cara Aitchison, Peter Hopkins and Mei-Po Kwan (eds) *Geographies of Muslim Identities: Diaspora, Gender and Belonging*, Aldershot: Ashgate, pp 189–200.

Hopkins, Peter (2009) 'Women, men, positionalities and emotion: doing feminist geographies of religion', *ACME: an International Journal for Critical Geographers*, 8(1): 1–17.

Hopkins, Peter (2011) 'Towards critical geographies of the university campus: understanding the contested experiences of Muslim students', *Transactions of the Institute of British Geographers*, 36(1): 157–169.

Hopkins, Peter (2016) 'Gendering Islamophobia, racism and white supremacy: gendered violence against those who look Muslim', *Dialogues in Human Geography*, 8(2): 186–189.

Hopkins, Peter (2019) 'Social geography I: intersectionality', *Progress in Human Geography*, 43(5): 937–947.

Hopkins, Peter (2021) *Scotland's Islamophobia: Report of the Inquiry into Islamophobia in Scotland by the Cross Party Group on Tackling Islamophobia*, Newcastle upon Tyne: Newcastle University.

Hopkins, Peter (2022) 'Afterword: spatializing hate – relational, intersectional and emotional approaches', in Edward Hall, John Clayton and Catherine Donovan (eds) *Landscapes of Hate: Tracing Spaces, Relations, and Responses*, Bristol: Bristol University Press, pp 238–246.

Hopkins, Peter (2024) 'Intersectionality, intergenerational relations, and relationality: revisiting youthful Muslim masculinities', in Lily Kong, Orlando Woods and Justin Tse (eds) *Handbook of Geographies of Religion*, Dordrecht: Springer, pp 533–540.

Hopkins, Peter and Smith, Susan J. (2008) 'Scaling segregation: racialising fear', in Rachel Pain and Susan J. Smith (eds) *Fear: Critical Geopolitics and Everyday Life*, Aldershot: Ashgate, pp 103–116.

Hopkins, Peter, Clayton, John and TellMAMA (2020) *Islamophobia and Anti-Muslim Hatred in North East England*, Newcastle upon Tyne: Newcastle University.

Hopkins, Peter, Botterill, Katherine, Sanghera, Gurchathen and Arshad, Rowena (2017) 'Encountering misrecognition: being mistaken for being Muslim', *Annals of the American Association of Geographers*, 107(4): 934–948.

Hörschelmann, Kathrin (2007) 'Youth and the geopolitics of risk after 11 September 2001', in Rachel Pain and Susan J. Smith (eds) *Fear: Critical Geopolitics and Everyday Life*, Aldershot: Ashgate, pp 139–156.

Hussain, Yasmin and Bagguley, Paul (2012) 'Securitized citizens: Islamophobia, racism and the 7/7 London bombings', *The Sociological Review*, 60(4): 715–734.

Hussein, Shakira, Bloul, Scheherazade and Poynting, Scott (2019) 'Diasporas and dystopias on the beach: burkini wars in France and Australia', in Irene Zempi and Imran Awan (eds) *The Routledge Handbook of Islamophobia*, London: Routledge, pp 263–274.

Hyokki, Linda (2022) 'Whiteness and anti-Muslim racism in Finland: the racialisation of Finnish Muslims', *Context: Časopis za interdisciplinarne studije*, 9(1): 61–86.

Hyokki, Linda and Cubelic, Danijel (2023) *Local Actions against Anti-Muslim Racism: Policy Recommendations for City Administrations and their Partners*, Heidelberg: European Coalition of Cities Against Racism.

Iftikhar, Arsalan (2016) *Scapegoats: How Islamophobia Helps our Enemies and Threatens our Freedoms*, Delaware: Holt Books.

Iftikhar, Arsalan (2021) *Fear of a Muslim Planet: Global Islamophobia and the New World Order*, New York: Skyhorse Publishing.

Iner, Derya, Mason, Gill and Asquith, Nicole L. (2022) 'Expected but not accepted: victimisation, gender, and Islamophobia in Australia', *International Review of Victimology*, 28(3): 286–304.

Itaoui, Rhonda (2016) 'The geography of Islamophobia in Sydney: mapping the spatial imaginaries of young Muslims', *Australian Geographer*, 47(3): 261–279.

Itaoui, Rhonda (2020) 'Mapping perceptions of Islamophobia in the San Francisco Bay Area, California', *Social and Cultural Geography*, 21(4): 479–506.

Itaoui, Rhonda and Dunn, Kevin (2017) 'Media representations of racism and spatial mobility: young Muslim (un)belonging in a post-Cronulla riot Sutherland', *Journal of Intercultural Studies*, 38(3): 315–332.

Itaoui, Rhonda and Elsheikh, Elsadig (2018) *Islamophobia in the United States: A Reading Resource Pack*, Berkeley: Hass Institute.

Itaoui, Rhonda, Dufty-Jones, Rae and Dunn, Kevin (2021) 'Anti-racism Muslim mobilities in the San Francisco Bay area', *Mobilities*, 16(6): 888–904.

Jangbar, Sakina (2022) 'The clock boy: an analysis of how news outlets used sources to conceal bias in new coverage of Ahmed Mohamed, a Muslim teen arrested for bringing a self-made clock to school', *Journal of Intercultural Communication Research*, 51(6): 581–594.

Jiwani, Yasmin (2022) 'Resisting Islamophobia through digital artifacts of mourning', *Islamophobia Studies Journal*, 7(2): 250–272.

Johnson, Boris (2018) 'The lovely Danes have got it wrong – a burka ban is not the answer; certain clothing may be oppressive and ridiculous, but Denmark (and others) are being too heavy-handed', *Daily Telegraph*, 5 August, p 4.

Jones, Rhys Dafydd (2014) 'University challenges: negotiating secularism and religiosity in higher education institutions', *Environment and Planning A: Economy and Space*, 46(8): 1983–1999.

Jones, Rhys Dafydd, Robinson, James and Turner, Jennifer (2012) 'Introduction – between absence and presence: geographies of hiding, invisibility and silence', *Space and Polity*, 16(3): 257–263.

Jones, Stephen H. (2022) *Islam and the Liberal State: National Identity and the Future of Muslim Britain*, London: IB Tauris.

Jones, Stephen H. and Unsworth, Amy (2024) 'Two Islamophobias? Racism and religion as distinct but mutually supportive dimensions of anti-Muslim prejudice', *British Journal of Sociology*, 75(1): 5–22.

Joseph-Salisbury, Remi and Connelly, Laura (2021) *Anti-Racist Scholar-Activism*, Manchester: Manchester University Press.

Kabir, Nahid Afrose (2023) *American Muslim Perspectives on Radicalization*, Cham: Palgrave Macmillan.

Kalmar, Ivan (2024) 'Islamophobia without Muslims? Not only in Eastern Europe', in Sahar F. Aziz and John L. Esposito (eds) *Global Islamophobia and the Rise of Populism*, New York: Oxford University Press, pp 132–150.

Kara, Seyfeddin (2012) 'Muslim youth at university: a critical examination of the British higher education experience', in Mohammad Siddique Seddon and Fauzia Ahmad (eds) *Muslim Youth: Challenges, Opportunities and Expectations*, London: Continuum, pp 144–162.

Karaman, Nancy and Christian, Michelle (2020) '"My hijab is like my skin color": Muslim women students, racialization, and intersectionality', *Sociology of Race and Ethnicity*, 6(4): 517–532.

Karcic, Hikmet (2023) 'Islamophobia in Bosnia and Herzegovina national report 2022', in Enes Bayrakli and Farid Hafez (eds) *European Islamophobia Report 2022*, Vienna: Leopold Weiss Institute, pp 149–169.

Karcic, Hikmet (2024) 'Islamophobia in Bosnia and Herzegovina national report 2023', in Enes Bayrakli and Farid Hafez (eds), *European Islamophobia Report 2023*, Vienna: Leopold Weiss Institute, pp 149–170.

Kassaye, Aida and van Heelsum, Anja (2020) 'Muslim organisations' response to stigmatisation in the media', *Journal of Muslims in Europe*, 9: 96–118.

Katz, Cindi (2007) 'Banal terrorism: spatial fetishism and everyday insecurity', in Derek Gregory and Allan Pred (eds) *Violent Geographies: Fear, Terror, and Political Violence*, London: Routledge, pp 349–361.

Khamis, Sahar (2023) 'Effective countering Islamophobia strategies in the digital age: three approaches', *Islamophobia Studies Journal*, 8(1): 25–41.

Khan, Kamran (2023) 'The perceptions of sharia: beyond words and intentions', in Salman Al-Azami (ed) *Media Language on Islam and Muslims: Terminologies and their Effects*, Cham: Palgrave Macmillan, pp 225–241.

Khandoker, Nasrin, Kuric, Dermana and Carr, James (2024) 'Rethinking gendered anti-Muslim racism in a relational matrix of race and gender', *Women's Studies International Forum*, 107: Article 102983.

Kirndörfer, Elisabeth (2024) 'Challenging the boundaries of exclusive Europeanisation: how young refugees unsettle normative spaces of urban citizenship', *European Journal of Regional Studies*, 31(1): 46–64.

Kiwan, Nadia (2023) 'Decolonial approaches to laïcité as a mode to re-think contemporary Islamophobia', *Modern and Contemporary France*, 31(2): 147–164.

Kiwan, Nadia and Wolfreys, Jim (2023) 'Confronting the politics of denial', *Modern and Contemporary France*, 31(2): 139–146.

Koch, Natalie and Vora, Neha (2020) 'Islamophobia and the uneven legal geographies of ethnonationalism', *Political Geography*, 83: Article 102187.

Koefoed, Lasse and Simonsen, Kirsten (2011) '"The stranger", the city and the nation: on the possibilities of identification and belonging', *European Urban and Regional Studies*, 18(4): 343–357.

Kozaric, Edin (2024) 'Are Muslim experiences taken seriously in theories of Islamophobia? A literature review of Muslim experiences with social exclusion in the West', *Ethnic and Racial Studies*, 47(5): 907–940.

Kumar, Deepa (2010) 'Framing Islam: the resurgence of Orientalism during the Bush II era', *Journal of Communication Inquiry*, 34(3): 254–277.

Kumar, Deepa (2017) 'Islamophobia and empire: an intermestic approach to the study of anti-Muslim racism', in Narzanin Massoumi, Tom Mills and David Miller (eds) *What is Islamophobia? Racism, Social Movements and the State*, London: Pluto Press, pp 49–73.

Kumar, Deepa (2018) 'See something, say something: security rituals, affect, and US nationalism from the Cold War to the War on Terror', *Public Culture*, 30(1): 143–171.

Kumar, Deepa (2020) 'Terrorcraft: empire and the making of the racialised terrorist threat', *Race and Class*, 62(2): 34–60.

Kumar, Deepa (2021) *Islamophobia and the Politics of Empire: Twenty Years after 9/11*, London: Verso.

Kundnani, Arun (2007) *The End of Tolerance: Racism in 21st Century Britain*, London: Pluto.

Kundnani, Arun (2015) *The Muslims are Coming! Islamophobia, Extremism and the Domestic War on Terror*, London: Verso.

Kundnani, Arun (2017) 'Islamophobia as ideology of US empire', in Narzanin Massoumi, Tom Mills and David Miller (eds) *What is Islamophobia? Racism, Social Movements and the State*, London: Pluto Press, pp 35–48.

Kundnani, Arun (2023) *What is Anti-Racism? And Why it Means Anti Capitalism*, London: Verso.

Kwan, Mei-Po (2008) 'From oral histories to visual narratives: re-presenting the post-September 11 experiences of the Muslim women in the USA', *Social and Cultural Geography*, 9(6): 653–669.

Kyriakidou, Maria (2021) 'Hierarchies of deservingness and the limits of hospitality in the "refugee crisis"', *Media, Culture and Society*, 43(1): 133–149.

Lajevardi, Nazita (2020) *Outsiders at Home: The Politics of American Islamophobia*, Cambridge: Cambridge University Press.

Larsson, Goran (2012) 'The fear of small numbers: Eurabia literature and the consensus on religious belonging', *Journal of Muslims in Europe*, 1: 142–165.

Law, Ian, Easat-Daas, Amina and Sayyid, Salman (2018) *Counter-Islamophobia Kit: Briefing Paper and Toolkit to Counter-Narratives to Islamophobia*, Leeds: Centre for Ethnicity and Racism Studies.

Law, Ian, Easat-Daas, Amina, Merali, Arzu and Sayyid, Salman (eds) (2019) *Countering Islamophobia in Europe*, Cham: Palgrave Macmillan.

Lean, Nathan (2012) *The Islamophobia Industry: How the Right Manufactures Hatred of Muslims*, London: Pluto.

Lean, Nathan (2017) 'Mainstreaming anti-Muslim prejudice: the rise of the Islamophobia industry in American electoral politics', in Narzanin Massoumi, Tom Mills and David Miller (eds) *What is Islamophobia? Racism, Social Movements and the State*, London: Pluto Press, pp 123–136.

Lean, Nathan (2019) 'The debate over the utility and precision of the term "Islamophobia"', in Irene Zempi and Imran Awan (eds) *The Routledge Handbook of Islamophobia*, London: Routledge, pp 11–17.

Lewis, Reina (2015) *Muslim Fashion: Contemporary Style Cultures*, Durham, NC: Duke University Press.

Lewis, Reina and Almila, Anna-Mari (2020) 'Muslim fashion, youth and belonging: an interview with Reina Lewis', *Youth and Globalization*, 2: 111–118.

Lippard, Cameron (2011) 'Racist nativism in the 21st century', *Sociology Compass*, 5(7): 591–606.

Listerborn, Carina (2015) 'Geographies of the veil: violent encounters in urban public spaces in Malmö, Sweden', *Social and Cultural Geography*, 16(1): 95–115.

Lloyd Evans, Sally and Bowlby, Sophia (2000) 'Crossing boundaries: racialised gendering and the labour market experiences of Pakistani migrant women in Britain', *Women's Studies International Forum*, 23(4): 461–474.

Lundsteen, Martin (2020) 'Conflicts in and around space: reflections on "mosque conflicts"', *Journal of Muslims in Europe*, 9: 43–63.

Mansson McGinty, Anna (2012) 'The "mainstream Muslim" opposing Islamophobia: self-representations of American Muslims', *Environment and Planning A: Economy and Space*, 44(12): 2957–2973.

Mansson McGinty, Anna (2014) 'Emotional geographies of veiling: the meanings of the hijab for five Palestinian American Muslim women', *Gender, Place and Culture*, 21(6): 683–700.

Mansson McGinty, Anna (2020) 'Embodied Islamophobia: lived experiences of anti-Muslim discourses and assaults in Milwaukee, Wisconsin', *Social and Cultural Geography*, 21(3): 402–420.

Mansson McGinty, Anna (2023) 'Lived Islam: embodied identities and everyday practices among American Muslim youth', *Annals of the American Association of Geographers*, 113(3): 756–770.

Mansson McGinty, Anna, Sziarto, Kristin and Seymour-Jorn, Caroline (2013) 'Researching within and against Islamophobia: a collaboration project with Muslim communities', *Social and Cultural Geography*, 14(1): 1–22.

Manzoor-Khan, Suhaiymah (2022) *Tangled in Terror: Uprooting Islamophobia*, London: Pluto Press.

Marranci, Gabriele (2004) 'Multiculturalism, Islam and the clash of civilisations theory: rethinking Islamophobia', *Culture and Religion*, 5(1): 105–117.

Marranci, Gabriele (2005) 'Pakistanis in Northern Ireland in the aftermath of September 11', in Tahir Abbas (ed) *Muslim Britain: Communities under Pressure*, Oxford: Zed Books, pp 222–234.

Marusek, Sarah (2017) 'The transatlantic network: funding Islamophobia and Israeli settlement', in Narzanin Massoumi, Tom Mills and David Miller (eds) *What is Islamophobia? Racism, Social Movements and the State*, London: Pluto Press, pp 186–214.

Massoumi, Narzanin, Mills, Tom and Miller, David (2017a) *What is Islamophobia? Racism, Social Movements and the State*, London: Pluto Press.

Massoumi, Narzanin, Mills, Tom and Miller, David (2017b) 'Islamophobia, social movements and the state: for a movement-centred approach', in Narzanin Massoumi, Tom Mills and David Miller (eds) *What is Islamophobia? Racism, Social Movements and the State*, London: Pluto Press, pp 3–32.

Meer, Nasar and Modood, Tariq (2019) 'Islamophobia as the racialisation of Muslims', in Irene Zempi and Imran Awan (eds) *The Routledge Handbook of Islamophobia*, London: Routledge, pp 18–31.

Meer, Nasar, Dwyer, Claire and Modood, Tariq (2010) 'Embodying nationhood? Conceptions of British national identity, citizenship, and gender in the "veil affair"', *The Sociological Review*, 58(1): 84–111.

Miller-Idriss, Cynthia (2020) *Hate in the Homeland: The New Global Far Right*, Princeton: Princeton University Press.

Miller-Idriss, Cynthia (2021) 'From 9/11 to 1/6: the war on terror supercharged the far right', *Foreign Affairs*, 100(5): 54–65.

Mills, Tom, Griffin, Tom and Miller, David (2011) *The Cold War on British Muslims: An Examination of Policy Exchange and the Center for Social Cohesion*, Glasgow: Spinwatch.

Mir, Uzma and Hopkins, Peter (2019) *Media Guidelines: Reporting on Muslims and Islam*, Edinburgh: Scottish Parliament.

Mirrlees, Tanner and Ibaid, Taha (2021) 'The virtual killing of Muslims: digital war games, Islamophobia, and the global war on terror', *Islamophobia Studies Journal*, 6(1): 33–51.

Modood, Tariq (2003) 'Muslims and the politics of difference', *The Political Quarterly*, 74(1): 100–115.

Modood, Tariq (2019) *Essays on Secularism and Multiculturalism*, London: Rowman & Littlefield.

Mohammad, Robina (1999) 'Marginalisation, Islamism and the production of the "other's" "other"', *Gender, Place and Culture*, 6(3): 221–240.

Mohammed, Marwan (2024) 'France's Islamophobic bloc and the "mainstreamization" of the far right', in Sarah F. Aziz and John L. Esposito (eds) *Global Islamophobia and the Rise of Populism*, New York: Oxford University Press, pp 112–131.

Mondon, Aurelien and Winter, Aaron (2019) 'Mapping and mainstreaming Islamophobia: between the illiberal and liberal', in Irene Zempi and Imran Awan (eds) *The Routledge Handbook of Islamophobia*, London: Routledge, pp 58–70.

Mondon, Aurelien and Winter, Aaron (2020) *Reactionary Democracy: How Racism and the Populist Far Right became Mainstream*, London: Verso.

Mondon, Aurelien and Winter, Aaron (2024) *Creating a Crisis: Immigration, Racism and the 2023 General Election*, London: Runnymede Trust.

Moosavi, Leon (2015) 'The racialization of Muslim converts in Britain and their experiences of Islamophobia', *Critical Sociology*, 41(1): 41–56.

Morgan, George and Poynting, Scott (2012) 'Introduction: the transnational folk devil', in George Morgan and Scott Poynting (eds) *Global Islamophobia: Muslims and Moral Panic in the West*, Aldershot: Ashgate, pp 1–14.

Munnik, Michael B. (2023) 'Islamic state: the political challenge of naming', in Salman Al-Azami (ed) *Media Language on Islam and Muslims: Terminologies and their Effects*, Cham: Palgrave Macmillan, pp 107–127.

Mythen, Gabe, Walklate, Sandra and Khan, Fatima (2009) '"I'm a Muslim, but I'm not a terrorist": victimisation, risky identities and the performance of safety', *British Journal of Criminology*, 49(6): 736–754.

Nagel, Caroline (2016) 'Southern hospitality? Islamophobia and the politicization of refugees in South Carolina during the 2016 election season', *Southeastern Geographer*, 56(3): 283–290.

Nagel, Caroline and Hopkins, Peter (2010) 'Spaces of multiculturalism', *Space and Polity*, 14(1): 1–11.

Najib, Kawtar (2021) 'Spaces of Islamophobia and spaces of inequality in Greater Paris', *Environment and Planning C: Politics and Space*, 39(3): 606–625.

Najib, Kawtar (2022) *Spatialized Islamophobia*, London: Routledge.

Najib, Kawtar (2024) 'Islamophobia in France: national report 2023', in Enes Bayrakli and Farid Hafez (eds) *European Islamophobia Report 2023*, Vienna: Leopold Weiss Institute, pp 285–316.

Najib, Kawtar and Hopkins, Peter (2019) 'Veiled Muslim women's strategies in response to Islamophobia in Paris', *Political Geography*, 73: 103–111.

Najib, Kawtar and Hopkins, Peter (2020) 'Where does Islamophobia take place and who is involved? Reflections from Paris and London', *Social and Cultural Geography*, 21(4): 458–478.

Najib, Kawtar and Teeple Hopkins, Carmen (2020) 'Geographies of Islamophobia', *Social and Cultural Geography*, 21(4): 449–457.

Narkowicz, Kasia and Pedziwiatr, Konrad (2017) 'Saving and fearing Muslim women in "post-communist" Poland: troubling Catholic and secular Islamophobia', *Gender, Place and Culture*, 14(2): 288–299.

Noble, Greg (2009) *Lines in the Sand: The Cronulla Riots, Multiculturalism and National Belonging*, Sydney: Institute of Criminology Press.

Omi, Michael and Winant, Howard (1986) *Racial Formation in the United States: From the 1960s to the 1990s*, New York: Routledge.

O'Toole, Therese, Meer, Nasar, DeHanas, Daniel Nilsson, Jones, Stephen H. and Modood, Tariq (2016) 'Governing through Prevent? Regulation and contested practice in state-Muslim engagement', *Sociology*, 50(1): 160–177.

Oza, Rupal (2007) 'The geography of Hindu right-wing violence in India', in Derek Gregory and Allan Pred (eds) *Violent Geographies: Fear, Terror, and Political Violence*, London: Routledge, pp 153–173.

Pain, Rachel (2001) 'Gender, race, age, and fear in the city', *Urban Studies*, 38(5–6): 899–913.

Pain, Rachel and Smith, Susan J. (2007) 'Fear: critical geopolitics and everyday life', in Rachel Pain and Susan J. Smith (eds) *Fear: Critical Geopolitics and Everyday Life*, Aldershot: Ashgate, pp 1–19.

Peek, Lori (2011) *Behind the Backlash: Muslim Americans after 9/11*, Philadelphia: Temple University Press.

Perry, Barbara (2019) 'Breaking the peace: the Quebec city terrorist attack', in Irene Zempi and Imran Awan (eds) *The Routledge Handbook of Islamophobia*, London: Routledge, pp 275–285.

Phillips, Deborah (1998) 'Black minority ethnic concentration, segregation and dispersal in Britain', *Urban Studies*, 35(10): 1681–1702.

Phillips, Deborah (2006) 'Parallel lives? Challenging discourses of British Muslim self-segregation', *Environment and Planning D: Society and Space*, 24(1): 25–40.

Phoenix, Ann (1997) 'The place of "race" and ethnicity in the lives of children and young people', *Educational and Child Psychology*, 14(3): 5–24.

Possamai, Adam, Dunn, Kevin, Hopkins, Peter, Amin, Faroque, Worthington, Lisa and Ali, Jan (2016) 'Muslim students' religious and cultural experiences in the micro-publics of university campuses in NSW, Australia', *Australian Geographer*, 47(3): 311–324.

Poynting, Scott (2020) '"Islamophobia kills" – but where does it come from?', *International Journal of Crime, Justice and Social Democracy*, 9(20): 74–87.

Poynting, Scott and Mason, Victoria (2007) 'The resistible rise of Islamophobia: anti-Muslim racism in the UK and Australia before 11 September 2001', *Journal of Sociology*, 43(1): 61–86.

Poynting, Scott and Briskman, Linda (2017) 'Terror incognito: black flags, plastic swords and other weapons of mass disruption in Australia', in Narzanin Massoumi, Tom Mills and David Miller (eds) *What is Islamophobia? Racism, Social Movements and the State*, London: Pluto Press, pp 137–162.

Poynting, Scott, Noble, Greg, Tabar, Paul and Collins, Jock (2004) *Bin Laden in the Suburbs: Criminalising the Arab Other*, Leichardt: Federation Press.

Rahman, Momin (2010) 'Queer as intersectionality: theorizing gay Muslim identities', *Sociology*, 44(5): 944–961.

Rana, Junaid (2016) 'The racial infrastructure of the terror-industrial complex', *Social Text*, 34(4): 111–138.

Rane, Halim, Ewart, Jacqui and Martinkus, John (2014) *Media Framing of the Muslim World: Conflicts, Crises and Contexts*, Basingstoke: Palgrave Macmillan.

Redclift, Victoria, Rajina, Fatima and Rashid, Naaz (2022) 'The burden of conviviality: British Bangladeshi Muslims navigating diversity in London, Luton and Birmingham', *Sociology*, 56(6): 1159–1175.

Ruez, Derek (2012) '"Partitioning the sensible" at park 51: Rancière, Islamophobia, and common politics', *Antipode*, 45(5): 1128–1147.

Runnymede Trust (1997) *Islamophobia: A Challenge for Us All*, London: Runnymede Trust.

Runnymede Trust (2024) *Islamophobia: The Intensification of Racism against Muslim Communities in the UK*, London: Runnymede Trust.

Sabir, Rizwaan (2022) *The Suspect: Counterterrorism, Islam, and the Security State*, London: Pluto Press.

Saeed, Amir (2007) 'Media, racism and Islamophobia: the representation of Islam and Muslims in the media', *Sociology Compass*, 1(2): 443–462.

Saeed, Amir (2017) 'Digital orientalism: Muslim youth, Islamophobia and online racism', in Sadek Hamid (ed) *Young British Muslims: Between Rhetoric and Reality*, London: Routledge, pp 134–150.

Saeed, Tania (2016) *Islamophobia and Securitization: Religion, Ethnicity and the Female Voice*, Cham: Palgrave Macmillan.

Said, Edward W. (1978, reprinted 1995) *Orientalism: Western Conceptions of the Orient*, London: Penguin.

Said, Edward W. (1997) *Covering Islam: How the Media and the Experts Determine How We See the Rest of the World*, London: Vintage.

Sakellarious, Alexandros (2019) 'Islamophobia in Greece: the "Muslim threat" and the panic about Islam', in Irene Zempi and Imran Awan (eds) *The Routledge Handbook of Islamophobia*, London: Routledge, pp 198–211.

Sanghera, Gurchathen and Thapar-Bjokert, Suruchi (2007) 'Because I am Pakistani ... and I am a Muslim ... I am political – gendering political radicalism: young femininities in Bradford', in Tahir Abbas (ed) *Islamic Political Radicalism: A European Perspective*, Edinburgh: Edinburgh University Press, pp 173–191.

Sanghera, Gurchathen and Thapar-Bjokert, Suruchi (2008) 'Methodological dilemmas: gatekeepers and positionality in Bradford', *Ethnic and Racial Studies*, 31(3): 543–562.

Sardar, Ziauddin (2009) 'Spaces of hope: interventions', in Richard Phillips (ed) *Muslim Spaces of Hope: Geographies of Possibility in Britain and the West*, Oxford: Zed Books, pp 13–26.

Sayyid, Salman (2003) *A Fundamental Fear: Eurocentricsm and the Emergence of Islamism*, London: Zed Books.

Sayyid, Salman (2014) 'A measure of Islamophobia', *Islamophobia Studies Journal*, 2(1): 10–25.

Sayyid, Salman (2018) 'Topographies of hate: Islamophobia in Cyberia', *Journal of Cyberspace Studies*, 2(1): 55–73.

Schenk, Christine Giulia, Gokariksel, Banu and Behzadi, Negar Elodie (2022) 'Security, violence and mobility: the embodied and everyday politics of negotiating Muslim femininities', *Political Geography*, 94: Article 102597.

Scott-Baumann, Alison, Guest, Mathew, Naguib, Shuruq, Cheruvallil-Contractor, Sanya and Phoenix, Aisha (2020) *Islam on Campus: Contested Identities and Cultures of Higher Education in Britain*, Oxford: Oxford University Press.

Selod, Saher (2015) 'Citizenship denied: the racialization of Muslim American men and women post 9/11', *Critical Sociology*, 41(1): 77–95.

Selod, Saher (2018) *Forever Suspect: Racialized Surveillance of Muslim Americans in the War on Terror*, New Brunswick: Rutgers University Press.

Selod, Saher (2019) 'Gendered racialization: Muslim American men and women's encounters with racialized surveillance', *Ethnic and Racial Studies*, 42(4): 552–569.

Selod, Saher (2024) 'Anti-Muslim racism and the rise of ethnonationalist populism in the United States', in Sahar F. Aziz and John L. Esposito (eds) *Global Islamophobia and the Rise of Populism*, New York: Oxford University Press, pp 56–72.

Selod, Saher, Islam, Inaash and Garner, Steve (2024) *A Global Racial Enemy: Muslims and 21st Century Racism*, Cambridge: Polity Press.

Shaheed, Ahmed (2021) *Countering Islamophobia/Anti-Muslim Hatred to Eliminate Discrimination and Intolerance Based on Religion or Belief: Report of the Special Rapporteur on Freedom of Religion or Belief*, Geneva: Office of the United Nations High Commissioner for Human Rights.

Shain, Farzana (2011) *The New Folk Devils: Muslim Boys and Education in England*, Stoke on Trent: Trentham Books.

Shaker, Reza (2021) '"Saying nothing is saying something": affective encounters with the Muslim Other in Amsterdam public transport', *Annals of the American Association of Geographers*, 111(7): 2130–2148.

Shaker, Reza, van Hoven, Bettina and van Lanen, Sander (2023) '"Just as much as there is Islamophobia, there is racism": corporeal encounters with the Muslim Other in Amsterdam', *Urban Geography*, 44(4): 570–590.

Sheller, Mimi and Urry, John (2006) 'The new mobilities paradigm', *Environment and Planning A*, 38(2): 207–226.

Shibli, Nawroos (2021) 'Political geographies of Islamophobia: Chinese ethno-religious racism and structural violence in East Turkestan', *Islamophobia Studies Journal*, 6(2): 150–166.

Sian, Katy P. (2010) 'Don't freak, I'm Sikh', in Salman Sayyid and AbdoolKarim Vakil (eds) *Thinking through Islamophobia: Global Perspectives*, London: Hurst and Company, pp 251–254.

Simonsen, Kirsten, de Neergaard, Maja and Koefoed, Lasse (2019) 'A mosque event: the opening of a purpose-built mosque in Copenhagen', *Social and Cultural Geography*, 20(5): 649–670.

Sirin, Selcuk and Fine, Michelle (2008) *Muslim American Youth: Understanding Hyphenated Identities through Multiple Methods*, New York: New York University Press.

Smith, Heather Jane (2021) 'Britishness and "the outsider within": tracing manifestations of racist nativism in education policy in England', *Prism: Casting New Light on Learning, Theory and Practice*, 3(2): 62–79.

Smith, Heather Jane (2024a) 'Deracialization', in Mitja Sardoc (ed) *Encyclopedia of Diversity*, Cham: Springer. https://doi.org/10.1007/978-3-030-95454-3_618-1

Smith, Heather Jane (2024b) 'Racist nativism', in Mitja Sardoc (ed) *Encyclopedia of Diversity*, Cham: Springer. https://doi.org/10.1007/978-3-030-95454-3_619-1

Smith Finley, Joanne (2019) 'Securitization, insecurity and conflict in contemporary Xinjiang: has PRC counter-terrorism evolved into state terror?', *Central Asian Survey*, 38(1): 1–26.

Smith Finley, Joanne (2021) 'Why scholars and activities increasingly fear a Uyghur genocide in Xinjiang', *Journal of Genocide Research*, 23(3): 348–370.

Smits, Amina (2024) 'Islamophobia in Belgium: national report 2023', in Enes Bayrakli and Farid Hafez (eds) *European Islamophobia Report 2023*, Vienna: Leopold Weiss Institute, pp 124–147.

Soltani, Anoosh, Johnston, Lynda and Longhurst, Robyn (2022) 'Fashioning hybrid Muslim women's veiled embodied geographies in Hamilton. Aotearoa New Zealand: #hijabiSpaces', *Gender, Place and Culture*, 29(3): 393–418.

Sziarto, Kristin, Mansson McGinty, Anna and Seymour-Jorn, Caroline (2014) 'Diverse Muslims in a racialized landscape: race, ethnicity and Islamophobia in the American city of Milwaukee, Wisconsin', *Journal of Muslim Minority Affairs*, 34(1): 1–21.

Tarlo, Emma (2010) *Visibly Muslim: Fashion, Politics, Faith*, Oxford: Berg.

Tarlo, Emma (2017) 'Re-fashioning the Islamic: young visible Muslims', in Sadek Hamid (ed) *Young British Muslims: Between Rhetoric and Realities*, London: Routledge, pp 151–170.

Taylor, Charles (1994) 'The politics of recognition', in Charles Taylor, Anthony K. Appiah, Jurgen Habermas, Steven C. Rockefeller, Michael Walzer and Susan Wolf (eds) *Multiculturalism*, Princeton: Princeton University Press, pp 25–74.

Tazamal, Mobashra (2024) 'Islamophobia: how the far right went mainstream in Britain', in Sahar F. Aziz and John L. Esposito (eds) *Global Islamophobia and the Rise of Populism*, New York: Oxford University Press, pp 94–111.

TellMAMA (2017) *A Constructed Threat: Identity, Prejudice and the Impact of Anti-Muslim Hatred – TellMAMA Annual Report 2016*, London: Faith Matters.

TellMAMA (2019) *Normalising Hatred: TellMAMA Annual Report 2018*, London: Faith Matters.

TellMAMA (2023) *A Decade of Anti-Muslim Hate*, London: Faith Matters.

TellMAMA (2024) *Manifesto Against Hate 2024*, London: Faith Matters.

Tesler, Michael (2018) 'Words of wisdom: Islamophobia in the 2016 election', *Journal of Race, Ethnicity and Politics*, 3: 153–155.

Thorpe, Holly, Ahmad, Nida, Marfell, Amy and Richards, Justin (2022) 'Muslim women's sporting spatialities: navigating culture, religion and moving bodies in Aotearoa, New Zealand', *Gender, Place and Culture*, 29(1): 52–79.

Titley, Gavan, Freedman, Des, Khiabany, Gholam and Mondon, Aurelien (eds) (2017) *After Charlie Hebdo: Terror, Racism and Free Speech*, London: Zed Books.

Tyler, Imogen (2020) *Stigma: The Machinery of Inequality*, London: Zed.

Uddin, Asma T. (2024) 'The politics of vulnerability: today's threat to American Muslims' religious freedom', in Sahar F. Aziz and John L. Esposito (eds) *Global Islamophobia and the Rise of Populism*, New York: Oxford University Press, pp 36–55.

UN Committee on the Elimination of Racial Discrimination (2024) *Findings on Belarus, Bosnia, Herzegovina, Iran, Iraq, Pakistan, United Kingdom, and Venezuela*, 23 August. https://www.ohchr.org/en/press-releases/2024/08/un-committee-elimination-racial-discrimination-publishes-findings-belarus

Vakil, AbdoolKarim (2010) 'Is the Islam in Islamophobia the same as the Islam in anti-Islam: or when is it Islamophobia time?', in Salman Sayyid and AdboolKarim Vakil (eds) *Thinking through Islamophobia: Global Perspectives*, London: Hurst, pp 23–43.

Vakil, AbdoolKarim and Sayyid, Salman (2023) 'Towards a grammar of Islamophobia', in Salman Al-Azami (ed) *Media Language on Islam and Muslims: Terminologies and their Effects*, Cham: Palgrave Macmillan, pp 29–56.

van der Kolk, Bessel (2014) *The Body Keeps the Score: Mind, Brain and Body in the Transformation of Trauma*, London: Penguin.

Verkaaik, Oskar and Tamini Arab, Pooyan (2016) 'Managing mosques in the Netherlands: constitutional versus culturalist secularism', *Journal of Muslims in Europe*, 5: 251–268.

Versi, Miqdaad (2023) 'Commentary: how theory can have a real impact – the practical realities of fighting Islamophobia in the media', in Salman Al-Azami (ed) *Media Language on Islam and Muslims: Terminologies and their Effects*, Cham: Palgrave Macmillan, pp 17–28.

Waikar, Prashant (2018) 'Reading Islamophobia in hegemonic neoliberalism through a discourse analysis of Donald Trump's narratives', *Journal of Muslim Minority Affairs*, 38(2): 153–178.

Walklate, Sandra and Mythen, Gabe (2015) *Contradictions of Terrorism: Security, Risk and Resilience*, London: Routledge.

Warren, Saskia (2019) '#YourAverageMuslim: ruptural geopolitics of British Muslim women's media and fashion', *Political Geography*, 69: 118–127.

Warren, Saskia (2022) *British Muslim Women in the Cultural and Creative Industries*, Edinburgh: Edinburgh University Press.

REFERENCES

Warsi, Sayeeda (2024) *Muslims Don't Matter*, London: The Bridge Street Press.

Wolfreys, Jim (2023) '"Avec vous?" Islamophobia and the Macron presidency', *Modern and Contemporary France*, 31(2): 165–182.

Young, Iris Marion (1990) *Justice and the Politics of Difference*, Princeton: Princeton University Press.

Younis, Tarek (2024) *The Muslim, State and Mind*, London: SAGE.

Zempi, Irene and Chakraborti, Neil (2015) '"They make us feel like we're a virus": the multiple impacts of Islamophobic hostility towards veiled Muslim women', *International Journal of Crime, Justice and Social Democracy*, 4(3): 44–56.

Zempi, Irene and Awan, Imran (2016) *Islamophobia: Lived Experiences of Online and Offline Victimisation*, Bristol: Policy Press.

Zempi, Irene and Awan, Imran (2019) *The Routledge Handbook of Islamophobia*, London: Routledge.

Zine, Jasmin (2022a) *Under Siege: Islamophobia and the 9/11 Generation*, Montreal: McGill-Queen's University Press.

Zine, Jasmin (2022b) 'The Canadian Islamophobia industry: Islamophobia's ecosystem in the Great White North', *Islamophobia Studies Journal*, 7(2): 232–249.

Index

References to tables appear in **bold** type.

A

absence as feature of Islamophobia 24–25, 40, 107
acts of Islamophobia 15, 16, 22–25
addressing Islamophobia 9–10, 12, 130, 139–153
affective acts of Islamophobia 99
Afshar, Haleh 34
Ahmed, Sara 24–25
airports 19, 45, 48, 53, 57, 63, 101–103
Akhtar, Sabeena 149
Al-Azami, Salman 87, 88, 105
Ali, Nadya 85
'Allahu Akbar' 86, 105
Allen, Chris **30**, 74, 119, 130
All-Party Parliamentary Group on British Muslims 3, 15
Al-Sabawi, Maryam 3, 149, 151
alternative terms for 'Islamophobia' 15, 17
Andrews, Kehinde 33
anti-black racism 15, 61
anti-immigrant discourse 40
anti-racism 5, 33, 108, 119, 147, 148–149
Arabic language 67
Arabs 36, 63, 109
asylum seekers 74, 98, 105, 107
Australia
  approvals for mosque development 113
  biased media 89
  'clash of civilizations' 41
  Cronulla beach, Sydney 108
  monitoring 4
  moral panics 42–43
  post 9/11 52
  public spaces 96, 99
  right wing politics 71, 72
  riots 108–109
  stereotypes 35, 36
Austria 44, 58–59, 118
Awan, Imran 22, 88
Aziz, Sahar F. 22, 23, 24, 37, 45, 60

B

Bagguley, Paul 56
Bangstad, Sindre 38, 109, 110
Bannon, Steve 78
Bayrakli, Enes 58–59, 71
Bazian, Hatem 13–14, 41
Bechrouri, Ibrahim 69–70
Belgium 85, 91, 93, 129
Beydoun, Khaled 20, 26, 27, 50, 54, 55, 59–60, 61, 62, 63, 64, 86–87, 117, 135, 136
Birt, Jonathan 7
blackness 18
Blackwood, Leda 102
blogs 77–78, 81
Bokhari, Saarah 86
Bonnett, Alastair 109, 143, 152
border controls 62, 74, 98, 102
Bosnia and Herzegovina 21, 118
Botterill, Katherine 130
Bowlby, Sophie 121
Bowler, Rick 74
Breitbart 78
Breivik, Anders Behring 2, 38, 43, 77, 81, 152
Brexit 44, 74, 105
Brice, Kevin M.A. 95
Briskman, Linda 72, 74, 86
Brown, Katy 106, 107, 146
burka 72
Butler, Judith 142
bystander action 100

C

Cada, Karel 35
CAGE 142–143
Campbell, Elaine 22
Canada 2, 4, 11, 79, 118, 122, 150, 151
capitalism 7, 23, 46, 48, 51, 143
caricatures 89
Carr, James 102, 145, 152

178

INDEX

categories of Islamophobia 25–29
census data 38
Center for Countering Digital Hate 88, 104, 106, 146
Center for Security Policy 78, 82
Centre for Media Monitoring of the Muslim Council of Britain 87, 88
Centre for Social Cohesion 82, 83, 84
Cesari, Jocelyn 41–42
chains of association 35
Chakraborti, Neil 98, 131
Chan, Wun Fang 94
charity donations 76–77
Charlie Hebdo shootings, Paris 8, 52, 86, 97
Chaudry, Izram 120, 141
Cheng, Jennifer 115–116
Chernick, Aubrey 81
children, interrogation of 125–126
China 11, 21, 41, 54, 64–68
  camps 66–67
  see also Xinjiang; Uyghur Muslims
Cho, Sumi 29
Christchurch attacks, New Zealand 2, 37, 89, 90, 91
Christianity 61, 76, 79, 97
circumventing Islamophobia 40–43, 147
civil society actors 85, 90, 148
'clash of civilizations' 41–42, 63
Clayton, John 112
Cohen, Stanley 42
collaboration, partnership, and collective working 148–151
collective responsibility 23, 93
colonialism 26
community cohesion policies 94
community engagement 150
community resilience 147
'conceptual Muslim' 85
Considine, Craig 19
conspiracy theories 10, 36–40, 85
  see also white genocide; Eurabia; great replacement
Council for American Islamic Relations 77, 80, 117
counter-narratives 147
counterterrorism
  airports 102
  disproportionate reactions 42
  effects at home 126
  five pillars of Islamophobia 27, 48
  'fundamental British values' 41
  'great replacement' theory 37
  hostility towards measures of 121
  interdisciplinary Islamophobia studies 7
  Prevent 25, 53, 57, 83, 126, 144
  racial profiling 18, 45
  radicalization 52–53
  and silencing 25

state-sponsored Islamophobia 55–60
surveillance 57
Crenshaw, Kimberle 28
Culcasi, Karen 97

D

David Horowitz Freedom Center 77, 106
Davis, Mark 36–37, 38, 39
definitions of Islamophobia 13–32
democracy 27, 35, 47, 63, 116
demographic change 37
Denmark 72, 93, 109, 110, 114
deracialization 40
deservingness of welfare/support 97
dialectical Islamophobia 26
Dinet, Etienne 13
discourse 19, 47, 75, 125, 145
discourse analysis 35
discrimination 3, 7, 22, 23–24, 95–96, 122
disease associations 68, 74, 89, 150
disenfranchised grief 142
dissidents 79, 80
Dobbernack, Jan 93
dress 24, 86, 96, 120, 122, 127, 130–135, 151
  see also headscarves; hijab
Dunn, Kevin 108, 109, 113, 114
Dwyer, Claire 132

E

Easat-Daas, A. 9, 29, **30**, 129
education spaces, Islamophobia in 41, 119–121
educational initiatives to tackle Islamophobia 149
Edwards, Sarah 107
Ehrkamp, Patricia 93, 96
Elahi, Farah 14
Elaud, Samantha 122
elections 73, 77, 78
Elsheikh, Elsadig 142, 149
embodied experiences of Islamophobia 12, 29, 31, 101, 102, 125, 127–130
  see also beards; headscarf; veil; dress; skin colour; face coverings
employment 24, 70, 121–122
English Defence League 81, 83
Esposito, John L. 22, 23, 24, 37, 45, 60
Essed, Philomena 31–32, 140
estate agents 95–96
ethnic and racial studies 7
ethnonationalism 21–22
etymology 13–14, 16
Eurabia 36, 38, 43
European Commission against Racism and Intolerance (ECRI) 74–75
European Commission Coordinator for Combating anti-Muslim hatred 4

European Islamophobia Report 58, 71
European Parliament 44
European Union Agency for Fundamental Rights 3, 29, 92, 95, 141
evangelical Christians 61, 76, 97
ex-Muslims 79, 80
extremism 37, 39, 43, 53, 55–56, 66, 89, 107–108
eye contact 101

F

face coverings 68, 72, 131, 132
Facebook 88, 89
far right
  alt-right 40, 120
  Christian far right 79
  conspiracy theories 36–37, 38, 39
  counterterrorism 53
  five pillars of Islamophobia 27
  France 44, 68, 69
  funding 106
  Ground Zero mosque 82
  Islamophobia industrial complex 49, 50
  mainstreaming 43–48, 106
  media 47, 75, 85, 106–107, 146
  riots 103–110
  Scandinavia 109
  tackling 145
Farage, Nigel 40, 44, 71, 105
fashion 151
FBI training 44
fear 75, 76, 80, 83, 108, 124, 141
feminist research 5, 8, 29, 127, 133
films/movies 87
Finlay, Robin 149
Finney, Nissa 95
five pillars of Islamophobia 27, 48–49, 55
flows of Islamophobia 19
forced deportations 110
forced incarceration 67
foreign policy 41, 60–64
Fox, Lawrence 105
framing 85, 142
France
  approvals for mosque development 116–117
  attacks on mosques 118
  attitudes towards Muslims 3
  bans on dress 131, 133–134
  Charlie Hebdo shootings, Paris 8, 52, 86, 97
  'colour blind' 68
  great replacement 37
  Islamophobia denial in 68–71
  right wing politics 39, 44, 68, 69
Frantova, Veronika 35
Fraser, Nancy 135
free speech 27, 45, 56, 120
funding 74, 75, 76, 77, 81, 83, 84, 106

G

Gaffney, Frank 78, 82
Gale, Richard 115
Ganesh, Bharath 19, 20, 75
gangs 42
Gardell, Mattias 118
Gatestone Institute 106
Gaza 24, 91, 107
Geller, Pamela 77–78, 81, 101, 106
gendered Islamophobia 29, 35, 56, 128–130
geopolitics 8, 9, 51, 74, 127, 133, 137
Germany 2, 3, 36, 85, 86, 98, 118, 129
Geronimus, Arline T. 140, 141, 142, 143
ghettoization 35, 93, 94
Gilliat-Ray, Sophie 119
global Islamophobia 51–73
Gökariksel, Banu 62–63
Goldmann, Fabian 118
'good'/'bad' Muslims 96–97
Gorman, Cynthia S. 97
Gove, Michael 82, 83, 107
graffiti 3, 18, 43
'great replacement' 2, 36, 37, 89
Greece 97
Green, Todd H. 3, 13, 14, 15, 86, 117
Griffin, Tom 83
Ground Zero mosque 11, 81–82, 112

H

Hafez, Farid 33, 38, 40, 51, 58–59, 71, 118, 126
Hajjat, Abdellali 70
halal 24, 69, 72, 85, 89, 121
Hamid, Sadek 121
Hamilton, Fiona 142
Hancock, Claire 68, 69, 116, 117, 133–134
Hanson, Pauline 71
harassment 24, 124, 134
hashtags 89, 146, 150, 151
Hassan, Oz 63
hate crime 22–23, 24, 26, 91, 107
headlines 87, 106
headscarves 63, 122, 128, 129, 131, 132
health and wellbeing impacts 57, 58, 59, 140, 142, 143
impact of Islamophobia 15, 139–143
Henry Jackson Society 82–83, 84, 87, 107, 142
hijab 59, 67, 96, 98, 102, 122, 128, 130, 132–134
Hilal, Mahu 27–28, 61
Hindu nationalism 21, 54, 109
historical Islamophobia 13, 25–26, 30, 48
home, Islamophobia at 124–138
homogeneity, assumed 34, 35, 63
honor killings 62
Hopkins, Katie 88
Hopkins, Peter 4, 5, 6, 8, 29, 99, 103, 131, 136, 146, 149

INDEX

'hostile environment policy' 74
housing 95
human rights 53, 79
humour 149
Huntingdon, Samuel 38, 41
Hussain, Yasmin 56
hypervisibility 132

I

identity markers 18, 63, 98, 102, 130–135, 142
  see also dress; fashion; headscarf; veil
Iftikhar, Arsalan 77–78, 85, 98, 118, 119, 122, 129, 131, 135
illiberal Islamophobia 27
impact of Islamophobia 15, 139–143
imperialism 20–22, 25
Independent Press Standards Organisation 88
India 21, 68, 109
Iner, Derya 99
infiltration 80
institutional factors 26, 30
institutional racism 95
integration 35, 56, 93–96
intellectual Islamophobia 27, 30, 40, 46, 50, 83
interdisciplinary Islamophobia studies 7
internalization of Islamophobia 27–28, 30
interpersonal Islamophobia 27–28, 30
intersectionality 9, 28–29, 30, 128–129
'invasion' rhetoric 69, 81, 114
Iqbal, Romin 80
Islamic State 88
Islamophobia industrial complex 33–50
  embodied experiences of Islamophobia 137–138
  mosques and institutions of education and employment 123
  and rioting 107
  riots 104, 105, 106, 111
  state-sanctioned Islamophobia 54
  tackling 144
  terminology 7
Islamophobia studies 7
Israel 89, 91
Italy 44
Itaoui, Rhonda 96, 98, 99, 100, 101, 108, 109, 119, 149

J

Jenrick, Robert 105
'jihad' 86
Jihad Watch 77
Jiwani, Yasmin 150
Johnson, Boris 72, 91, 107
jokes 120
  see also humour
Jones, Rhys Dafydd 119, 120
Jones, Stephen 3, 121

K

Kara, Seyfeddin 120
Karcic, Hikmet 21, 118
Kassaye, Aida 85
Katz, Cindi 52, 54
Khamis, Sahar 89, 149, 150, 151
Khan, Amir 150
Khan, Ghazala 151
Khan, Kamran 86
Khan, Omar 14
Kirndörfer, Elisabeth 98
Kiwan, Nadia 70
Koch, Natalie 21
Kumar, Deepa 20–21, 53, 63, 74, 78, 79, 81, 82
Kundnani, Arun 17, 21, 34, 49, 55–56, 90, 92–94, 95, 148
Kwan, Mei-Po 124, 135
Kyriakidou, Maria 97

L

Lajevardi, Nazita 64
Lane, D. 37
Larsson, Goran 38
Law, Ian 143–144, 147
Le Pen, Marine 39, 41, 44, 68, 71
Lean, Nathan 16, 72, 74, 75, 76, 77, 78, 80, 84
left wing politics 71, 117
Lewis, Bernard 38, 41
Lewis, Reina 122
liberalism 27, 45–46, 49, 78, 94, 120
Linge, Marius 109, 110
Lippard, Cameron 40
Listerborn, Carina 132
lived experience, research based on 9–10, 31–32, 56–57
Lloyd Evans, Sally 121
local officials reporting on Muslims 66
London, Ontario 2, 150, 151
'lone wolf' discourse 3, 39, 43
'low-level' discrimination/harassment 31, 124
Lundsteen, Martin 115

M

MacArthur High School, Irving, Texas 1–2, 126
Macron, Emmanuel 70, 71
mainstreaming of Islamophobia 43–48, 85, 145
Mansson McGinty, Anna 12, 29, 127, 128, 133
Manzoor-Khan, Suhaiymah 7, 10, 25, 48, 60, 82, 84, 125–126, 131, 142–143, 144, 148, 153
Marranci, Gabriele 52
Marusek, Sarah 74, 76
Massoumi, Narzanin 26–27, 48, 50, 53, 54, 55, 57
matrix of anti-Muslim racism 79
media 74–91
  blogs 77–78, 81
  far right 47, 75, 85, 106–107, 146

films/movies 87
framing 85, 142
Islamophobia industrial complex 49
and issues of dress 134
post 9/11 52
representational Islamophobia 28
riots 103–104, 106
role of 84–91
stereotypes 85, 87, 145–146
tackling 145–146
men
 beards 66, 67, 102, 136
 dress 102, 122, 135
 gendered Islamophobia 130
 research on 6
 stereotypes 53, 62, 129
microaggressions 23, 32, 120
Middle East 35, 61, 63
Middle East Forum 82, 106
migration 7, 21, 26, 29, 34–35, 36, 40–41, 44, 62
Miller-Idriss, Cynthia 37, 38, 39, 40, 43, 44, 48, 74, 107, 147
minarets 115–116
Mir, Uzma 146
misinformation 74, 77
misogyny 68, 131
misrecognition 9, 18, 23, 52, 63, 90, 109, 125, 135–137
Mobillion, Virginie 133–134
Modood, Tariq 34
Mohamed, Ahmed 1–2, 126
Mohammad, Robina 94
Mohammed, Marwan 70
Mondon, Aurelien 27, 44, 45, 46, 47, 48, 106, 107, 145, 146
monitoring 3, 22, 57, 58, 145
 see also surveillance
moral panics 42, 51, 56, 117
Morgan, George 42, 43, 51
mosques
 approvals for mosque development 113–117
 attacks on 21, 104, 112, 117–119
 Ground Zero mosque 11, 81–82, 112
 mosque attendance 67
 protecting 152
 symbolism of 112
 universities 119–120, 121
 vandalism 23
Munnik, Michael B. 88
Murray, Douglas 83, 105
Muslim Milwaukee Project 148

N

Nagel, Caroline 97
Najib, Kawtar 70, 118, 131
names 24, 67

national identity 34
national security 37, 52, 54
naturalization applications 116
neoconservative movement 27, 49, 79, 83
neo-fascism/neo-Nazis 44, 120
Netherlands 3, 39, 71, 72, 81, 99, 114, 128, 129
new atheist movement 27, 49
New Zealand 2, 37, 129, 132
Newcastle upon Tyne 152–153
9/11 6, 8, 43, 45, 52, 55–56, 65, 81–82, 124, 133
niqab 72, 130, 134
Noble, Greg 108
non-religious Muslims 18
Northern Ireland 52
Norway 2, 38, 43, 78, 109–110, 131

O

Obama, Barack 22, 48, 60, 74, 82, 97
Omi, Michael 17
online Islamophobia 88–90, 146, 150
oppression framework 22, 25
Orientalism 20–22, 63, 102
Oslo 2, 43, 81, 91
othering 20–22, 36, 42, 108
O'Toole, Therese 144
Oza, Rupal 109

P

Pain, Rachel 141
Palestine 54, 76, 89
Paludan, Rasmus 110
PEGIDA (Patriotic Europeans against the Islamization of the West) 47–48, 98
performative acts of Islamophobia 99
Phillips, Deborah 95
'phobia' 7
Pipes, Daniel 82
planning permission 113
platforming 80, 81, 106, 146
Policy Exchange 82, 83, 84
policy making 77, 78
political and community activism 151
politics and politicians 49, 59, 71–73, 105, 106–107, 110
 see also Donald Trump; Nigel Farage; Barack Obama; Marine Le Pen; Michael Gove; Pauline Hanson; Anas Sarwar
populism 47, 105
Poynting, Scott 2, 35, 36, 41, 42, 43, 51, 52, 72, 74, 86
Prevent 25, 53, 57, 83, 126, 144
private Islamophobia 26, 27
processes of Islamophobia 15
progressive politics 27, 45
pro-Israel groups 76, 83
propaganda 37, 76, 77

INDEX

pro-war groups 27, 49
public intellectuals 46, 49, 50
public spaces 98–101, 124, 132–133
public transport 98–101, 133, 152–153
'Punish a Muslim Day' 12, 126–127, 152

Q

Quran burnings/desecration of 11, 67, 109–110

R

race equality policies 40
racial profiling 19, 45, 65, 102
racialization 17–20, 36, 40–41, 53–54, 68, 100, 135–136, 146
racism
  absence in public policy 40
  counterterrorism apparatus 53
  in definitions of Islamophobia 14–15, 17–18, 40
  everyday racism 31–32
  Ground Zero mosque 82
  institutional racism 95
  liberal racism 45–47, 79
  mainstreaming of 44
  online Islamophobia 89
  post 9/11 52
  in property buying 95
  structural racism 27
  'war on terror' 52
radicalization 52–53, 55–56, 62, 69, 121
Rana, Junaid 33, 48, 54
Rauf, Feisal Abdul 81
Razak, Amina 74
Redclift, Victoria 141
Reform UK 40
refugees 62, 96–98
religious practices 59–60, 66, 67
religious profiling 102
religious studies 5
religious symbols 131, 133
  see also dress
representational Islamophobia 28, 30
researching Islamophobia 4–6
Rigby, Lee 90, 137
right wing politics and organizations 50, 71–73, 75–77, 78, 81, 82
  see also far right
riots 2, 11, 45, 52, 91, 94, 103–109, 153
Robert, Naima B. 149
Robertson, Rev Pat 85
Robinson, Tommy 105, 106
Runnymede Trust 1, 2, 14, 16

S

Sabir, Rizwaan 57, 126
Saeed, Amir 120, 150
Said, Edward W. 20, 84–85
Sakellarious, Alexandros 117
San Bernardino, California 60, 97
Sanghera, Gurchathen 18
Sardar, Ziauddin 94
Sarwar, Anas 5
Sayyid, Salman 34
Scandinavia 109–110
scapegoating 16, 23, 42
schools 70, 94, 119, 125–126, 137
Scotland 5, 136, 146
Scott-Baumann, Alison 121
securitization 55–56, 66, 79, 120, 130, 134
segregation versus integration 35, 93–96, 113, 114
Selod, Saher 1, 14, 17, 18, 19, 22, 33, 52–53, 54, 65, 68, 81, 102, 130, 135, 144
sexism 62, 63, 114
sexual predator tropes 35
Shaheed, Ahmed 1, 3, 15, 23, 87, 112, 117
Shaker, Reza 99, 128
Sharia law 36, 38, 76, 86, 116
Sheller, Mimi 100
Shibli, Nawroos 64, 65, 66, 68
Shillman, Robert 106
Sikhs 18, 135, 136–137
silencing 24–25, 107
Sillwood, Anas 151
Simonsen, Kirsten 114
Simpson, Ludi 95
Sisemore, Basima 142
Smith, Heather Jane 41
Smith Finley, Joanne 64–65, 66, 67, 68
Smits, Amina 91
social media 39, 77, 88–90, 103–104, 106, 110, 118, 146, 151, 153
  Facebook 88, 89
Soltani, Anoosh 129, 132
Southport attacks 103–104
Spain 115
spatialized Islamophobia 29, 30, 100–101
Spencer, Robert 77, 81, 106
state roles 48, 51–73, 107, 145
stereotypes
  aggressive stereotypes 35
  approvals for mosque development 113
  'clash of civilizations' 63
  countering 114
  counter-narratives 147
  dialectical Islamophobia 26
  dress 130–131, 132
  embodied experiences of Islamophobia 125
  fundamentalism 34
  gendered Islamophobia 62, 129, 130
  Ground Zero mosque 81
  housing 96
  Islamophobia industrial complex 10
  media 85, 87, 145–146
  modalities of Islamophobia 16

Orientalism 20–21
  post 9/11 52
  refugees 97
  in schools 119
  segregation versus integration 94
  simplistic stereotypes about Muslims and Islam 34–36
  stigmatization 23
  terminology 86
  terrorism 35, 45, 135, 136
  Trump's Muslim ban 62
  women 23, 35, 62, 129
stigmatization 22, 23, 24, 121, 122, 125, 141
'stop and search' 45
Stop Islamization groups 76, 81, 109, 110
'Stop the Boats' 43, 44, 107
structural Islamophobia 26, 30, 48
structural racism 27, 32
structural violence 139–140
'subject of interest' status 57, 58, 59
surveillance 33, 54, 56, 58, 78, 101, 117, 118–119, 121, 129
Sweden 109, 110, 118, 132
Switzerland 115–116

T

Tamini Arab, Pooyan 114
Tarlo, Emma 131–132, 151
Tarrant, Brenton 2
Taylor, Charles 135
TellMAMA 4, 72, 74, 90, 91, 104, 124, 127
terminology 6–7, 13–16, 86
terror industrial complex 33, 48, 53, 54
terrorism
  'banal terrorism' 52, 55
  definitions of Islamophobia 26
  films/movies 87
  'great replacement' theory 37
  against Muslims 23
  Prevent 25, 53, 57, 83
  stereotypes 35, 45, 135, 136
  Trump's views on 62
  white supremacists 39
Tesler, Michael 60
Texas 1–2, 38, 126
Thapar-Bjokert, Suruchi 18
think tanks 49, 78, 79, 82–84, 106
transnational networks of Islamophobia 11, 75–84
transnational politics 8, 9, 62
trauma 59, 140
trigger events 90–91
Trump, Donald 11, 44, 60–64, 78, 83, 86–87, 97, 151
trustworthiness ranking 66
Tyler, Imogen 23, 141

Types of Islamophobia
  embodied 12, 29, 31, 101, 102, 125, 127–130
  gendered 29, 35, 56, 128–130
  global 51–73
  historical 13, 25–26, 30, 48
  intellectual 27, 30, 40, 46, 50, 83
  interpersonal 27–28, 30
  online 88–90, 146, 150
  representational 28, 30
  structural 26, 30, 48
  spatialized 29, 30, 100–101

U

UK
  7/7 London 8
  All-Party Parliamentary Group on British Muslims 3, 15
  approvals for mosque development 115
  attacks on mosques 117
  August 2024 riots 2, 45, 91, 103–108, 117
  Bradford, Burnley and Oldham riots 52
  British values 41, 94
  counterterrorism 25
  far right 44
  levels of Islamophobia 2–3
  mistaken identity as Muslim 137
  right wing politics 39, 40, 71
  schools 119
  stereotypes 36
  universities 119–121
  workplace cultures 121–122
under-reporting 3, 145
United Nations (UN)
  General Assembly 4
  International Day to Combat Islamophobia 4
  Special Rapporteur on Freedom of Religion or Belief 1, 74–75, 90, 112, 117
  UN Committee on the Elimination of Racial Discrimination (2024) 108
United States (US)
  alt-right 40
  attacks on mosques 117, 118
  attitudes towards Muslims 3
  Barack Obama 22
  counterterrorism 53, 59
  Department of Homeland Security 53
  embodied experiences of Islamophobia 128
  far right 44
  foreign policy 21
  Ground Zero mosque 11, 81–82
  Islamophobia industrial complex 77–81
  misrecognition 135–136
  Muslim ban 60–64, 78, 83, 86–87, 97
  New York 81
  'threats to American way of life' 97
  transnational networks of Islamophobia 11, 75

INDEX

Trump, Donald 44
universities 120
veils 133
'white genocide' theory 37–38
workplace cultures 122
universities 57, 70, 119–121, 134
Uyghur Muslims 11, 54, 64–68

V

Vakil, AbdoolKarim 14, 15
van der Kolk, Bessel 140
van Heelsum, Anja 85
veils 68, 69, 131, 132, 133, 134
Veltman, Nathaniel 2
verbal abuse 27, 99, 124, 132, 152
Verkaaik, Oskar 114
Versi, Miqdaad 87–88
violence
  addressing Islamophobia 152
  assumed aggressiveness 35, 63, 68
  conspiracy theories 37
  dialectical Islamophobia 26
  and dress 134
  fear 80, 108
  interpersonal Islamophobia 27
  local, neighbourhood issues 124
  online Islamophobia 89
  performative acts of Islamophobia 99
  post 9/11 52
  Scotland 1992 5
  on those who look Muslim 63
  white supremacists 39
  women 129, 134
visual imagery 85
Vora, Neha 21

W

Waikar, Prashant 62
'war on terror' 2, 11, 12, 26, 45, 48, 52, 54–55, 65, 144–145
Warren, Saskia 151
weathering 139, 140, 140–143
'white genocide' theory 2, 36, 37–38
white supremacists 2, 39, 44, 48, 108, 120, 127
'whitewashing' 87
Wilders, Geert 39, 71, 72, 81, 106
Winant, Howard 17
Winter, Aaron 27, 44, 45, 46, 47, 48, 145
Witham, Ben 85
Wolfreys, Jim 69, 70
women
  concealing identity 142
  dress in France 68–69
  exclusion from Muslim 'types' 52
  gendered Islamophobia 29, 128–129
  identity markers 130–135
  public spaces 152
  rights 27
  securitization 120
  stereotypes 23, 35, 62, 129
  workplace cultures 121–122
workplace cultures 121–122

X

Xinjiang (Uyghur) Autonomous Region (XUAR) 64–68

Y

Yezza, Hicham 57
Young, Iris Marion 22, 125, 141
Younis, Tarek 15–16, 18, 68, 118

Z

Zemmour, Eric 68
Zempi, Irene 22, 88, 98, 129, 131
Zine, Jasmin 2, 15, 23, 25, 31, 54, 74, 75, 77, 79, 80, 120, 122, 148, 151
Zionism 27, 49, 76, 79

www.ingramcontent.com/pod-product-compliance
Lightning Source LLC
Chambersburg PA
CBHW051547020426
42333CB00016B/2131